AFRICA'S QUEST FOR A
PHILOSOPHY OF
DECOLONIZATION

VIBS

Volume 153

Robert Ginsberg
Founding Editor

Peter A. Redpath
Executive Editor

AFRICA'S QUEST FOR A PHILOSOPHY OF DECOLONIZATION

Messay Kebede

Amsterdam - New York, NY 2004

Cover Design: Paul Pollmann

The paper on which this book is printed meets the requirements of "ISO
9706:1994, Information and documentation - Paper for documents -
Requirements for permanence".

ISBN: 90-420-0810-5
©Editions Rodopi B.V., Amsterdam - New York, NY 2004
Printed in the Netherlands

CONTENTS

EDITORIAL FOREWORD

If you have time to read only one book to learn about the intricacies of African philosophy, then read *Africa's Quest for a Philosophy of Decolonization*. The author, Messay Kebede, was raised in Ethiopia, and received his Ph.D. at the University of Grenoble (France). Returning to Ethiopia he chaired the Department of Philosophy at the University of Addis Ababa; he is currently teaching in the United States as associate professor of philosophy at the University of Dayton. He writes and lectures knowledgeably about the status of philosophy in Africa.

The beauty of this volume is Kebede's clear presentation and thoughtful evaluation of each of the main schools in African philosophy. The book begins with a criticism of traditional Western views on Africa. In these treatises the presumption is that Western philosophy alone is rational, and since African sages do not match Western standards of rationality, African thinking is inferior to Western thought. Kebede studies the arguments of this racist approach and by using dissident trends of Western philosophy respectfully disagrees about Africans being less rational than the "white man."

The first scholar Kebede treats is Placide Tempels, who shows that the Bantu's rationality serves a different function than Western rationality. Though pursuing different goals, the philosophy of the Bantu tribe has a rational underpinning. Accordingly, African philosophy is not in a prelogical, primitive stage that will eventually mirror what modern and contemporary Western philosophers have been expounding. Instead of irrationality, difference from established European philosophy correctly defines Bantu thinking.

A major stand on African otherness is negritude. Negritude is a race-based philosophy that differs from tribal grounded views. Negritude presupposes a core African philosophy exists that has its essence in being black, which philosophy is necessarily distinct from white philosophies. For instance, precolonial negritude is community based and has its own epistemological orientation that depicts the world by means of emotional antennae. The gist of these views is that philosophy is pluralistic, and that African thinkers, while different from Eurocentric thinkers, are not backward.

Other African philosophies exist that reject negritude and propound a more European philosophy, such as Marxism. There are also those of postmodernist inspiration that accept the African difference but reject the definition of negritude. Kebede attempts another approach. He follows Henri Bergson in giving myth a prominent place in the generation of rational thinking. His basic argument is that the antagonism between myth and rationality on account of which Africans are stigmatized as primitive is anything but true. Western thought has had a mystical period in the Middle Ages that set the stage for Cartesian and other modern philosophies; similar claims have been made for the origins of Greek philosophy. The idealism that permeates Western thought is based upon myth; worldliness and heroic individualism are grounded on mythical conceptions. These unacknowledged foundations are different from the myths that permeate African thinking. If the West would stop oppressing Africa and the third world, and cease downplaying the value of alternate myths, then Western thinkers might learn the virtues of dialogue with a culture that is imbued with a different set of myths.

The book is an intellectual tour through African philosophy. Western discourses are not debunked, and Kebede does not side with any particular African school. The author remains the philosopher examining all sides, and setting up a construct within which pluralistic schools can flourish without giving way to relativism. African philosophy needs to be taken seriously, and Western rationality ought to be respected as the important tool that it is. Let the debate continue.

I have known Kebede for five years. As colleagues we have discussed many issues and I deeply appreciate his keen insights and breadth of knowledge. He has studied philosophy in three cultures and shares his synthesizing wisdom in these pages. I believe his book will be taken seriously in the West as yet another instance of African philosophy that explodes the cruel oppressive stigma of primitive thinking. African philosophers will surely cherish Kebede's even-handedness and rational analysis, and hopefully this balanced study will pave the way for a more pluralistic Western attitudinal opening to our brothers and sisters in this emerging continent.

Joseph C. Kunkel
University of Dayton

PREFACE

The central theme of this book is the study of the African philosophical school known as ethnophilosophy. As such, the book exposes itself to the objection that African philosophy is not reducible to ethnophilosophy, which objection is stronger today as new and better-equipped schools of thought have appeared on Africa's philosophical scene. My answer underlines that the most recent of such schools still define their positions in relation to ethnophilosophy, which therefore remains in full actuality. Moreover, the study of other schools as various reactions to the ethnophilosophical discourse provides an interesting perspective pointing to what is really at stake in the African philosophical debate.

As is customary, the study contrasts two main trends: the school of ethnophilosophy, mainly represented by the works of Placide Tempels, John S. Mbiti, and the thinkers of negritude on the one hand, and the school of "professional philosophers," represented by such thinkers as Paulin Hountondji and Marcien Towa on the other. While ethnophilosophy defends the existence of philosophy in traditional Africa by unraveling the philosophical foundation of traditional beliefs, the term "professional philosophers" refers to the strong opposition of a group of African thinkers to the equation of philosophy with culture and folk thinking and, by the same token, to the idea of African otherness. The book also discusses the position of those philosophers who attempt to strike the middle course by presenting more acceptable notions of African philosophy and difference. Ranging from the hermeneutical orientation to the deconstructionist school, these attempts present the common characteristics of rejecting the negritude definition of blackness, without however succumbing to the universalist stand of "professional philosophers."

A perspective centering ethnophilosophy diminishes neither the richness nor the scope of African philosophical debates. Since none of the major schools is excluded, the book portrays, if not an exhaustive view of African philosophy, at least the major moments of its development. Thus, the opponents of ethnophilosophy are analyzed and evaluated with the intention of showing to what extent their own philosophical positions overcome the alleged weaknesses of ethnophilosophy or succeed in proposing alternative views. The outcome of the analysis confirms not so much the irrelevance of the ethnophilosophical school as the need to better understand its persistent significance. The analysis suggests that the objections against ethnophilosophy will become interesting only to the extent that they succeed in integrating it. By depicting the major weakness of ethnophilosophy, the study lays the ground for such a salutary integration.

The study assigns an important place to Western discourses on Africa for the obvious reason that much of what passes for African philosophy is a reaction to those discourses. However, it avoids giving a monolithic idea of Western views by remaining attentive to the fact that ethnophilosophy as well as various African philosophical schools have tapped many of the findings of anthropologists.

Even though the issue of the existence of a precolonial African philosophy and the subsequent debate on the otherness of the African subject constitute the major themes of the book, reflections are not restricted to a speculative treatment of these themes. On the contrary, the book directly tackles the issue of African modernization and development, and so ventures into political and sociocultural problems with the firm intention of showing how philosophical concepts permeate such problems. Under the banner of the imperative of modernization, it discusses the issue of elitism as well as the tension between the nation-state and ethnicity, just as it probes into questions of culture change and construction of identity.

But more yet, in conjunction with the problem pertaining to the existence of African philosophy, the book delves into the tremendous issue of the foundation of civilization. In particular, it asks the question of knowing what makes a given civilization viable and sustainable. Taking the misfired modernization of Africa as an indication of its inability to create a viable civilization, the book diagnoses the problem as the failure to bring together myth and rationality and attributes the inability mainly to the paralyzing effect of the colonial discourse on the African mind. The diagnosis assumes that myth confers a transcendent meaning on existence with the consequence that rationality is understood as a device for going after the promised transcendence. The split and subsequent misunderstanding between ethnophilosophy and professional philosophy as well as the notorious gap in Africa between theory and practice are the most salient manifestations of the paralysis of the African mind.

Philosophy becomes an important key to understanding Africa inasmuch as all the impediments point to the necessity of decolonizing the African mind. The rethinking of philosophical concepts in the direction of deconstruction for the purpose of achieving mental decolonization teams up modernization with philosophical questions. Nothing can be accomplished in the direction of overcoming marginality unless Africa repositions itself by means of philosophical premises free of Eurocentric conditionings. Decolonization is primarily a philosophical problem, given that the emancipation of the African mind from the debilitating ascendancy of Western *episteme* is its inaugural moment.

Acknowledgments

Special thanks go to my dear friend Robert Ginsberg, who encouraged me to write this book while he was Executive Editor of VIBS. His encouragement was one of the motives that sustained my effort to write the book. I also express my deep gratitude to a dear colleague Joseph C. Kunkel, who applied his consummate skill of editor to significantly improve the book both in terms of clarity and correctness. I take this opportunity to thank Paul Benson, the Chair of the Department of Philosophy, for his administrative support, and Linda McKinley for all her professional assistance in the preparation of the camera-ready copy of the book.

One

WESTERN DISCOURSES ON AFRICA

The first condition to understand the problems and contents of African philosophy is to refer to the colonial narrative about Africa, there being no doubt that African philosophical reflections are all attempts to refute the degrading views developed in the West to justify slavery and colonialism. Central to the colonial discourse and the justification of colonial rule is the hierarchical notion of human races with its blunt promulgation of the superiority of the white race over all other peoples. However, another facet of this Western discourse proved nagging in default of being equally influential. It came out against the colonial idea of hierarchy through the rejection of the notion of human races or the affirmation of non-gradable pluralism. This chapter studies these two aspects of the Western conception of Africa with the view of laying the theoretical ground for the African responses.

1. The Invention of the "White Man"

Let me begin by underlining that the Western attempt to degrade Africans has required the prior embellishment of the "white man." Grant that the notion of primitive Africa is a construct of Eurocentric concepts, and the logical precedence of the invention of the "white man" over the invention of Africa springs to mind, given that the inventors must first believe lies about themselves before they give credence to the demeaning descriptions of Africans.

A. The Prelogical as Opposed to the Rational

No need to go into fussy research to lay hands on the method used to invent the "white man." All the ingredients are found in the thinker who is universally believed to have codified the colonial discourse, namely, Lucien Lévy-Bruhl. One of the leading French ethnologists of his time, Lévy-Bruhl is the author of *Primitive Mentality* and *How Natives Think*, two books in which by an array of arguments and alleged facts he endeavors to draw a line of demarcation between the West and non-Western peoples. The leitmotif running through his analyses is that the dominance of logical thinking distinguishes the "white man" from the rest of humankind. Let us briefly review the main arguments.

To herald the radical nature of his study, Lévy-Bruhl begins by stating the need for a new terminology. If we suppose that similar mental functions are found in all human aggregates, the same terminology can be used with the understanding that "'savages' have minds more like those of children than of adults."[1] But if we assume that otherness instead of immaturity characterizes the non-Western peoples, then the terms and classifications derived from the mental study of Westerners "are not suitable for those which differ from them; on the contrary, they prove a source of confusion and error."[2] Confusion dissipates if the notion of "*mystic*" or "*prelogical*" mental activity is opposed to the logical thinking of the West.[3]

One reason for not assimilating the thinking of non-Western peoples to childlike mentality is their similarity to the "white man" in terms of physiological development. "Undoubtedly they have the same senses as ours . . . and their cerebral structure is like our own," concedes Lévy-Bruhl.[4] Better still, outside the collective representations, that is, when the primitive is taken as an individual, he finds that the primitive "will usually feel, argue and act as we should expect him to do."[5] To get hold of the difference, we must venture, beyond the physical constitution or properties, into the manner of thinking, into the strange laws governing the mind of the primitive.

What is most striking to Lévy-Bruhl about the mystic, prelogical character is the subsequent inability of the primitive mind to think of the physical as physical. This means the prevention of pure cognitive representations in favor of collective representations in which the cognitive element "is found blended with other elements of an emotional or motor character, coloured and imbued by them, and therefore implying a different attitude with regard to the objects represented."[6] Whereas in the West pure intellectual concepts are obtained through the retention of the cognitive element to the detriment of the affective side, in non-Western societies some such purification is not sought so that a cognitive attitude toward objects is never achieved. The mixture of intellectual elements with affective reactions postulates occult forces, which hinder the apprehension of material phenomena in a physical and causal fashion. Not only are these mystic entities imperceptible to the senses, but they also induce the mind to arrange concepts with a total disregard for the elementary laws of logic. Thus, the same entity can be classified both as a person and an animal, just as the same person can be simultaneously in two different places, or be objectively active in reality as well as in dreams.

For Lévy-Bruhl, prelogicality and mysticality are "two aspects of the same fundamental quality, rather than two distinct characteristics."[7] The first aspect refers to the contents of the thought, that is, to the permeation of the physical with mystic powers incarnating the fear, hope, and religious awe of the primitive. The second aspect concerns connections between ideas, which because they implicate occult forces, operate independently of logical laws. The social and technological retardation of native peoples is wholly due to this inability to think physically and logically. Some such turn of mind is adamantly opposed to scientific thinking and technological orientation; it is only fit to wallow in magic, thereby perpetuating the subordination of natives to mysterious forces. In the words of Lévy-Bruhl, "the prelogical mind does not objectify nature thus. It *lives* it rather, by feeling itself participate in it, and feeling these participations everywhere."[8]

The statement according to which colonialism portrayed Africans as an inferior race to justify the need for a tutor, however disparaging, was somewhat optimistic and condescending. Through prolonged tutorship, Africans could hopefully acquire, though in a reduced version, the moral and intellectual virtues of the West. In refusing to derive the inferiority of colonized peoples from immaturity, Lévy-Bruhl, for his part, ascribes their backwardness directly to alterity. Their mind does not work like its Western counterpart; nor does it follow the same principles. The whole purpose of colonialism becomes problematic, since the possibility of closing the gap with the West, the so-called civilizing mission of colonialism, is thereby lost. The service that inferior races owe to the superior one is all that is left. The idea of other races being slaves by nature to the superior race could not have been better intimated.

What is quite astonishing is the existence of scholars—African or Western opponents of colonial methods—who readily endorse the claims of the colonizer. In the debate over the existence of African philosophy, the term ethnophilosophy designates the position of those African scholars who assent, directly or indirectly, to the idea of African otherness. Because it provides "a revamped version of Lévy-Bruhl's 'primitive mentality,'" ethnophilosophy is accused of being nothing less than a "secret accomplice" of colonial and neocolonial designs.[9]

Be it the idea of vital force as the supreme ontological principle of Bantu thinking, as expounded by Placide Tempels, or the predominance of emotion in the African thinking process, as upheld by Léopold Sédar Senghor, the truth remains that these definitions of African mental attitudes do no more than bolster Lévy-Bruhl's allegations. What is to say that for the Bantu force "is inseparable from the definition of 'being'" if not to soak reality in a mystical ambience?[10] In what sense does Senghor's statement that the European has toward the object "an objective intelligence," whereas the African Negro "*feels* it," differ from the descriptions of Lévy-Bruhl?[11] In all these assertions, emotion and occult forces do pervade the African perception of reality to the point of obstructing the rise of rational thinking.

The coming chapters will deal with the real meaning of this apparent endorsement of the colonial discourse. In the meantime, let us concentrate on the task of exposing the considerable part of self-illusion inflating the belief in the exclusive rationality of the "white man." For prior to the attempt of refuting what colonialism and anthropology said about Africa, we face the question of knowing whether the self-portrait of Europe is not itself an invention. The question sets the proper stage for revealing the strengths and side-slips of the ethnophilosophical discourse, given the correlation between the Western definition of the "white man" and the African response.

B. The Myth of the "White Man"

Limiting again my investigations to Lévy-Bruhl's formulations, many instances show that we are dealing with an illusive idea of the West. To begin with, his definitions abound with contradictions denoting now his hesitations, now his involvement in pure fantasies. Already, the rage with which the idea of the distinction of the "white man" is pursued betrays so idiosyncratic a notion that it repels rationality by abjuring universality. Hardly is it possible to pin the label "rational" on an entity that so loudly cries for exclusiveness. Further, the theory of primitive peoples frankly hesitates between linear and divergent conceptions of evolution.

When Lévy-Bruhl dismisses the identification of the primitive with a child, his conception seems to espouse the idea of different types of human beings. However, sometimes he reverts to a linear, stage-type of difference. Such is the case when, speaking of the perception of reality, he says: "ours [the Western perception] has ceased to be so," that is, of being impregnated with mystic notions.[12] It cannot cease to be mystic unless it was once mystic, and this brings back the usual evolutionary gap between the civilized and the primitive. Likewise, the provision that without the collective representations, the primitive, taken as an individual, is quite able to behave rationally seems to conceive of primitiveness less as a natural state than as an accumulated product of bad habits and misguided thinking.

Though Lévy-Bruhl expresses the need to forge new concepts to portray the primitive, he comes up with commonplace notions, such as, collective representations, mystic and prelogical thinking. Is not prelogical a stage-notion, implying lateness, immaturity in lieu of alterity? As a matter of fact, Lévy-Bruhl does not succeed in thinking the otherness of the primitive: his comparative method cannot but translate difference into superiority and inferiority. Because the primitive is constantly defined negatively, the purpose of the exercise is not so much objective apprehension as the elevation of the "white man" to the rank of the chosen race.

Where the part of invention becomes overwhelming is in the attempt to reduce, if not eliminate, the influence of irrational, mystic thinking in the West. Consider, for instance, what Lévy-Bruhl says about the place of dreams. Unlike civilized Europeans, primitives have full faith in dream. For them, far from being illusory, dream is even "a provision of the future," and so has "far greater significance than to us."[13] The tendency to minimize the part of the irrational to decorate the "white man" with the honors of rationality becomes obvious when we recall how little the affirmation is supported by facts. Whether we take the Bible, the foundation of European Christianity, or the ordinary belief of the Westerners, the role of dreams as revelation of profound truths is largely accepted.

What, then, should we say when a thinker, such as Sigmund Freud, who is the product of Western rationality, pleads for the need to take dreams seriously? Interestingly, Freud notes, "the view of dreams which came nearest to the truth was not the medical but the popular one, half involved though it still was in superstition."[14] So his purpose is not to question the relation of dreams to reality; it is to wipe out the part of superstition by raising the interpretation of dreams to the level of science. While this may mean that dreams are not caused by demoniac and divine powers, still it preserves the important idea of dreams being revelations of deeper truths that are inaccessible to conscious life. Through his conviction that dreams are *"disguised fulfilments of repressed wishes,"* Freud salvages much of the popular belief of the West, which is similar to that of "the primitive."[15]

In addition to refuting the assertion that the "white man" does not give credit to dreams, the position of Freud suggests that the attribution of greater significance to dreams, and not its dismissal, is rationally justified. In light of rationality turning out to be the acceptance of irrationality, Lévy-Bruhl's attempt to lessen the place of dreams in the "white man's" thinking appears as an overstatement of rationality that is backfiring. Blaise Pascal warns: "he who would play the angel plays the beast."[16]

We can call upon the critical views of Karl Marx as well as those of Friedrich Nietzsche to strengthen the idea that rationality begins with the acceptance of irrationality. The merit of both philosophers is to have exposed how much of the history of the West is the story of irrational beliefs putting on the mask of rationality. Take the history of philosophy itself: does it not relate the manner occult beliefs are paraded as rational statements, as exemplified by the rationalization of religious beliefs in all idealist philosophy? To brag about being rational on top of being unable to recognize the initial irrationality of Western thinking constitutes a double failure that throws the thinking far away from rationality. Genuine rationality begins with the recognition of irrationality, not its denial. This genuineness is then understood as a conquest obtained by the development of a critical relationship with oneself. The main condition to achieve such a critical view is the surrender of all self-flattering images, a condition that Lévy-Bruhl hardly meets.

Similarly, the emphatic affirmation that primitives do not obey the principle of non-contradiction does not pay attention to the controversies generated by the same principle in the history of Western philosophy. Just as many philosophers considered the principle of non-contradiction as a sacrosanct law of correct thinking, so too philosophers who disclose its limitations, some going so far as to suggest the creation of another logic, are not hard to find. A case in point is Heraclitus, who is famous for defending the unity and struggle of opposites, saying, for instance, that "the path up and down is one and the same," or "as the same thing there exists in us living and dead and the waking and the sleeping and young and old: for these things having changed round are those, and those having changed round are these."[17] Closer to our times, Georg Wilhelm Friedrich Hegel and the Marxists contrast metaphysics with dialectics, which they credit with superior intelligence and consider as the apex of Western thinking. Unlike metaphysics which, to quote Friedrich Engels, declares that "a thing either exists, or it does not exist," or that "it is equally impossible for a thing to be itself and at the same time something else," dialectics holds:

> motion itself is a contradiction: even simple mechanical change of place can only come about through a body at one and the same moment of time being both in one place and in another place, being in one and the same place and also not in it.[18]

Granted that those called "primitives" did not have the same understanding when they were transgressing the law of non-contradiction, nonetheless under pain of relegating much of Western philosophical breakthroughs to primitive thinking, the apparent flexibility of "primitives" about contradictions should not be called prelogical.

The mere neglect of the various facets of Western thinking is not the only issue. The strong impregnation of idealist concepts with mystic notions can be established without endorsing the Marxist critique of idealism. For example, what else is at work but a mystic thinking when Plato speaks of the objective existence of a world of ideas? In general, the constant references of idealist philosophers to the role of God and the autonomy of the spiritual together with the use of such notions as the "noumenal world," "the vital impetus," the transcendence of "the idea," show to what extent Western philosophy is fraught with mystic notions, to say nothing of the truth contained in the accusation that much of Western philosophical energy originates from the necessity of rescuing Christian mysticism and ideals from the attacks of science.

The reality about the West is not so much rationality versus irrationality as the coexistence and interaction of the two. May it not be, then, that in the primitive mentality too the two coexist, maybe with the difference that the dominion of irrationality is greater over the "primitive" than the "civilized." At any rate, the denial of irrationality, the stubborn care to reserve rationality for the West and irrationality for the rest of humankind, authorizes us to speak of the invention of the "white man." What is more, the more obstinate the denial, the higher is the irrationality of the classification.

So great is the blinding power of the alleged Western specialness that it prevents Lévy-Bruhl from asking simple though essential questions. If primitive peoples are so completely shrouded in mystic notions that they ignore the laws of logic and causality, the crucial question becomes that of knowing how they manage to survive in so inhospitable a natural environment. From the descriptions of primitives, what we gather is their total powerlessness *vis-à-vis* nature, given their failure to take into consideration its most elementary laws. Had this been true, they would have been wiped off the face of the earth long ago. Lévy-Bruhl cannot recognize this fact because it objects to the myth of the unique rationality of the West.

This survival is exactly what Henri Bergson underlines in his refutation of Lévy-Bruhl's thesis. Without the confidence in the invariability of natural laws, the primitive, according to Bergson, "would not rely on the current of the river to carry his canoe, nor on the bending of his bow to shoot his arrow, on his hatchet to cut into the trunk, on his teeth to bite, on his legs to walk."[19] In all the cases discussed by Lévy-Bruhl, none really stipulates the indifference of the primitive to causal laws. Instead, occult causes are supervenient phenomena: they intervene to explain, not the physical effect as such, but "its *human significance* . . . its importance to man, and more especially to a particular man."[20] Bergson concludes: "there is nothing illogical, consequently nothing 'prelogical' or even anything which evinces an 'imperviousness to experience.'"[21] Better still, he asks us to take note of the "striking . . . resemblance between the mentality of the civilized and of the primitive man when dealing with facts such as those . . . [of] death, illness, serious accident."[22]

Nowhere in the world has magic ever been a substitute for causality. In reality, concerning things that are within their mechanical reach, human beings rely on mechanical laws to obtain or counter material effects. As these effects depend also on wider material connections that are outside their control, they tend to evoke occult forces whose significance is to humanize nature. To be susceptible to human solicitations and influenced by rituals, reality "must appear animated with a purpose."[23]

The function of spiritual entities is this provision of reality with purpose. As scientific knowledge progresses, the mechanical circle grows to the detriment of the magical one, without however displacing it entirely. In short, as an expression of the natural, irrationality remains the forced companion of rationality. Lévy-Bruhl's attempt to draw a hard and fast line of demarcation between the rational and the irrational comes under the heading less of objective study than of self-deceiving thinking. Apart from being a falsification of reality, the rejection of irrationality particularizes and isolates "the white man" from the rest of humankind. So exclusive a rational attribute shakes off universality, and contains its refutation.

C. Anthropology: Myth and Reality

Nietzsche's critical study of Western idealism shows how an ideal world is constructed and projected onto the real world. The result of this projection is the depreciation of the real world: termed "appearance" as opposed to truth, the visible world becomes the realm of change and deceit while the ideal world is described as eternal and perfect. Nietzsche finds that moral ideals provide the ultimate justification for the separation and opposition of the two worlds. Behind the construction of the ideal world as unchanging, immaterial, and perfect is a moral aspiration of an ascetic type that takes delight in declining sensuous life. What knowledge portrays as the opposition of truth to falsity, of essence to appearance is, therefore, the aspiration for a morality hooked on an ascetic ideal. The visible being untrue, the good cannot reside in the senses. The purpose of metaphysics, and by extension of its main product, the concept of reason, is to refute the reality posited by the human body. Nietzsche recapitulates the thinking of the metaphysicians thus:

> The senses, *which in other things are so immoral*, cheat us concerning the true world. Moral: we must get rid of the deception of the senses, of Becoming, of history, of falsehood. . . . And above all, away with the *body*, this wretched *idée fixe* of the senses, infected with all the faults of logic that exist, refuted, even impossible, although it be impudent enough to pose as if it were real![24]

Lévy-Bruhl's analyses are all impregnated with the same type of evaluation. Primitives are peoples dominated by passions; their body occupies the central place in their thinking to the extent of stifling rational thinking. Reason has not yet established its power over the body so that emotion dominates even in operations that are supposedly intellectual. According to Western canons of evaluation, this preponderance of the body denotes a lower rank in the hierarchy of being. To call primitives prelogical is the same thing as saying that they are sensuous. Their inability to control sensuousness explains their failure at dissociating the intellectual from the emotional. The superiority of the "white man" is thus supposedly first and foremost moral. Instead of being a question of more or less, such moral superiority involves the quality of the mind.

In thus harnessing Lévy-Bruhl's position to the mainstream of idealist thinking, we secure the means to solve the riddle of anthropology. When African scholars criticize anthropological discourse, more often than not they consider it as a deliberately falsified discourse intent on justifying colonialism. For Paulin J. Hountondji, anthropology is a "pseudo-science."[25] For V. Y. Mudimbe, anthropological statements "speak about neither Africa nor Africans, but rather justify the process of inventing and conquering a continent."[26] The notion of invention brings out the confounding dichotomy between the claims of anthropology as a science and its unsubstantiated findings. So fixed a dichotomy is bound to raise numerous questions.

The dichotomy does not, for instance, explain why European thinking could be so lured as to give credibility to a fictitious discourse. The question is legitimate as African scholars borrow much of their critical weapons against anthropology from Western scholars. Marx, Freud, Nietzsche, and the various schools of structuralism are known to provide the critical apparatus. This raises the question of knowing how the same Western culture could at once produce the imaginary discourse on Africa and the critical concepts exposing its fallacies. More generally, seeing that the same culture produced both anthropology and the scientific method with its tested objective results, under pain of losing a coherent view of the human mind, we must show how anthropology fits into the scientific practice.

To resolve the problem, the first condition is to cease contrasting science with myth. Just as metaphysics inspired rationality and science, so too the myth of the "white man" can set off a scientific practice intent on validating its belief. This suggests that the same process of construction and objectification is active in the scientific study of nature as well as of human societies and cultures. However, while natural objects passively conform, in the Kantian sense of the word, to the process of objectification, human beings can protest against objectification, thereby nullifying its procedure and outcomes. Through such protest, human beings invent themselves anew so that transcendence defines them better than the possession of fixed characteristics.

Jean-Paul Sartre gave a striking formula for this transcendence when he said that in the case of human beings "existence precedes essence."[27] Unfortunately, more often than not people let themselves be defined externally; in such cases, they surrender their freedom and give in to submission. For the purpose of objectification is to bring the object under control, which when applied to human beings amounts to the negation of subjectivity. Even so, subjectivity does not go away. Sartre judiciously remarks, "if I do not choose, I am still choosing" by refusing to choose.[28]

The ineluctability of choice sets the purpose of Lévy-Bruhl's dichotomy: it elevates the white race above the other races and calls for a hierarchical combination, the very one that justifies the ascendancy of the logical over the prelogical. That is why going beyond mere difference, his definition establishes a contrast between the primitive and the "white man." Such a binary opposition invites an articulation in which the hegemony of the logical race supplements the deficiencies of the primitive. According to most theories, economic reasons explain in the last instance the colonial conquest of Africa. Far from me to deny the importance of economic drive, still some theories suggest that Europe could have obtained higher economic returns if it had avoided the cumbersome and inhuman practice of political and cultural subjugation and opted for the development of the continent through free economic exchanges. The soundness of the argument indicates how feasible the idea was. But, the theory of colonialism retorts, the rivalry between the major

European powers obstructed the option for free economic relations with Africa: the protection of economic interests favored the possession of colonies. No sooner is this argument accepted than it goes counter to the principles of liberalism. When, in the name of the free market, some people praise Europe for having destroyed all internal barriers, strange is the way they say simultaneously that Europe had encouraged colonization.

To avoid the contradiction, theoreticians of colonialism must concede that the "white man" is a myth, an invention, and as such in need of substantiation. The trend toward colonial conquest and anthropological discourse thus crops up from the core of the myth. One thing cannot be taken away from the myth, to wit, its compulsion to look for validation. So that, the justification for subjugating non-Western peoples instead of engaging in free economic exchanges emanates from the perceived otherness of these peoples, which otherness justifies the hegemonic position of the West. The myth of the "white man" calls for the attribution of otherness to non-Western peoples, and subjugation constitutes its validation following the scientific criterion of successful practice as a confirmation of truth. While anthropology establishes the otherness of non-Western peoples, conquest confirms materially the superiority of the "white man."

To understand the possibility of this inversion of myth into rationality, we must brush aside the idea of a deliberate falsification of reality. The concept of ideology, of false consciousness, as conceptualized by Marx and Engels, is liable to bring clarification into the matter. According to Engels:

> ideology is a process accomplished by the so-called thinker consciously, it is true, but with a false consciousness. The real motive forces impelling him remain unknown to him; otherwise it simply would not be an ideological process.[29]

Ideology is then an internal deception unnoticed by the author. It is no lie because individuals who lie know they are lying. Ideology is not a mere fantasy either, since it has connections with reality. The illusion is not about the object; it is first of all in the consciousness thinking the object. This consciousness has illusions about itself, about its motives and nature. As a result, what such a consciousness does materially does not coincide with its thinking. The thinking interprets practice differently, more exactly, ideally. Thus, it veils economic pursuits with lofty ideals, and private property becomes a natural right, the state of the ruling class the defender of the general interest, and colonialism a civilizing mission.

This concealment was apparently the state of mind of Europe when it undertook the conquest and study of native peoples. The myth of "the white man" invents otherness as the lower rank of human essence while anthropological studies and colonialism provide the concrete practices of its confirmation. This false consciousness explains both the sincerity of the belief in the superiority of the white race and the possibility of an objectification of Africa. After all, the achievement of objective results in the pursuit of mythical ideas is not infrequent. The development of rational thinking in an atmosphere heavily loaded with idealism is the very history of Europe. The ideality of the false consciousness explains the birth of an objectivist and conquering practice. Thus, through the dualistic conception of mind and body—an idea that goes back to Christian beliefs—René Descartes fostered the necessary detachment enabling him to grasp matter as a mechanical reality.

This idealist inspiration of Western philosophy highlights the main purpose of my approach, which is to exhort Africans to reconcile themselves with mythical thinking if they mean to play any meaningful role in the world. W. E. B. Du Bois wrote: "no people that laughs at itself, and ridicules itself, and wishes to God it was anything but itself ever wrote its name in history."[30] The realization that the so-called European exclusive rationality is more an invention than a distinct characteristic should liberate Africans from the need to define themselves in terms acceptable to the "white man."

African critique of anthropology boils down to a denial of its descriptions of Africans on account of nonconformity with the criteria set by the "white man." As a result, the illusion of the "white man" is reproduced; worse, Africa is suppressing all its driving impulses just to conform to an idea of humanity whose censorship of irrational drives is anything but true. The characteristics of the "white man," such as, wholly rational, ascetic, and conquering, become models of behavior that Africans must imitate by surrendering their right to freely define themselves. Some such exhortation transpires in Hountondji when, refusing the notion of African alterity, he asks for the inauguration of philosophical systems which are African only by "the geographical origin of the authors rather than an alleged specificity of content."[31] Is it surprising if, as a result of this ideological emasculation, Africa becomes unable to cope with the modern world?

Take the critique of ethnophilosophy by those African philosophers called "professional philosophers." Whether they refer to Tempels's attribution of the notion of vital force to Africans, or John Mbiti's exclusion of the future from the African notion of time, or Senghor's view on the predominance of emotion in African thinking, none of these thinkers escapes the charge of endorsement of colonial discourse. Instead of inciting further research, the slightest suggestion of African difference arouses indignation. Yet such should not have been the reaction of African scholars, given their propensity to liken the idea of the "white man" to a false image. Whatever the idea may otherwise signify, for sure it cannot be used to define the humanness of Africans. In return, Africans should have suspected that what the "white man" despises probably contains a grain of truth for everybody else. Once the idea of the "white man" is taken seriously as an invention, a wide possibility of defining themselves in a creative way opens to Africans. As we shall see, despite its numerous shortcomings, negritude was the first attempt to bend the anthropological discourse in the direction of self-creation.

2. Western Attempts to Make Sense of Africa

Lévy-Bruhl's assimilation of primitive mentality to a prelogical form of thought was bound to generate objections in Western academic circles. Though few in number, these objections represented remarkable efforts to intersperse the triumphant march of Eurocentrism with a pluralist notion of human beings. A clear demarcation of these efforts from the evolutionist trend of thought helps to bring out the remarkable influence that these Western scholars had on African thinkers in their responses to the colonial discourse.

A. Demystifying Reason

No sooner had the Western triumphant and confident march toward progress recorded its first impressive victories than doubts were heard as to the intrinsic validity of the whole project. The two notions on which the Enlightenment had build its philosophy of history, to wit, the idea of reason and the progressive march toward freedom, which stood for the unquestionable superiority of the Western model of life, were never entirely successful in dismissing doubts and interrogations. A most memorable moment of this skepticism is the dissenting position of Jean-Jacques Rousseau on the notion of progress. To the question in 1750 by the French Academy of Dijon of whether the restoration of the sciences and the arts had served to purify or corrupt manners and morals, Rousseau flatly responds in a notorious discourse: "our souls have become corrupted in proportion as our Sciences and our Arts have advanced toward perfection."[32]

Rousseau defends his objection against the belief in progress by a comparative study of modern life with the life of those called primitives whose noticeable trait is their apparent indifference to the ideal of science and the refinement of civilization. While these peoples, "protected against this contamination of vain knowledge, have by their virtues wrought their own happiness and the model for all other Nations," modern civilization merely multiplies and expands the vices of greed, luxury, and inequality.[33] Consequently, the modern human being is completely unhappy. The submersion of human life in ever-increasing vices simply annuls the benefits of technological advances. The proliferation of vices and the engulfment in an artificial and frenzied style of life give evidence of estrangement from the right path to human fulfillment.

Rousseau's defense of the primitive peoples rests on the assumption that nature created human beings good so that the closer human societies remain to nature the better their chance is of fulfilling the end of human life. Hence the need of the modern person to fall back on the primitive peoples to understand the real aspirations of human nature. Let alone being a retarded race, primitive peoples represent the prototype of the human essence, the pure form before the deformation imparted by the so-called civilization. Rousseau insists: "it was not owing to stupidity that they [simple peoples] preferred other forms of exercise to those of the mind."[34]

The claim that native peoples are good because they are ignorant or innocent, as children are, does not see their goodness as a positive and deliberate choice. The truth is that while modern human beings opted for the artificial life called civilization, thereby biding farewell to the advantages of natural life, wiser peoples have preferred to stay close to nature, which harbors the secrets of human happiness. Their goodness is not due to their undeveloped nature, but to the positive understanding that since "man is naturally good," the best mode of life is the one that follows nature.[35]

Anticipating the dismissal by some contemporary anthropologists of the Western discourse as a tissue of inventions whose purpose is to marginalize non-Western peoples, Rousseau reiterates his suspicions about the credibility of the description of primitive peoples given by Western travelers. In one of his replies to objections, he characterizes these travelers as "more interested in filling their purses than their heads," and adds that "all of Africa and its numerous inhabitants, as remarkable in character as they are in color, still remain to be studied; the whole earth is covered with Nations of which we know only the names, and yet we pretend to judge mankind!"[36] Contrast this appeal to study other peoples and learn from them with the Eurocentric arrogance of Hegelianism and evolutionism. By insisting that the alleged superiority of the West only hides moral degradation and a wandering course, Rousseau imputes the major omission of human happiness to the whole Western civilization.

With deep roots in Rousseau's thinking, the other tradition of Western philosophy that challenged the haughtiness of the West is the spiritual movement known as romanticism. One facet of this complex movement believes that Immanuel Kant's *Critique of Pure Reason* correctly establishes the limits of rational knowledge while corroborating the existence of a true reality beyond the phenomenal world. The main upshot of this limitation is that rational knowledge is only a superficial, external view of the world, exclusively driven by the need to manipulate objects from outside. However, though Kant is right in saying that the deeper reality of things escapes reason, he forgets that human beings have other possibilities as well, for instance, sentiments and intuition. The latter seem perfectly equipped to penetrate the deeper reality of the noumenal world better than the faculty of reason. Thus, for Arthur Schopenhauer, unlike the superficial view of perception and reason in which the world appears as discontinued collections of separate objects, intuition grasps the world as will, and so views objects as integrated and coordinated sources of activity.

The best illustration of this will is our body. As an object of representation, our body appears as a thing existing in various spatio-temporal relations with other objects. As apprehended from within, we feel it as will. "This will constitutes what is most immediate in his [the individual] consciousness, but as such it has not wholly entered into the form of the representation, in which object and subject stand over against each other," says Schopenhauer.[37] This immediateness involves a different faculty than the intellect, and is properly called intuition. The revelation of the power of intuition protests in advance against the hierarchy established by Lévy-Bruhl: rational thinking is not the highest mental ability; intuition or feeling obtains a deeper view of reality, especially of spiritual realities. This role of feeling endows art with a greater cognitive dimension than science and speculation.

The romantic inspiration has continued through various forms in the West right up to the twentieth century. A case in point is Bergson's philosophical stand in favor of the irreplaceable role of intuition, which alone can go beyond the limitations of rational knowledge. After a series of systematic contrasts, Bergson finds that "*the intellect is characterized by a natural inability to comprehend life*," while "it is to the very inwardness of life that *intuition* leads us."[38] Another important trend is the existentialist protest against the dominance of rational thinking. From Søren Kierkegaard to Sartre, the protest insists on the extent to which reason has little to say concerning the important questions related to the meaning of life.

To limit the protest to Kierkegaard, he notes that the ideal of objective knowledge excludes, by definition, the subject; none of the terms used to describe the world objectively answers the deep concerns of the subject. Hence the imperative to become subjective: it counters the tendency of objectivism to turn the truth into an object. In this way, meaning returns to truth, since "for a subjective reflection the truth becomes a matter of appropriation, of inwardness, of subjectivity, and thought must probe more and more deeply into the subject and his subjectivity."[39]

The existentialist drift into subjectivism was spurred on by the spectacle of the civilized world being dragged into the insanity of two successive and most destructive world wars, with at its peak the rise of fascistic theories and regimes. In light of the butchery of these modern wars, the naive belief in progress became indefensible; nay, the harrowing question of knowing whether Western civilization is really representing an ascending and progressive course came into sight. This doubt persuaded many scholars into challenging the characterization of non-Western peoples as inferior and arrested peoples.

Both the rise of the romantic inspiration and the multiplication of protests suggest that the issue of rationality versus non-rationality is a debate internal to the West itself. The diverse outcries against an excessive rationalist trend suppressing the role of sentiments and intuition together with the attempt to rehabilitate the so-called primitive peoples attest to the internality of the debate. The dispute has to do with the place of reason and, by extension, of science in the complex issue of civilization and human fundamental aspirations. That Western trends of thought rose against the dominance of reason pleads for a nuanced reception of the identification of the West with rationality.

B. The Discovery of Western Idiosyncrasy

Predictably, the thinkers who judged the trend of Western civilization as far from being satisfactory were warming to the idea of other civilizations as alternatives. The notion of a Western breakthrough was not for them a convincing idea, for they noted progress in some directions but also regress and loss in other equally important aspects of life. So released from the belief in the civilizing mission of the West to which most Westerners were attached, they came to conceive of ethnology as a spiritual voyage, an acquaintance with the diversity of human nature, and a discovery of new and alternative modes of life. As one author explains, "dissatisfied at home and questing abroad," the anthropologist "is a scout sent out by a civilization in turmoil to find a resting place and learn the lay of the land."[40]

Implicit in this quest for the primitive is the belief that what in the West passes for universal is only an idiosyncratic development. After the arrogant glorification of Eurocentrism, comes the time of critical evaluation and radicalism. No school of thought incarnates better this critical project than postmodernism, given that "the most general characterization of postmodernism is that its emphasis is on calling into question the foundational concepts at the heart of Western philosophy."[41] For many scholars, the origin of postmodernism lies in "the profound influence of Nietzsche and Heidegger on contemporary Western intellectual life."[42] This influence grows stronger as many Western intellectuals become increasingly disenchanted with socialism and Marx's ideas of socialist revolution without, however, recovering any attachment to capitalism. Postmodernism essentially reflects the "sociopolitical pessimism" stemming from the clear impression of a civilization caught in a deadlock.[43] In addition to undermining the confidence of the West, the conviction encourages the belief that Eurocentrism offers no other outlets than the frenzy of capitalist pursuits. In light of this disillusionment, the trend of thought so far followed has to be altered: abnormality shifts from other cultures to that of the West and it becomes "increasingly tempting to contrast the West as a whole with the rest of the world as a whole."[44]

Such repeated references of Martin Heidegger to "the end of philosophy" and to the primacy of "questioning," together with his recurring allusions to "the oblivion of Being" and his diagnosis of the West as having "exhausted its possibilities," describe a situation of deep crisis that reaches a stalemate. Instead of extolling Europe's advanced stage—behind which the rest of the world is lagging—the diagnosis depicts an abnormal trend, which, on top of being singular, forces the rest of the world into a futureless process. The Western deadlock entails the rehabilitation of Africa by stripping the West of its pretension to be a model. No need for Africans to engage in the defense of Africa: the West is pleading guilty and the disparagement of Africa is only a misrepresentation of its phantasms.

Heidegger corroborates the idiosyncrasy of the West by a sustained analysis of its mode thinking. For him, the essence of the West lies in its particular way of thinking being, which explains its uncommon technological leaning. As Richard Rorty elucidates, this particular way flows from

> the separation between the "what" and the "that." This separation between what a thing is in itself and the relations which it has to other things engenders distinctions between essence and accident, reality and appearance, objective and subjective, rational and irrational, scientific and unscientific and the like—all the dualisms which mark off epochs in the history of an increasing lust for power, an increased inability to let beings be.[45]

These dualisms inaugurate the age of the world picture, an age in which Westerners entirely surrender all other possible relationships with being except the one targeting power and conquest. This pathological lust for power and domination defines the essence of Western idiosyncrasy. As such, the lust invalidates the promotion of the West to the rank of the most advanced stage, just as it rejects the idea of a unilinear process of universal evolution. That the goal, the *raison d'être* of humanity is the conquest of nature can never be proven. Other cultures define humanity's relationships with nature in different terms, and their definition is no less valid than the goal of conquest. The definition is even wiser, given the Western impasse.

Specifically, what explains the shift in the West of the question of ontology from the fact of being to that of a picture or a representation is none other than the precedence of the preconceived idea or project to the bare reality of being. In the words of Heidegger, world picture

> does not mean a picture of the world but the world conceived and grasped as picture. What is, in its entirety, is now taken in such a way that it first is in being and only is in being to the extent it is set up by man, who represents and sets forth.[46]

Even the approach most committed to studying things objectively, namely, the scientific approach, implicates this kind of projection. Contrary to the received idea describing scientific experiment as the process of learning from nature, Heidegger shows that the particularity and power of modern science derive from studying nature through a projected plan. The whole purpose of an experiment is to see the extent to which facts of nature either verify or deny the preconceived idea. This precedence of the plan in the Western dealings with nature demands the reversal of the historical order. Though modern technology is admittedly a product of modern science on the grounds that science chronologically preceded the production and use of machines, from the viewpoint of imparting the inspiration, modern technology is "historically earlier" to science.[47] How otherwise could we understand the primacy of the world picture over the fact of being if not as evidence of nature being interpreted through a preconceived project, the very one handing it over to a Promethean inspiration?

What is wrong, we may ask, with this desire for empowerment? According to Heidegger, its major drawback is that the way being is conceived impacts on the manner human beings understand themselves. The desire to conquer nature entails the conception of human beings as a subjectivity whose consequence is that everything appears as a human construct. The revelation at the heart of knowledge of a preconceived plan turns all human conceptions into subjective views with no bearing on reality and truth. Such is the adversity of the lust for domination that "it seems as though man everywhere and always encounters only himself."[48]

To admit that the price for domination is the relativization of knowledge is to open our thought to the idea that other ways of relating with the world exist as well as to acknowledge the different choices that sustain them. Though these other ways may not be as efficient in providing control over nature as the Western orientation, they may reveal ways of being and thinking that drag human beings out of their narrow subjectivity. For instance, unlike the conquering model, poetry suggests a different mode of revealing being: by letting things be, it discovers and glorifies their inner beauty, and so incites the mind to transcend the mere desire to control and dominate. This incitement to transcend subjectivism reconverts the human essence from "the lord of beings" to "the shepherd of Being."[49]

This Heideggerian analysis draws much of its inspiration from Nietzsche's anatomy of the Western mental orientation. What makes Nietzsche's insights particularly original and illuminating is the demonstration of the extent to which the lust for domination engulfs the human person as well. Western ethical and religious ideas are so many ways of establishing within the human person the antinomy of domination and servitude. The dualisms of mind and body, pleasure and duty, nature and culture, good and evil, are nothing but the manner one aspect of the human person, considered superior, noble, and good, is set against another part, considered inferior, low, and evil. In this uninterrupted conflict between the two components of the same person, ethical life is how the superior part maintains its dominance over the lower part. The opposition of true being (soul, spirit) to false or apparent being (the body), characteristic of the metaphysical form of thinking, authorizes this mode of evaluation. Thus metaphysicians say:

> things of the highest value must have a different origin, an origin of *their own*—in this transitory, seductive, illusory, paltry world, in this turmoil of delusion and cupidity, they cannot have their source. But rather in the lap of Being, in the intransitory, in the concealed God, in the 'Thing-in-itself'—*there* must be their source, and nowhere else!—[50]

The goal of dominance has brought about the admiration of the warrior, but even more so the veneration of the priest. With his resolution to achieve a complete victory over sensuous life, the priest represents the highest model of mastery, the greatest demonstration of the power of the immaterial and the abstract over the material and the sensuous. What is venerated through the priest is the highest value of the West, to wit, the "ascetic ideal."[51] Because asceticism combines metaphysics and morality, it is the consummation of the victory over false being and sensuousness. No better way exists to denounce falsity than to say no to life even as it promises pleasure. The secret of this denial is none other than the achievement of a greater sense of power through the generation of an inner conflict that unleashes, in the words of Nietzsche, "the resentment of an insatiate instinct and ambition, that would be master, not over some element in life, but over life itself."[52]

C. Postmodernist Inferences

The understanding of Western culture as a particular and aggressive drive reiterates the eccentricity of Western mental orientation and mode of life. In particular, if, as emphasized by both Nietzsche and Heidegger, what passes for reason and universality is a product of an idiosyncratic inspiration, the conclusion that knowledge, including scientific knowledge, is an objective apprehension of things can no longer be made. This lack of objectivity is not caused by a faulty usage of the mind; it is due to the fundamental fact that all knowledge is a construction, that the so-called objective reality is a made up, subjective product. Alluding to the deconstruction theory, Michael Paul Gallagher writes:

> all reality is like a text, open to a myriad of conflicting interpretations. Instead of the "modern" assumption that objectively correct answers are possible, we are all caught in a "prison house of language," where rela-

tivism replaces any rationally ordered world. Meaning, if it exists at all, is created by us and is always in flux.[53]

If a material fact implicates construction, then how much more so may it be with social and cultural realities. Such a deep-going relativism of concepts and views spares nothing; it even challenges the entrenched belief in personal identity. In place of the humanism of the Renaissance and the Enlightenment, both based on the centrality of human beings and on the permanence of individual identity as source of human freedom, "postmodernism proposes the 'death of man', in the sense of a radical scepticism about subjective approaches and about the importance given to personality and self-consciousness in Western culture."[54]

Once personal identity as a defining feature of individuals is challenged, the very foundation of Western religious and ethical ideas as well as political systems is seriously shaken. The challenge is greater to the foundational beliefs of modernity. Notably, the universal and progressive course of history by which the Enlightenment had justified and popularized the view of human history as a goal-oriented process implicating distinct stages of realization becomes an untenable belief. Branded universal, these stages were believed to denote the transition from the simple and inferior state of human freedom and knowledge to complex and superior moments of realization. This gradual scheme led to the supposition that Europe represents the highest stage of this evolution with the consequence that European history reveals the course that lagging societies must follow to resume the progressive course of history. Stated otherwise,

> Third World cultures are falsely identified as moving along the same historical evolutionary path as the West, propelled by the same cultural ideals and the same dynamic forces. Both the liberal and Marxist systems subsume Third World cultural processes under universalist theories of evolution that do not apply universally.[55]

The reduction of concepts to constructs seriously undermines this scenario by suggesting that the vision of a universal and unilinear evolutionary course is nothing else than the fraudulent manner Europe so constructs its continuity as to assume the exclusive leadership of the historical process. Otherwise known as Eurocentrism, the true essence of this vision is usurpation, which usurpation is caused by the phantasms of a culture greedy for self-glorification and conquests.

The denunciation of Eurocentrism entails the untenability of the concepts used to describe non-Western societies. As noted by D. A. Masolo, "the historical merit of the postmodernist critique arises out of its questioning of the validity of taking the Western model of rationality as the yardstick for judging others."[56] Such expressions as primitive, backward, and traditional express the fact of other cultures being forcefully taken in tow by the Western path, arbitrarily elevated to the rank of advanced model. Besides decentering other cultures, the towing has the characteristic effect of misconstruing their understanding. In light of relativism urging us to speak of "Western categories," "Western *episteme*," and "Western principles," other cultures emerge "as 'creations' or representations of Western social science."[57]

Because these representations take the West as the model, a major consequence of this usurpation is that "the traditional approaches in Western philosophy systematically exclude and marginalize some stories and experiences."[58] The net result of erecting a model can only be the marginalization of other cultures, their depiction as inferior and lagging cultures. The promotion is a malicious construct in that it authorizes the characterization of non-Western peoples as primitive and savage by placing Europe at the center of everything.

From the marginalization of non-Western cultures, there emerges the justification of domestication, the civilizing mission of the West. This domestication promises the progressive removal of the accumulated obstacles to progress through the assimilation of Western methods and values. Be it noted that the project does no more than revive the premises of Western *episteme* and ethical principles. Just as the separation of essence and appearance in knowledge prepares the dethronement of the apparent being, so too Westernization replaces the false "man" of native cultures with the real "man" as revealed in the West. The operation is how the spiritual principles and rational norms of the West endeavor to take control of a life engulfed in sensuousness, magic, and emotion as a result of failing to emancipate itself markedly from nature and instinctive behaviors.

The highly auto-critical impact of postmodernism achieves more than the disgrace of colonialism through the denunciation of its phantasms; it also moves toward the rehabilitation of the marginalized cultures. Once the universality of the Western trend is contested, the way is wide open to understanding other cultures as legitimate and equally valid alternative forms of life. According to Rorty, once more Heidegger shows the way by suggesting that "the opposite of metaphysics is Openness to Being, something most easily achieved in a pretechnological peasant community with unchanging customs."[59] The paradox is that postmodernism becomes a backward movement that calls for the reevaluation of traditional societies: the disillusionment with the West entails a *de facto* rehabilitation of other cultures. Instead of being backward, these cultures represent different modes of life, other ways of connecting with Being. In misreading and colonizing these cultures, the West was obeying its impulsive urge to make things conformable to its representations. This urge should not come as a surprise: the West could not let these cultures be, any more than it let things be.

All these critical views on Western modernity converge on the major discovery of postmodernism, to wit, pluralism. By denouncing Western universalism and the subsequent imposition of sameness, "postmodernism has rediscovered 'difference' as a key value and relishes in the seeming anarchy of cultural diversity."[60] The radical nature of the postmodernist discovery must be clearly stated. Especially, we must distinguish the discovery from the type of pluralism that refrains from characterizing other cultures as false or backward while considering them as largely commensurate. Because this mitigated pluralism still harbors universalist creeds, it takes differences as superficial deviations against the background of deeper similarities.

Radically different is postmodernism: it takes other cultures as valid alternatives to the Western course. Thus, Ruth Benedict spoke of cultures as being "incommensurable," for "they are traveling along different roads in pursuit of different ends."[61] The rehabilitation of other cultures is thus total, without any restriction, for no culture has a universal status. The commitment to radical relativism implies that all cultures are views taken from different perspectives, and not from different spots or moments of the same line of evolution. As such, they are incommensurable. Postmodernism denounces all forms of reductionism as well as all forms of ranking. The ranking of cultures becomes impossible once the unilinear and evolutionary scheme is rebuffed. When the basis for the defense of Western superiority is removed, a pluralistic view of history forces its way. This pluralistic view of history says that third world countries were following their own course until they were brutally interrupted by the West and taken in tow. May it not be, then, that the explanation for the great difficulties that these countries face in coping with modernity lies in this fundamental disorientation imparted by the Western intrusion?

The discovery of relativism and pluralism gives a strong backing to ethnophilosophy. From the viewpoint of postmodernism, it makes sense to speak of non-Western philosophies, better still of the philosophies of cultures alien to technological drive. The irony is that such philosophies may well be more authentic than the Western one, given their endeavor to escape subjectivity, to let being be. At any rate, besides setting aside the temptation to deny any philosophical dimension to traditional cultures, the rise of postmodernism shows how ethnophilosophy crops up from the heart of Western philosophy, from the tear generated by the encounter with relativism. Other ways of knowing and being inaugurate the plurality of philosophy, and so their equal dignity in a decentered world. This filiation of ethnophilosophy to Western philosophy testifies to the seriousness of the African ethnophilosophical school. The precipitation to dismiss ethnophilosophy as an endorsement of colonial discourse should be resisted. The next chapters study some representative moments of African ethnophilosophical trend.

Two

BETWEEN EVOLUTIONISM AND PLURALISM: TEMPELS'S PATH TO HUMAN SAMENESS

The views of Lucien Lévy-Bruhl perfectly explain why many African scholars consider Placide Tempels, a Belgium priest who published a book titled *Bantu Philosophy* in 1945, as "a real revolutionary, both in philosophy and in anticolonial discourse."[1] To the question why an apparently innocuous attribution of philosophy to an African tribe, the Baluba, among whom Tempels did missionary work, is credited with the tremendous effect of having shaken the whole colonial world when all the attribution says is that a group of human beings is exchanging philosophical views, the answer is, of course, to be found in the justification of colonialism.

Conceptualized as a civilizing mission, the colonial rule rests on the assumption of the inferiority of the colonized, who are consequently offered the benefit of a tutorial that would pull them out of their primitive life. Philosophy counts as a compelling piece of evidence, since the inferiority is established on the strength of the total absence of rational thinking among native peoples. What can provide greater evidence of irrationality and immaturity than the ineptitude to philosophize because Bantu thinking is not developed enough to use rational and logical canons? Considering this colonial denigration of natives, a book on Bantu philosophy is undoubtedly a clap of thunder in the serenity of the self-righteous colonial world.

The purpose of this chapter is to examine the motives that bring a missionary around to the idea of accrediting philosophical thinking to native peoples. Given that the zeal for the expansion of civilization and the dissemination of Christianity incites the missionary to "impose the law of God that he incarnates" rather than to "enter into dialogue with pagans and 'savages,'" Tempels's turnaround constitutes a puzzling outcome.[2] One sure way of making the reversal intelligible is to suggest that it is a product of the scruples that Tempels feels about his missionary work. In showing how the proselytizer becomes the convert, the study hopes to demonstrate why the religious motive discards the implications of evolutionism and why this same religious goal cannot be content with pluralism.

Tempels is as much eager to show the originality of Bantu philosophical thinking as he is committed to defending the universality of human nature. In his eyes, the success of the missionary work depends on the full rehabilitation of the colonized, which rehabilitation requires, in turn, the recognition of particularism and universalism as two inseparable facets of human existence.

While particularism underscores the historicity of human identities, universalism testifies to the doctrine of monogeny, alone suitable to the Creator. Embracing ethnophilosophy with the understanding that it is not condemned to espouse otherness: such is Tempels's dissident pronouncement.

1. Logic and Conversion

Tempels is quite aware of the difficulty besetting his discovery of an African philosophy. He expects little support and understanding, for high interests are at stake and the conviction of the colonial world about the primitive nature of Africans remains strong. D. A. Masolo says that he "confesses not to be able to convince his readers—the missionaries and colonial administrators—'that a true philosophy can exist among the natives and that there is sense in searching for it.'"[3] To show the contrast between his conviction and the deep-seated prejudice of the colonial world, Tempels gives a clear and straightforward analysis of the exact meaning and implications of his discovery. He writes:

> This "discovery" of Bantu philosophy is so disconcerting a revelation that we are tempted at fist sight to believe that we are looking at a mirage. In fact, the universally accepted picture of primitive man, of the savage, of the proto-man living before the full blossoming of intelligence, vanishes beyond hope of recovery before this testimony.[4]

This loaded awareness, in addition to showing that it is the product of a reflective attitude, also points to a cause that transcends the African issue. No doubt, Tempels is telling us that his discovery refutes the dominant though mistaken view about the primitive nature of Africans. But the insistence and the sense of triumph imply that much more is at stake, of the kind suggesting that his discovery also upgrades the battle for religion in the West. We will not understand the enthusiasm with which Tempels defends his idea of Bantu philosophy unless we read into the defense of Africans the defense of religiosity in general, the connecting link being the encounter with beliefs not yet contaminated by materialist premises.

One facet of this defense begins with an assessment: missionary work in Africa is far from being a success. Tempels agrees with the conclusion of a conference, which "announced the failure of the missionary work of Christianity."[5] However, the fact of failure does not incite Tempels to call for upgraded efforts of conversion. He prefers to reflect on the real cause of the failure. His diagnosis is as simple and direct as it is perplexing: the denial of the existence of a native philosophy is the main reason for the failure of missionary work in Africa. True, Tempels is not alone in making this assessment.

Nor is he the last one to put the blame for the failure of evangelization on the repudiation of African philosophy.

John Mbiti, an African clerical thinker, arrives at the same conclusion. He too speaks of "the tragedy of establishing since the missionary expansion of the nineteenth century only a very superficial type of Christianity on African soil."[6] His diagnosis also tallies with Tempels's view: convinced that "Africans have their own ontology, and to understand their religions we must penetrate that ontology," Mbiti attributes all the derogatory qualifications of African religions, such as, animism, superstition, and witchcraft, to the denial of African philosophical ideas.[7] These derogatory qualifications are responsible for the wrong path taken by the missionary work. Because missionary work failed to respect and understand Africans, it could only offer them a cheap Christianity.

How does Tempels concretely connect the failure of evangelization with the denial of philosophy? In his eyes, the problem resides less in the African resistance to conversion than in the repeated relapses of the convert into traditional beliefs. This continuous resurgence of old beliefs and practices testifies to a superficial conversion that failed to get to the root of Bantu soul. The real meaning of the relapses becomes patent when we note that they are associated with moments of crisis caused by intense sufferings or threats to life. This existential sense of the relapses indicates the depth of the reaction and is evidence of the powerful impact of traditional beliefs on the natives. The relapses mean that the natives tend to rely on traditional beliefs rather than on the lessons of Christianity when real challenges crop up.

The attribution of this defeat of Christianity to an outburst of emotional reactions is the easy trap that analysts must avoid. If Christianity is overtaken by traditional beliefs, the explanation is more logical than emotional. Everything appears as though a repressed mode of thought comes to the rescue of the Bantu because it makes better sense of serious plights and gives more control over them. What resurfaces then is not so much an emotional reaction as an enhanced ability to interpret and face up to a challenging situation. This defensive role of the relapses of the Bantu extends to the relationships with the colonizer. Besides coming to the rescue of the Bantu in times of crisis, traditional beliefs supply them with a protective layer: their sudden irruption disrupts the calm process of acculturation, and so changes the recipient into an enigmatic figure liable to discourage the molding zeal of the "civilizer."

Tempels notes that the same resurgence is observed in the European who gives up Christian beliefs. Such a European "quickly returns to a Christian viewpoint when suffering or pain raises the problem of the preservation and survival or the loss and destruction of his being."[8] How are the relapses of Europeans explained? Even though a great conscious effort to emancipate from spiritual beliefs is exerted, moments of severe crisis are said to conjure up relapses because such beliefs are liable to offer assistance. They enable

Europeans to interpret the situation in such a way that the threat to their life is at once accepted and denied.

We recognize the operation of the philosophy upholding the Christian belief in the survival of the spiritual principle by guaranteeing its autonomy from bodily existence. To quote Tempels, "this view of the visible and invisible world is too deeply ingrained in the spirit of Western culture, not to rise up again irresistibly when the great crises of life occur."[9] While scholars readily concede that the relapses of the African denote a similar resurgence of traditional beliefs, the presence of a philosophy in these traditional beliefs is nevertheless strongly disputed. In the case of the Bantu, the return of irrational and uncoordinated beliefs in lieu of philosophy is maintained.

Tempels is tireless in his efforts to show the untenability of this position. Relapses are impossible if what is resurfacing is not itself a well-ordered, coordinated, and systematic thought. The power of resurgence depends effectively on the characteristics of logicality and systematicness. A pile of unco-ordinated, irrational, and disjoined beliefs could neither return nor overtake the Christian teachings. Seeing how enlightenment easily dissolves disparate ideas, the resurgence manifests a power uncharacteristic of superstition or ignorance. So that, the presence of logical characters points to a transcending view, a paradigm conditioning Bantu beliefs and practices, in a word, a complete philosophy, a conception of life. Assessing the force of resurgence of Christian as well as Bantu beliefs, Tempels writes:

> The persistence of these [Christian as well as Bantu] attitudes through centuries of simultaneous evolution can only be satisfactorily explained by the presence of a corpus of logically coordinated intellectual concepts, a "Lore." Behaviour can be neither universal nor permanent unless it is based upon a concatenation of ideas, a logical system of thought, a complete positive philosophy of the universe, of man and of the things which surround him, of existence, life, death and of the life beyond.[10]

Overlooking of the philosophy underlying traditional beliefs and practices commits the missionary to a mistaken method of conversion that gives primacy to the dismissal of the traditional baggage. The method wrongly thinks that the realization of spiritual vacuum activates the receptivity of the native to Christian teachings. This project to inflict a *tabula rasa* is a consequence of the view describing the African legacy as a collection of "stupid customs, vain beliefs, as being quite ridiculous and devoid of all sound sense."[11] Yet exchange this view for the one that recognizes the presence of a philosophy, and the strategy of conversion automatically changes. Conversion is conceptualized more as an outcome of dialogue than as the molding of a dispossessed soul.

The immediate effect of the recognition of philosophy is to stimulate the disposition to dialogue. Since the possession of a philosophy turns the other into a rational being, the proselytizer naturally sets the exchange at the level of logical discourse. This is to admit that the exposure to the persuasive arguments of Christianity, and not the mere imposition of creed, is alone suitable to a rational being. The first negative impact of the tendency to disparage the heritage of the natives is, therefore, the prevention of communication. Such prevention corrupts the process of conversion by demobilizing the cognitive faculties of the natives. Even though people feel an urgent need to understand as well as to be understood, conversion grows into a shocking and self-defeating monologue. If one does not understand Bantu philosophy, Tempels repeats, "one is entering into no spiritual contact with them. One cannot make oneself intelligible to them, especially in dealing with the great spiritual realities."[12]

We may retort by saying that Tempels's recommendation is hardly unprecedented. Missionary work stresses from the start the need to understand the life and customs of native peoples. So much is this the case that it specifically recommends that "a missionary really needs to become an anthropologist in order to be a good missionary."[13] Going beyond the mere external acquaintance of customs and beliefs, missionaries should strive to get an inner knowledge of the native soul. And they cannot approach native people without becoming familiar with their outward life (language, history, social customs, physical environment) and, most of all, without the knowledge of the inner subjectivity of the native, including "his philosophy of life and—most vital of all—his religious beliefs."[14] All this groundwork intimates nothing less than the transformation of the missionary into an anthropologist.

The imperative to engage in anthropological studies reveals the attitude of missionaries who are no longer equating the beliefs of the natives with mere superstition. Since they take the trouble to study these beliefs, the safest conclusion is to say that they intend to initiate a dialogue. For Tempels, even this revised attitude is not radical enough; it does not really insist on the knowledge of the philosophy. It speaks of philosophy in a weak and loose manner, in the reduced sense of a philosophy of life, not in the strong sense of the presence of a corpus of logically coordinated intellectual concepts. The dialogue must be established at the logical level because logic commands the whole process of understanding and exchange.

Add to this need of logical discourse the fact that mere anthropological studies bring out the alterity of Bantu thinking by the use of a descriptive method committed to underscoring differences. By contrast, the philosophical approach is obligated to dissolve alterity because it pushes for a logical understanding. The task of the philosophical approach is to make a set of beliefs intelligible. It cannot do so without revealing the inner logic of the thinking, and hence getting over its alterity. The Western belief in life after death would have been irrational without the ontological distinction between the visible and the invisible. In the same way, understanding the philosophy of the Bantu is grasping why they act and think as they do so that they cease to be bizarre or folkloric. Tempels concludes:

> ethnology, linguistics, psycho-analysis, jurisprudence, sociology and the study of religions are able to yield definitive results only after the philosophy and the ontology of a primitive people have been thoroughly studied and written up.[15]

Conversion misses its target so long as the right attitude toward the natives is not reached. Take the colonial ideology of treating Africans as children. Had Africans been really children, the failure of the missionary work would have been unexplainable. Just as children are highly malleable, so too would Africans be impressionable and ready to absorb whatever they are told. However, Africans are not children. The presence of the traditional legacy prevents the missionary work from being tantamount to baptizing children. As Tempels clarifies, "it is quite another problem to reeducate men fully formed—or misinformed, if you will—than to begin the education of infants, receptive to any and every impression."[16]

Tempels does not hesitate to unravel all the disastrous implications of the Western attitude. He summarizes them in the statement: "anyone who claims that primitive peoples possess no system of thought, excludes them thereby from the category of men."[17] In what sense is the denial of philosophy a denial of the humanity of Africans? For one thing, the propensity to treat Africans as children is how their full human nature is contested, since grownups cannot remain children without a characteristic deterioration of their nature. For another, this way of treating Africans has the distinctive effect of disfiguring their humanity to the point of making them unable to understand and receive the teachings of the missionary. In a word, the denial of philosophy is a disabling act.

The Western conception and method have been efficient only in creating uprooted people. In their pursuit of a *tabula rasa*, missionaries obtain a mind increasingly impervious to religious appeal, not a fresh, decontaminated mind. The obvious impact of being cut off from the legacy of tradition is the loss of the religious sense; it is not openness to a higher religious appeal. Tempels draws up the balance sheet and concludes: "Of *déracinés* and degenerates the number is legion. Of materialists who have lost their foothold in ancestral tradition without having grasped Western thought and philosophy there are not a few."[18]

This paradox of the missionary work resulting in the propagation of irreligiousness is a consequence of uprootedness, squarely defined as the death of the humanity of Africans. In losing touch with their roots, identity, and history, Africans forfeit all those spiritual organs by which they could understand the teachings of the missionary. In becoming ghosts of themselves, they grow deaf to spirituality. Just as any cultural phenomenon, spirituality exists only insofar as it is transmitted. The assassination of the human is embedded in this negation of the historicity of the African, in this obstinacy to force the African to start from zero. Tempels sees no "graver offence" than this determination to "deprive peoples of their own patrimony, which is their only possession able to serve as the starting point of a higher civilization."[19]

This mordant analysis of uprootedness essentially applies to the educated Bantu, known as the *evolués*, the civilized. Tempels "hated the *evolués*, whom he considered to be bad copies of Europeans," because they represent the final, finished product of the civilizing mission, which for Tempels turns out to be a dehumanizing mission.[20] As an outcome of dehumanization, the *evolués* retain all the evil tendencies of the colonizer in default of being able to assimilate the positive aspects of Western civilization. Failing to reconcile their new way of life with their former native philosophy, which remains intact just below the surface, despite a resolute rejection, the *evolués* are also particularly prone to relapses. Having lost the meaning of life and having no firm footing in Christian beliefs, small wonder great crises cause the irruption of traditional beliefs.

To sum up, missionary work in Africa has only succeeded in spreading confusion and irreligiousness instead of a steady ascent to a firm belief. In light of the *evolués* representing the finished product of what Tempels calls the assassination of "'the man' in the Bantu," the conclusion that missionary work fails in Africa because it generates people who are basically immune to its teachings is unavoidable.[21] In denying the logic of the Bantu, Christian missionaries commit themselves to such illogical outcome. The death of the "man in the Bantu" is also the death of religion.

2. Mysticism and Rationality

Mounting perplexities and suspicions assail Tempels the more he reflects on the unfairness of the treatment of Africans. According to the proponents of African otherness, once the denial of philosophy has firmly established that Africans are not up to rational thinking, the next step is to define the nature of their thinking. As we saw, Lévy-Bruhl could find no other term to make palpable the distance separating Africans from the Western type of rational thinking than to characterize their "mental activity" as "a *mystic* one."[22] Tempels inquires how this demarcation has been justified. He finds that the demarcation between the mystical and the rational is established in reference to an empirical yardstick. That such is the criterion is confirmed by Lévy-Bruhl's further specification: the term "mystic," he says, does not refer to "the religious mysticism of our communities, which is something entirely different," but to "the strictly defined sense in which 'mystic' implies belief in forces and influences and actions which, though imperceptible to sense, are nevertheless real."[23]

Why is Lévy-Bruhl exonerating Western religious beliefs from mystic depravities? And what is his justification for characterizing African beliefs as strictly mystic? The empirical criterion provides the answer. Africans believe in forces and actions that have no empirical reality, whereas the beliefs of Westerners dissociate the realm of the invisible from that of the visible. In avoiding the confusion of the two realms, Western thinking asserts its inner rationality and thus is not mystic, even if it believes in non-empirical entities. For Lévy-Bruhl, the strict demarcation between the empirical and the non-empirical defines rationality.

A separation of this kind does not entail that Western thought is free from mystical leanings. On the contrary, Western thinking argues in favor of the transcendence of the spiritual, thereby elevating the autonomy of philosophy and religion beyond empirical and scientific criteria. Tempels asks: "Is our philosophy based upon scientific experiment? Does it depend upon chemical analysis, on mechanics, or on anatomy?"[24] The answer is "no" because of the generally accepted distinction in the West between the empirical and the transcendental, the visible and the invisible, the concrete and the abstract, essence and appearance, facts and values. The strong contrast established by Lévy-Bruhl between the rational and the mystic is, therefore, anything but persuasive. Both modes of thinking coexist in the Western mind, let alone the one rejecting the other. In the words of Tempels, "the tool of empirical science is sense experience of visible realities, while philosophy does off into intellectual contemplation of general realities concerning the invisible nature of beings."[25]

An important portion of Western philosophy came into being before the birth of scientific knowledge, "at a time when . . . experimental scientific knowledge was very poor and defective, if not totally erroneous."[26] Even so, no scholar characterizes this prescientific philosophy as irrational under the pretext of lacking in scientific backing. Even when a philosophical system openly contradicts scientific theories, no one concludes that the contradiction reflects on its rationality. It remains as valid on its own terms as any other philosophy, so deep-seated is the conviction that "natural sciences can no more refute a system of philosophy than they can create one."[27] True, a philosophy that completely contradicts the empirical laws would be hard to justify, and such philosophy does not exist. The net result of all this is that philosophy transcends the empirical so that the latter cannot be used to question the rationality of philosophy.

If scientific criteria are neither prerequisites nor refutations of philosophical thinking, how comes it, then, that they are used to deny the rationality of African thinking? Obviously, only recourse to a gross subterfuge can justify the denial. When African beliefs are scrutinized according to scientific criteria and declared unfit and savage, while those of the West are allowed to soar above such criteria, the real purpose of this discriminatory treatment is the denigration of the African mind. As far as science is concerned, the bulk of Western philosophy is pure mysticism, since non-empirical principles are used as explanatory notions.

Even in terms of empirical support, Tempels is not prepared to concede. He finds that Bantu philosophy is as realist and critical as any Western philosophy can be. If critical philosophy means a philosophy founded upon observation of reality and deductions, then "Bantu philosophy is, from their [the Bantu] point of view . . . a critical philosophy as rightly so called in our western systems."[28] A little reflection on the implications of the opposite assertion provides the reason. One major implication would be that the Bantu, turning their back on a realistic attitude, have deliberately invented a whole system of thought with no bearing on reality. But why would they burden themselves with a mere fancy? Most of all, from where would this fancy draw its power if it does nothing for them? In order to give credence to one belief in lieu of another, practical and empirical considerations must somehow creep into the choice. If such considerations are presumed absent, then the attachment of the Bantu to a particular set of beliefs remains unexplained. No belief could obtain the confidence of the Bantu without the provision, however narrow and fragile, of a framework of observation and critical evaluation.

Tempels readily considers as legitimate the question of knowing whether the observations and critical deductions of the Bantu are correct. Still, the judgment that the Bantu are alien to critical thinking cannot be inferred even if the observations were entirely false. To be critical is never synonymous to being true; otherwise only one system of philosophy would have existed, and it would have been intolerable that "differing systems of thought should have the word 'philosophy' applied to them."[29] Since to be "critical" does not signify unanimity or exclusion, the fact that the Bantu possess a different system of explanation does not authorize the denial of critical thinking. The Bantu can be critically-minded without being critical of the same phenomena or converging on the same conclusions as the West.

This recognition of the critical side of Bantu thinking has the paramount implication of going against the opinion of those African philosophers who accuse Tempels of endorsing the view of Lévy-Bruhl by conceding a mystical philosophy to Africans. A case in point is Paulin Hountondji, who finds that the very notion of a collective philosophy is how Tempels "was indirectly confirming the contentions of Lévy-Bruhl."[30] More generally, many scholars maintain that, according to Tempels, there are two modes of thought or systems of rationality and two philosophical systems derivable from them: one Western, the other Bantu or African. The former is scientific and proper, the latter intuitive, magical, and contradictory.[31]

Even V. Y. Mudimbe, who understood the real purpose and procedure of *Bantu Philosophy* more than anybody else, warns us that in the book "the affirmation and promotion of African philosophy meant a claim to an original alterity."[32] This imputation explains Mudimbe's reservation as to the import of the book, which, he says, "paradoxically opened some holes in the monolithic wall of colonial ideology."[33] Even though the book questions the Western claim to superiority and the classical method of conversion, the affirmation of otherness could not but reinstate the mission to civilize the Bantu. Because the alleged alterity of the Bantu entails their inability to progress by themselves, the radical departure, Mudimbe concludes, could not go beyond a mere revision of colonial policy.

To be more specific, Tempels's depiction of vital force as the cardinal concept of Bantu philosophy is responsible for the charge of otherness. The concept of vital force seems to place Africans on the opposite side of Western philosophy, since unlike the Western notion of a given and static object, a mysterious and active force appears to animate the African notion of being. For Westerners, as a mere predicate, force is not identified with being. Of all the qualities and features of objects, only the fact of being is not predicable for the obvious reason that any kind of characterization presupposes being. That is why being is the most abstract and universal concept. This method of conceiving qualities and features as attributes sets being as the underlying support, or to quote Aristotle, "the ultimate subject which is not predicated of something else."[34] The reduction of being to a substratum, to a supportive role inaugurates a static and individualized conception of objects that paves the way for a form of knowledge harboring a manipulative intent.

Such is not the manner Africans conceive of being; for them, "force is the nature of being, force is being, being is force."[35] This determination of being as force betrays a conception making qualities and features into attributes of force. Since hierarchy is the mode of existence of force, the conception grasps things and their characteristics as interrelated through a hierarchical order. The universe is thus like one huge tree: as the same vital force emanating from the roots animates all the components of a tree, so too a single force internally differentiating itself according to the order of "primogeniture" runs through all the animate and inanimate phenomena of the world.[36] Just as a seed possesses superior power to the developed organism, generative forces have supremacy over their offspring. The primacy of primogeniture establishes God as the ultimate source of force. It also justifies the cult of ancestors, the power of the old over the young, and of parents over children.

This dynamic, vital link between things and people upholds the belief that a superior force can influence a lower force without any mechanical contact, as postulated by magic, which is then a logical product of the dynamic conception of being. The main implication of the interposition of force is to block the static conception of things. To the extent that force is not an attribute while being an active principle, it turns into an imponderable agency that escapes human control. Hence the charge of mysticism and prelogicality: the identification of being with force substitutes a mysterious entity for the Western notion of extended and manipulable object.

Let us ask ourselves whether a philosophical difference of this nature can really inaugurate the African otherness. Differences on the nature of being proliferate in Western philosophy without thereby invoking the idea of otherness. Starting from the pre-Socratic philosophers, who identified being with water, fire, and the indefinite, up to Plato and the whole trend of idealist philosophers, the arguments have been that what is said about being is truer the less being is extended or equated with the visible. And what should we say about the insistence on the dynamic conception of being of the school of thought known as vitalism? In agreement with the Bantu, this Western school thinks that an inner force animates things beyond their static and extended appearances. This is so true that D. A. Masolo suggests that, despite differences, "Tempels's theory of vital force finds its filiation in the philosophy of Henri Bergson, which is characterized by dualism and dynamism."[37] Clearly, there is not enough to make up otherness on the basis of philosophical differences concerning the nature of being. The entire philosophy of Martin Heidegger is a plea for a new conception of being. Does this suggest that otherness should define Heidegger's philosophy?

In stressing the ontological difference, Tempels was denoting not so much the otherness of Africans as the presence of a universal human attribute endowing Africans with a philosophy of their own. The philosophical difference points to the underlying rational process even as it results in particularized philosophical views. If the colonial denial of African philosophy signified otherness, the negation of that denial annuls otherness. Furthermore, the very attempt to show that the Bantu have a philosophy directs Tempels toward the elucidation of their philosophical difference. No other way exists to refute the colonial denial of philosophy than to display their philosophical originality.

The recognition does not dismiss the philosophical difference, but insists that the disparity stems less from a different mind than from a different conception or interpretation of experience. As a product of reflection, it exhibits philosophical divergences within a shared mentality. *Bantu philosophy*, let us admit, restores to the Bantu what was taken away from them, namely, their humanity, and throws away what was merely pasted onto them, namely, otherness.

A recurring theme in *Bantu Philosophy* is the need to recognize the profound mysticism of Western rationality, which goes even further than the African mysticism by splitting the invisible away from the visible. What does this recognition really mean? It means that in contrast to Léopold Sédar Senghor's assertion that "the *emotive attitude* towards the world . . . explains all the cultural values of the African Negro" instead of reason, Tempels is assuring us that mysticism is Western as much as it is African.[38]

Take the case of Plato. He incarnates Western rationalism, even though he posits the necessary existence of an invisible, non-empirical world. Plato's invisible world is an ontological reality and a principle of explanation of the visible world. In view of this forceful assertion of the independence of the spiritual, is the classification of the Bantu as exclusively mystical and of Plato as wholly rational really legitimate? And what should we say about George Berkeley? According to Lévy-Bruhl's criterion, Berkeley's statement that things being ideas, "the absolute existence of unthinking things without any relation to their being perceived . . . is perfectly unintelligible," should constitute a characteristic expression of a thinking dominated by mysticism.[39] Yet even this complete dissolution of the physical into the spiritual is not enough to deny the rationality of Berkeley's process of thinking. A system of thought can be rational even if it rejects the distinction between the spiritual and the material.

We must yield to the facts: Tempels's target is less the otherness of Africans than their sameness. What he wants to establish is the universalism of mysticism, not the African speciality in mystical beliefs. He denounces the alleged contrast between Africans and Westerners, together with the specification that "in spite of all the abuses and deviations of beliefs, we can trace among them [the Bantu] the operation of sound universal human commonsense."[40] This language in terms of universality and human common sense little supports the idea of African otherness.

To fully appreciate the importance of this universalist conception, we must refer to the philosopher who, to all appearances, has profoundly influenced Tempels, namely, Henri Bergson.[41] In the previous chapter, we saw how, in his effort to refute Lévy-Bruhl's thesis on the prelogical stage of primitive mentality, Bergson came to conceive of mysticism and intelligence as complementary functions, and not as different stages of the evolution of the mind. Accordingly, defining evolution as a progressive elimination of mysticism by intelligence is not correct. Nor is the attribution of intelligence to one category of human beings and mysticism to another category acceptable.

The persistent interaction of intelligence with mysticism in various ways and at different levels is the mode of functioning of the human mind. The net outcome of this conception is that the primitive is not different from the civilized: "the mind works just the same in both cases."[42] If at all costs we must pinpoint differences, we will find them in the amount of knowledge, especially scientific knowledge, which the civilized possess in comparison with the primitive, and not in the way of thinking. So "let us not then talk of minds different from our own. Let us simply say that they are ignorant of what we have learnt," says Bergson.[43]

For Tempels, this amounts to saying that mysticism, a tendency intrinsic to all human beings, grows into philosophy because it inevitably generates the need to connect the visible with the invisible. The task of philosophy or rationality is not to deny the connection or the reality of the invisible, but to articulate the two worlds so as a set of observable, practicable, and knowable objects protrudes from the articulation. The extent and the accuracy of the deployment can vary from one philosophy to another, though its logical and rational nature is common to all the philosophies of the world. That is why the dismissal or refutation of the deployment makes no sense. Whatever be its range, the deployment always signifies an empowerment of human beings through the unlocking of being. The reality of the empowerment cannot be contested; it can only be expanded or exchanged for a different one with the understanding that the old is no less rational than the new.

Both Africans and Westerners draw their inspirations from a mystical source, which becomes philosophy as a result of rationalization. The universal way of achieving rationalization is through the distinction between the invisible and the visible. However, while the West adjoined a secular thinking thanks to a dualistic approach, the African trend was instead prone to emphasize the spiritual side. The dualistic position gave birth to science and the scientific method, leading to an objectification of reality that allows greater control and manipulation. The African rationality proceeded in the direction of inner spiritual reinforcement through the opening of spiritual channels. Some such disparity does not resurrect the African otherness. Both trends are derivations of the same mystical inspiration and both use the same kind of rationality. Instead of analyzing the African difference in these integrating and cross-cultural terms, the West hurried on to give an evolutionary interpretation by turning rationality into an advanced stage reachable only by the surrender of previous lower stages of thinking.

3. Getting Over Evolutionism: Evangelization as Purification

Of all the philosophies and religions of the world, the Christian doctrine should have been the least susceptible to endorse the evolutionary interpretation. Founded on a solid "monogenism" loudly stating: "all men have a common origin," no other belief was better situated to draw all the implications of this essential unity of human beings than Christianity.[44] Tempels had to identify the real culprit that led the Christian missionary astray. His finding is that evolutionism seduces Christian peoples because it flatters their passion. Thanks to his energetic rejection of all those evolutionary expressions suggesting the inferiority of the Bantu, such as, "childish and savage customs," "stupid and bad," and "great children," Tempels puts his finger on the real explanation for the perplexing sympathy of Christian Europe for evolutionary assumptions: the rise of arrogance in Europe.

Arrogance alone prevented the method of conversion to Christianity from being consonant with Christian love. Conversion would have been the work of love, and as such heading for success, had it not imposed a *tabula rasa* on the Bantu under the perverting influence of arrogance. Unless we decide "to love the man as he is, to understand him, to put ourselves in his place, to acquire his mental outlook . . . unless we give proof of this humane love, how can we 'educate' him, or gain his confidence?" asks Tempels.[45] There is no escaping the fact that conversion failed because the proselytizers are no longer impelled by Christian love.

Christian missionaries, Tempels insists, would not have been seduced by evolutionism to the point of disbelieving the fundamental equality and consanguinity of human beings without the spur of arrogance. Because Westerners are "puffed up with pride," they imprudently look down on Africans and invent disparaging expressions to characterize them.[46] The spectacle of Christian missionaries busy with the work of debasing human beings is the product of arrogance flattering itself by the adoption of evolutionism. Is not the scheme of an evolutionary ascent from animism (countless spirits) to monotheism (one supreme God) via polytheism (major spirits) assuring the highest place to Christianity? The more missionaries relegated African religions to animism, superstition, and witchcraft, the higher, they thought, the place of Christianity became. Their insensibility to the anti-Christian nature of their approach was caused by their belief painting the disparagement of African beliefs as an exaltation of Christianity. Narcissism, then, explains why evolutionism seduced the missionary.

The imputation of narcissism clarifies why Tempels expects great corrective effects from the assertion of African philosophy. One sure way of pulling Westerners out of evolutionism is through the deflation of their arrogance. No better avenue exists to obtain a maxim of deflation than to prick on the claim of exclusive rationality. The demonstration that Africans too partake in philosophical thinking should strike at the heart of the Western citadel. Once the arrogance is lowered, it becomes possible to explain to the missionaries why they "should speak 'from one school of wisdom to another,' 'from one ideal to another,' 'from one conception of the world to another conception of it.'"[47] The conviction that Africans have their own philosophy should talk missionaries into saying: "the gods are dethroned, the disinherited stand before us as equals."[48]

Assume for one moment that the gods are dethroned. There follows the complete transformation of the method as well as the goal of conversion. In particular, the sight of the pitiful *evolués* dissuades the missionary from seeking the Westernization of the Bantu. Shifting to the method of dialogue, the missionary will consequently pursue two interrelated objectives: the correction of some of the glaring deviations of the Bantu and the preservation of those beliefs and practices that are healthy and crucial to the Bantu. In this way, conversion orients itself toward the purification of Bantu beliefs the end result of which is the generation of a modern Bantu civilization. In the words of Tempels:

> we must proceed with the Bantu towards its sources to the point at which "the evolution of primitive peoples" was led into a false path by false deductions; and, taking this as our point of departure, help the Bantu to build their own Bantu civilization, a stable and noble one of their own.[49]

Needing emphasis is that missionary work becomes a kind of assistance given to the Bantu in their effort to purify their traditional beliefs. In view of the admittance of failure, only the rudeness of arrogance delayed the salutary shift from the wrong method of emptying the Bantu mind—so as to staff Western beliefs into it—to the practice of a critical regeneration of Bantu beliefs. As though to hammer the obstructing presence of arrogance into the mind of the missionary, Tempels reiterates his question:

> Why do we not assist them to perceive the true Bantu wisdom hidden within its present errors? Why do we not educate them to discover and to venerate the ancient elements of truth ever present in their traditions? Why have we not assisted forward their evolution from this wholesome Bantu starting-point?[50]

One question comes to mind: What is to become of evangelization if the missionary work is thus focused on the task of purifying and salvaging Bantu beliefs? The question provides a glimpse into Tempels's deepest conviction, to wit, his confidence that the purification of Bantu beliefs will converge on the basic tenets of Christianity. Doubtless, the infamous scheme postulating an evolution from animism to monotheism via polytheism is all against the assumption of convergence. As no common denominator exists between the superior Christian beliefs and the savage stage of African religions, the only way to reach the higher stage is through the complete eradication of the lower stage.

Tempels reminds the reader that this evolutionary interpretation has never been proven. To the great dismay of ethnologists of the evolutionary school, serious empirical studies "have revealed that it was amongst the most primitive peoples, those least civilized, that the purest and most sublime idea of a monotheistic God was to be found."[51] Nothing could better expose the narcissistic inspiration of evolutionism than this fact of humanity starting with monotheism, which is then the mark of the Creator. The discovery dismisses the allegation that Africans believe in a remote and indifferent God. The allegation is yet another attempt to confirm at all costs the evolutionary scheme; in reality, the African God is quite active and present, and nothing happens without divine permission. According to the Bantu, God is "the causative agent, the sustainer" of the world and of all its events.[52]

Interestingly, the grant of monotheism as a starting point explains why some elements of Bantu beliefs turned out anti-Christian, such as, magic and witchcraft. If monotheism is the beginning, then antimonotheistic beliefs must have originated as a result of decline or deterioration. This analysis contains the reason why Tempels defends the civilizing mission while criticizing its method and goal. The controversy between the opponents and defenders of Tempels stems from the fact that the opponents are offended by his zeal to civilize the Bantu, while the defenders are sensible to his rehabilitating effort. The point is that both aspects exist, and the oversight of their correlation is responsible for the contradiction describing Tempels now as a promoter of colonial ideology, now as an exponent of African otherness. All one-sided reading fails to see how for Tempels the act of civilizing is also a rediscovery of human oneness.

Tempels's duality is an invitation to reflect on the meaning that he attributes to the word "primitive." What is certainly most unexpected is that Tempels, who so vehemently criticizes the treatment inflicted to Africans, never questions the word "primitive." Far from challenging the expression, he uses it quite extensively. One possible answer is to suggest that Tempels could be thinking of reconciling his respect for the Bantu with his mission to civilize if, instead of the evolutionary sense of inferiority or backwardness, the word "primitive" is made to denote a state of decline or deterioration of a disposition, which was originally fully furnished. This concept of deterioration clears God of any accusation of injustice for creating inferior human beings. It also gives sense to the civilizing mission, which is then a kind of assistance rescuing Africans from a state of decline. The following statement from Tempels can serve as evidence for this interpretation:

> Their [Bantu] original simple philosophy of the influence and strengthening of beings has taken the road to more and more magical applications, which have over-developed and smothered the simple clan community life and clan ancestor worship. We see now more and more individual practices, or practices of life-strengthening, outside and apart from the clan hierarchy. In many Bantu tribes we are confronted with deviations contradicting the original concept of vital influence and of the strengthening of life.[53]

All the more reason for ascribing the theory of degeneration to Tempels is that the theory ties him to those Christian thinkers who thought that the attribution of the retardation of primitive peoples to a degenerative chute is the best way to counter the premises of evolutionism. As one such scholar says, the theory "refutes the sterile and materialistic theories of the evolutionists with the majestic truth of Holy Writ."[54] It preserves the unity of humankind in line with the original Christian doctrine, while putting the blame for backwardness on evil developments occasioned by the straying of some human groups from the right path.

Still, the mere reduction of Tempels's position to the theory of degeneration, appealing though it is, is not consistent with his overall position. It hardly agrees with his outright defense of Bantu philosophy. Why would Tempels make such a fuss of Bantu philosophy if he had assumed that it is a product of degeneration? Two things must be clearly stated here: according to Tempels, (1) the deviations contradict the basic and original beliefs of the Bantu, and (2) most of them are of recent origin so that the core of Bantu beliefs is sane and perfectly admissible. To quote Tempels:

> It would seem, in fact, that the erroneous deviations from and inadequate applications of Bantu philosophy noted in the body of this book are generally of recent date. Older Bantu thought, healthier and more certain, can still be discovered in its most exact form among the most conservative tribes.[55]

These reservations indicate that Tempels has too complex a conception of the primitive to simply adhere to the theory of degeneration.

Since Tempels's conception of evangelization depends on his assessment of the impact of magic on Bantu beliefs, a full clarification is in order. If the Bantu are now inclined to give in to magic and witchcraft more than ever before, the fault, Tempels accuses, falls on the dehumanization of colonial rule. Western arrogance and domination have so diminished and overpowered Africans that they seek refuge in magical beliefs. When people are at bay, their vulnerability to magical beliefs intensifies.

This recent frenzy can all the more be attributed to the European presence since the Bantu had begun by depicting Europeans in terms of force and strengthening of forces. Seeing the extent to which the European seemed to control natural forces, the Bantu had naturally mobilized their own categories of forces and hierarchy of forces to comprehend the European power, thereby exalting it even further. In the face of such display of force, only one aspiration could get hold of the Bantu: "to be able to take some part in our superior force."[56] What should be then the deception and the subsequent fear and despair of the Bantu when they realized that, on top of concealing their secret, Europeans were using their power against them? In this matter, the evidence is overwhelming. Besides the great number of disillusioned *évolués*, Tempels finds that "even among the tribes of the interior, some are to be found who seem to have lost the courage to live."[57] This "intense despair" perfectly explains the outbreak of magical frenzy.[58] The colonial attitude of displaying yet refusing to share power can land sane and reasonable people in the hysteria of magic.

So long as their aspirations are denied, "the masses will founder, in even greater numbers, in false applications of their philosophy; that is to say, in degrading 'magical' practices."[59] The gist of the charge is unmistakable: colonialism drives peoples to magic and then accuses them of being prone to irrational explanations. The proliferation of magic is a dreadful effect of colonial domination, an appalling outcome of the deep disturbance of Bantu soul. Before Tempels, studies of the degrading aspects of colonial rule had denounced uprootedness and the loss of self-confidence as well as of pride, but none, to my knowledge, had mentioned the explosion of magic as an outcome of colonial domination. For these studies too, magic was already out there, extensive and feared. Tempels suggests that this extension and exaggeration are recent and imputable to the very nature of colonial rule. The Europeans have made into a legacy of African culture what was their own fabric, the outcome of their inhuman rule.

The reduction of magic to mere irrational and emotional reactions would be a truncated view. Deep-down, recourse to magic is a perfectly rational act of self-defense and survival. It seeks to counter the attempt to dehumanize the Bantu by broadening the distance between the colonizer and the colonized. Magic is how the Bantu defies Western rationality by refusing to reciprocate in rational terms so long as the demeaning behavior continues. In thus rendering the Bantu incomprehensible to the colonizer, magic offers them an escape from colonial objectification. In a real sense, then, rather than the Bantu Europeans are acting irrationally when they deny or are unable to recognize the rationality of the Bantu.

In light of the recent upsurge of magical practices, Tempels concludes that the method of purification is enough to bring the Bantu to Christianity. Such a method points out to the Bantu that magical deviations contradict and spoil their original beliefs. It insists on the need to return to the purity of the original monotheism, thereby preparing the ground for the encounter with Christianity. In direct contrast to the method of denigration, purification activates a powerful calling, the very one depicting Christianization as an expression of higher fidelity to Bantu traditional beliefs so that conversion is released of the stress of betrayal of tradition. As Tempels writes:

> We arrive, therefore, at the unheard conclusion that Bantu paganism, the ancient wisdom of the Bantu, reaches out from the depths of its Bantu soul towards the very soul of Christian spirituality. It is in Christianity

alone that the Bantu will find relief for their secular yearning and a complete satisfaction of their deepest aspiration. . . . Christianity—and especially Christianity in its highest and most spiritual form—is the only possible consummation of the Bantu ideal.[60]

Tempels reminds us that his proposal is a re-enactment of the method of evangelization applied formerly to the then pagan Europeans. Indeed, who can deny that European Christianity was built on the synthesis of Christian teachings, local views and manners, and Greco-Roman legacy? Not only was no attempt made to empty the pagan Europeans of their legacy, but also Christian teachings were used to purify and enhance the legacy. A characteristic example is the monumental effort of Thomas Aquinas to reconcile the ancient world with the evangelic spirit. The success of Christianity in Europe is largely due to this method of fitting local beliefs into the new spirit. Tempels is of the opinion that no reason exists to proceed otherwise with Africans.

All the more reason why conversion should not adopt a different method is the agreement on many crucial points of Bantu philosophy and culture with Christian beliefs. Already the fact that monotheism was the point of departure of religious beliefs militates strongly in favor of the existence of a common stock of beliefs in all the religions of the world. What happened is not what the evolutionists want us to believe, that is, the growth of higher and complex notions from lower and simple ones. Instead, a process of divergence leading to the dispersion and particularization of the common stock of beliefs occurred. Viewed as crystallized forms which have branched out from a common trunk, the different religions exhibit a deep kinship and hence a wide context for dialogue.

Take, for instance, the African belief in vital force. At first look, this notion seems as far removed from Christian teachings as anything can be. The belief centers on the idea that vital force is a kind of variable entity that can increase and decrease according as superior forces are benevolent or not. The determination to increase vital force has understandably become the motive and the profound meaning of all Bantu practices. Yet, this belief, which seems both singular to the Bantu and responsible for their mistakes, has its equivalent in Christian faith, since "the internal and intrinsic growth of being, in the way in which the Bantu teach it, is precisely what is taught by the Christian doctrine of Grace, founded on the assured rock of Revelation."[61] Christians too expect from their union with God a supernatural uplifting resulting in the intensification of their forces and the inner growth of their life. The belief in vital force is a philosophical translation of similar spiritual expectation on the part of the Bantu.

How is that the Bantu belief appears as irrational and primitive while the Christian one has no such predicaments? Once more, the hideous face of

Western narcissism transpires, all the more so as Westerners know that this aspect of their belief lacks the support of science. In the eyes of "rationalistic Western science," Tempels notes, the Christian doctrine "remains just a hypothesis, an unproved theory."[62] Because the doctrine of grace is not a rationally established fact, Western Christianity justifies it through faith in revelation. Precisely, while the separation of faith and reason is granted to Western beliefs, a similar right is refused to Bantu beliefs every time they are required to present the sanction of reason for their beliefs.

This unfair treatment can only be the work of narcissism. We saw that colonizers and missionaries get involved in the enterprise of denigrating African beliefs because they thought that in so doing they were exalting and promoting Christianity and Western civilization. Tempels is amazed by how short-sighted this thinking is. Western believers do not see that the denigration of African beliefs can easily change into laughter at Christianity itself. When the right attitude should have been the solidarity of believers, strange is the way Westerner believers remain blind to the real implications of their alliance with the proponents of evolutionary theory.

The real target of evolutionism when it disparages primitive religions is actually the so-called advanced or higher religions. No sooner do Western believers admit that primitive religions constitute the simple and lower forms of religious beliefs than whatever is said about the lower forms becomes applicable to the higher ones. If primary religions are irrational, prelogical, and illusory, so too are the higher ones, there being no doubt that the superior product can never emancipate itself totally, however improved it may be, from the characteristics of its roots. This understanding of the real meaning of the attack on primitive religions affiliates Tempels with many scholars coming from different sectors and having different preoccupations. A point in case is E. E. Evans-Pritchard who, echoing a position similar to that Tempels, says:

> If primitive religion could be explained away as an intellectual aberration, as a mirage induced by emotional stress, or by its social function, it was implied that the higher religions could be discredited and disposed of in the same way.[63]

In view of the attacks on primitive religions targeting Christianity, what is called for is solidarity with African religions. The demonstration that Bantu religious beliefs are based on sound philosophical principles endows religiosity in general with a solid rational foundation. Evolutionism is refuted if even the less sophisticated and the most remote and decried beliefs are shown to have a rational and logical foundation. The explanation according to which higher forms evolve from lower and cruder ones loses its confidence as soon as the lower stages are shown to possess already all the positive quali-ties—if not superior ones—of the higher forms.

We can now resolve the pending question of Tempels's usage of the term "primitive." We noted that primitiveness is not merely an outcome of deterioration, although there is some such meaning. The suggestion is that, in terms of religion, regress instead of evolution took place. Modern human beings have lost many of the spiritual antennae of their ancestors so that their depiction as advanced is a one-sided and false statement. To be sure, the modern human being knows more than the primitive, just as the primitive had greater access to spirituality than human beings today. Wrong, therefore, is the view that the modern grew from the primitive. Primitiveness was instead a divergent direction imparted by the accentuation of some faculties to the detriment of others, which were consequently undeveloped.

This correction allows us to discard evolutionary interpretations while preserving the term "primitive." Primitiveness no longer stands for a backward stage; instead, it denotes an original state of endowment or assets in terms of spiritual resources, a common starting stock. It means initial, inaugural, primary, or fundamental. To the extent that the Bantu, through magical inflections, have departed from this initial impulse, they have blemished their primitiveness. To the extent that they are still nearer to it than their Western counterparts, they are rightly called primitive.

This understanding of primitiveness is not unique to Tempels. It reminds us of Jean-Jacques Rousseau's equation of the primitive with the natural and the simple, as opposed to what is acquired, artificial, and unnatural. We saw how from this equation Rousseau deduced that civilization is the main source of the vices disfiguring the modern human being. Criticizing Thomas Hobbes's assimilation of the state of nature to that of perpetual war of all against all, Rousseau writes:

> Since the state of nature is the state in which the concern for our self-preservation is the least prejudicial to that of others, that state was consequently the most appropriate for peace and the best suited for the human race.[64]

This thinking of Rousseau still reverberates because it recalls the enormous change of significance when the imperialist era twisted the meaning of primi-tiveness into inferiority. The change meant the abandonment of the concept of the primitive as a search for the natural human being. "Regarded as remote in time and space," primitive characteristics became "the base of the evolution towards civilization; and civilization . . . [was] identified as a unilinear, inevitably progressive movement."[65]

What is original to Tempels, however, is his understanding that the alleged inferior characteristics of the primitive people are those that bear witness to the proximity of the divine. The Western version of the modern human being has squandered this proximity. Worse yet, modern conception has interpreted the depletion as a measure of progress and advancement. For those scholars who still doubt that for Tempels primitive means natural, I ask them to reflect on his characterization of the Bantu as a people who "know and accept Natural Law as it is formulated in the Ten Commandments."[66] This reference to natural law indicates that for Tempels the Bantu represent the closest image of the human being as created by God. This is so true that the laws of God exist in them as a natural disposition and not as an external command.

Each time the primitive is decried, insulted, and pushed aside in the name of civilization, the natural, the original human being in each Westerner is mistreated. This maltreatment suppresses all those sensitivities that reveal to us the closeness of the divine. The alleged all-round advancement of the West in relation to the Bantu is in need of serious examination. Tempels is little impressed by the technological achievements of the West. A true assessment of the value of a civilization depends less on its material prowess than on the manner the human person is treated. Though improvements of the material conditions of life are necessary and most welcome, the crucial question is still: "do they constitute 'civilization'? Is not civilization, above all else, progress in human personality?"[67] Tempels's verdict makes no concession: despite all its material achievements, the West "has misunderstood man and neglected him."[68] The misunderstanding and the neglect are embedded in the characterization of the Bantu as inferior and backward people, which characterization is how a human dimension inherent in Westerners is trampled underfoot.

4. Beyond Evolutionism and Relativism

What has been said so far suggests that Tempels's views echo the romantic protest against Western civilization. Like that protest, he is involved in the critique of his own Western civilization that he accuses of converting the human person into an object, just as he seems to be searching for an alternative, for a fresh and unspoiled notion of the human being. Since an important dimension of modern anthropology continues the romantic inspiration, a full clarification of Tempels requires that we determine his position in relation to the anthropological school of thought that came out in defense of pluralism through the rejection of evolutionary interpretation.

An additional reason for making the clarification is that Tempels shares many points of agreement with the school of pluralist anthropology. His critiques of Western civilization, his open dissatisfaction with its excessive immersion in material pursuits and comforts, his defense of non-Western cultures, his anti-evolutionary position, all place him in the trend of thought of pluralist anthropology. Notably, Tempels's defense of the primitive meets the goals of pluralist anthropology, including its commitment to find a historical contrast to the Western type of civilization, which it judges intolerable and disastrous. The primitive offered an ideological alternative to the harmful technical conquest of the planet by Europeans, who themselves are disfigured by an aggressive culture. But more than a mere agreement on the criticism of Western civilization is at stake. Tempels's statements concur with the views defended by such scholars as Franz Boas and Ruth Benedict, even concerning the issue of Western superiority. Benedict's assertion that "no basis for the presumption of Western superiority" exists certainly sides with Tempels's position.[69] May it be, then, that Tempels is, as the relativist anthropologist, in search of another civilization because he is dissatisfied at home?

There would be no objection to the parallel, were it not that Tempels departs from the relativists on the crucial issue of pluralism. For Benedict, cultures are incommensurable because they are moving along different roads in pursuit of different goals. The goals of one culture are not qualified to judge those of other cultures.[70] Not so for Tempels, who maintains that Africans and Europeans partake in the same rationality. The demonstration of the existence of African philosophy confirms the participation of Africans in the same process of reasoning as the West. Moreover, Tempels does not behave as a scout searching for a different mode of life; he is attached to the civilizing mission of the West. He is in Africa not so much as a learner as an educator. Should we, then, speak of inconsistency between Tempels's rejection of Western superiority and his resolution to civilize the Bantu?

What stops Tempels from crossing into cultural relativism is once more his religious goal. His missionary inspiration takes the lead. He remains committed to the civilizing mission, to the spreading of Christianity. However, this statement remains true only if Tempels's other commitment, to wit, his belief in the universality of monotheism is added to the commitment to civilize. This fundamental communion of all human beings controls his approach to human differences and justifies his reading of Christianity as the secret aspiration of all religions. We already know that he gives a guarded support to the theory of degeneration, as though to suggest the possibility of steering between degenerationism and relativism. The full implication of the universality of monotheism does more than assert the compatibility between Bantu culture and Christianity; it turns Christianity into an aspiration of Bantu culture. At any rate, the implication shows that differences are variations on the same common theme, not real disparities. They are different vestments, appearances due to external factors. The weakness of relativism is to present the West and Christianity as incompatible with African identity and aspirations.

Let me illustrate Tempels's position by contrasting it with the interpretation of Dominique Zahan. In opposition to the supernaturalism of Western religions, Zahan thinks that African religion is "a kind of humanism" championing "an individual and social ethic whose normal development culminates in mystical life."[71] Put otherwise, for African religions the human being "is not the 'king' of creation but rather the central element of a system on which he imposes a centripetal orientation."[72] The purpose of this analysis is to make tangible the extent to which African religions differ from Western beliefs. Zahan does not infer the inferiority of African beliefs; on the contrary, the study wants to show the incommensurability of worldviews and the need to defend and protect their originality. Such is not Tempels's approach. He is committed to showing how a closer look at said differences reveals deeper cross-cultural themes. Because these themes echo to the Christian message, conversion turns into an actualization of a latent disposition.

The point is that cultural relativism comes up against the very notion of mission by contesting the universality of the Christian message. Since one culture cannot be judged by the norms of another culture, to speak of a civilizing mission is an aberration. For Tempels, cultural relativism has thus two defects, both opposing the purpose of missionary work. It denies the universality of Christianity and presents cultures as closed entities.

Tempels is not in favor of the notion of conversion seeking the eradication of the recipient culture, but neither is he ready to concede that the respect for local cultures entails the surrender of the missionary task. He defines the missionary work as a purification pursuing the elimination of those beliefs and practices—mostly due to superstitions and fear—that have come to corrupt the purity of the original inspiration. When this happens, Africans become Christians. This is what relativism cannot grasp, confined as it is in cultural exclusiveness. It is also what degenerationism cannot allow as a result of being unable to construe conversion as activation of a primary and for that matter indestructible inspiration. Human beings differ by their deviations and mistakes; they grow incomprehensible to one another in proportion to their wanderings from human nature. As in any human conduct, evil should account for deficiencies.

Once more, an appeal to Bergson is likely to clarify Tempels's concepts and position. To conceptualize the relationship between primitive religions and Christianity, Bergson defines primitive religions by the generic term of "static religion," while using the term "dynamic religion" to characterize Christianity. The choice of these terms is specifically meant to denounce "the mistake . . . that it is possible to pass, by a mere process of enlargement or improvement, from the static to the dynamic."[73] The impossibility derives from the fact that nature can neither be destroyed nor displaced. The dynamic religion has no other choice than to mold its message into the structure of the static religion.

This "translation of the dynamic into the static" enables society to accept the new inspiration and to stabilize it by education.[74] Any attempt to proceed otherwise, as, for instance, to destroy the static religion so as to replace it by the dynamic, is bound to fail. This Bergsonian postulation of a universal and indestructible human nature multiplies similarities among human beings in direct opposition to evolutionary theory and relativism, both too inclined to overrate disparities. What these two schools have in common despite their divergent goals is their equal determination to dig walls between human beings, the one through the notion of stages of human existence, the other through the notion of dispersion. That the one speaks in temporal and the other in spatial terms should not conceal the common trait that both sanction human disparity to the point of dissolving the very concept of human nature.

In many ways, Tempels's philosophy of conversion reproduces the Bergsonian conception of the connection between the natural and the dynamic. The postulate of an indestructible human nature enables Tempels to underscore, unlike the method of pluralist anthropology, the sharing of some fundamental assumptions. As we saw, his understanding of African philosophy and religion is motivated more by the need to show their congruence with the West than their difference, since even the idea of vital force is a belief concurrent with Christian beliefs. The supposition of a static human nature defies relativism as much as it discards the evolutionary method of eradication. Conversion is not condemned to chase an empty mind, any more than it is thwarted by the exclusiveness of cultures. Much of what is Christian finds acceptance by all the cultures of the world through the stubborn presence of human nature.

The path of the true missionary, as Tempels envisions, lies between pluralism and evolutionism. Inspired by love and little impressed by Western material conquests, this religious attitude is reluctant to compare and rank civilizations. Instead, it pays attention to the foundational role of human nature and to the proximity of "primitive" peoples to that role.

The consideration establishes the matchless value of primitive religions, the very one acclaiming them as what human beings were able to achieve without the help of revelation. Properly called natural religions, primitive religions institute a structural truth, a proof of the innateness of the divine, beyond any sophistication and ornament. But then, the relationship between the revealed religion and primitive religions becomes one of response to a calling. In a situation of expectation, higher notions do not remove lower ones; nor does peculiarity obstruct openness. Abeyance inaugurates a relationship of fulfillment such that the recipient culture remains the indispensable and extant foundation of the response. Primitive religions are what human beings have been able to reach on their own, so to speak. The leap to Christianity is obviously the result of divine intervention. This revelation takes religion further without invalidating the natural basis. As the saying "grace presupposes nature" intimates, revelation should be conceived of as an ennoblement, a crowning, a consecration of the natural.[75]

The full meaning of conversion as purification appears clearly when we note that, during their long existence, primitive religions have been saddled with additions that overlaid the real primitive, original inspiration. Mostly due to superstitions and local colorations, these additions have so covered the original monotheism that many scholars are misled into thinking that animism is the starting point of religion. The act of purification is then the work of excavating the original bedrock; it is an exacting archaeological work that pursues the removal of the artificial and acquired layers so that the original calling resounds again, this time the right answer close at hand. The closeness of primitive religions to natural belief warrants a rapid and biased opening to Christianity.

Any suggestion that Christianity should dismiss primitive religion, by falling into the trap of evolutionism, fails to understand that primitive religions call for the revealed religion and that the revealed religion, in turn, presupposes the primitive religion. This mutual grounding is how the supernatural connects with the primitive, "how the Word becomes flesh in successive cultures and traditions."[76] Just as the higher skill of poetry presupposes prose, so too is the sense of the divine of primitive religions necessary to understand the very meaning of revelation. As Evans-Pritchard writes, "nothing could have been revealed about anything if men had not already had an idea about that thing."[77] The intention of evolutionism is to deny revelation by suggesting that it is an outgrowth of the evolution of primitive religion. The countering reply is that no transition exists from the natural to the revealed religion. The latter is the result of a breakthrough, an intervention of the supernatural.

Relativism too is pushed aside as soon as revelation is construed as an expectation of the natural religion. Tempels could not hear the calling of the natural religion without assuming that "one aspect of Christian responsibility was to convert humanity to the revealed truth."[78] The expectation that he reads into primitive religions entails his responsibility to propagate the revealed truth. Those who happen to be aware of the truth would be committing the greatest crime if they kept the revelation to themselves. No external imposition or disrespect, however, is involved thereby, as one simply relays an awaited message.

That is why the revealed truth must be adapted to the local culture. For the revealed religion to appear as a dismissal of the primitive religion, which is the soil on which revelation erects itself, does not make sense. Dismissal of the native religion is just the surrender of the "bridgehead, by means of which natives can attain without hindrance all that we have to offer them in respect of stable, true civilization."[79] Since the relationship between a primitive religion and the revealed one is one of response to a calling, the callers cannot make the response intelligible unless it is acclimatized to their local language.

Only in this way can Bantu religion reach out to Christianity, and inversely, only in this way can Christianity reach out to the Bantu.

To conclude, the powerful message of Tempels says that the West cannot convert the Bantu to a Christian faith commensurate with its hailed greatness unless Christianity respects the Bantu and recognizes their rationality. The main qualification for the propagation of the true message of Christianity is the surrender of Western arrogance embedded in the evolutionary theory. The success of the civilizing mission depends on the West discovering the virtues of humility and love. The West must be reborn into Christianity to be worthy of converting Africans. Put otherwise, *Bantu Philosophy* is also a manifesto for the re-Christianization of Europe. It directs the civilizing mission toward Europe itself: the West must be first humanized, re-Christianized to be able to convert the Bantu. The conversion of the Bantu is not a problem; the real problem is that the proselytizers are no more Christian. When this problem is resolved, conversion becomes a two-way street, a reciprocal process, a celebration of sameness, of convergence on the unifying values of Christianity.

More exactly, nobody is really converting anybody. Conversion is how both civilizations discover the human in their inherent fabric. Unfortunately, instead of leading to the re-Christianization of Europe, conversion became the occasion to give vent to anti-Christian vices. The characterization of the primitive as inferior and the use of evolutionary premises as method of conversion have only reinforced Western arrogance and materialism. Yet conversion should have led to the discovery and revival of the primitive in the civilized, and hence to a return to Christian sources and subsequent changes. The missionary work resulting both in the miscarriage of African Christianity and in the further de-Christianization of Europe is the distressing news that *Bantu Philosophy* is breaking to the self-satisfied European Christianity. The mistake is corrected if human disparities are perceived as embroideries on the canvas of human nature.

Tempels's characterization of Africans resolutely backs down from ascribing differences to racial attributes. Yet the characterization does not minimize differences insofar as it insists that the humanity of the Bantu largely draws on the particularity of their legacy. Human beings are as much the outcome of the attributes of their species as they are products of their historicity, which is their own invention. The importance of the historical dimension persuaded Tempels to speak of Bantu philosophy, that is, to endorse the idea of thought peculiar to an ethnic group, but in the context of ethnic particularity mobilizing universal faculties and aspirations. Instead of being an inherent racial specialization, particularism branches out from a stock of common attributes. Even so, the impact of the acquired characteristics should not be underestimated: just as the particular grows from the universal, so too the universal needs the life force of particularism to become concrete.

The next chapter studies a version of ethnophilosophy that argues for a distinction reaching the level of racial disparity. According to this school, the full rehabilitation and renaissance of Africans require nothing less than the display and defense of their racial specialty. One must go beyond Tempels by showing that the philosophical disparity of Africa, such as the belief in vital force, implicates more than just a difference in conceptions: it is first and foremost a different way of being and understanding the world. The difference flows from racial otherness, and so soars above philosophical disagreements. We recognize the main theme of negritude whose study is the purpose of the coming chapter.

Three

THE HOLY GRAIL OF OTHERNESS

This chapter studies two different trends of ethnophilosophy developed by scholars who are natives of Africa. Their resolute commitment to otherness differentiates their views from those of Placide Tempels. They also raise particular questions, since they invest otherness with the task of defending and rehabilitating Africans. What is more, they make the success of modernization dependent on the African dedication to otherness. Let us begin with the most influential of the two trends, to wit, negritude.

1. The Complementariness of Otherness: Negritude and the Idea of Race

The prominent role of negritude in shaping and determining the course of African philosophical discourse is hardly contested. Even those African thinkers who feel an instinctive aversion to its philosophical positions consider the formal refutation of negritude as an inaugural act of their philosophical career. The attribution of this unavoidable presence of negritude to the defense of extremely controversial ideas would be unfair, given that many scholars are sympathetic to what they perceive as an attempt to provide an alternative view of things. The best approach is to define negritude as a counterpart to Eurocentrism by underlining its attempt to reverse the marginalizing impact of the notion of race into an inspiring and liberating commitment. Contrary to Kwame A. Appiah's linkage of the notion of race with "disabling labels," the conviction is that race can become a springboard for a representative universalism in lieu of the one imposed by Eurocentrism.[1]

A. Otherness versus Savagery

The main thrust of negritude is to explain the technological lag of black Africa in terms undetrimental to African pride and confidence. Though the negritude thinkers take the lag as an undeniable fact, they strongly dismiss all evolutionary explanation, just as they refrain from searching for and taking pride in the glory of a past civilization in the manner of Cheikh Anta Diop. Diop develops the thesis of black Egypt to refute G. W. F. Hegel's assertion that black Africa "is no historical part of the World," that "it has no movement or development to exhibit."[2] Diop argues that Egypt was essentially an African civilization in the precise sense that its founders and sustainers belonged to the racial group that is currently dominant in Sub-Saharan Africa. Given that "Greece borrowed from Egypt all the elements of her civilization, even the cult of the gods, and that Egypt was the cradle of civilization," the demonstration that Egypt is part of Africa both racially and culturally establishes black leadership in the genesis of European civilization.[3]

The method of negritude expressly declines any pioneering role of black peoples in the field of technology and science. In attempting to shake off the stigma of backwardness while declining the benefit of a posthumous recognition, the negritude movement puts itself in the dilemma of making the best of the concept of race. In this regard, most provocative is the bold choice of the main thinker of negritude, namely, Léopold Sédar Senghor, to define African otherness by the predominance of emotion over rationality. Senghor's assumption is clear enough: the ascription of a different mental orientation to the black essence, and that alone, is liable to give a non-derogatory explanation of the African technological lag. This strategy of rehabilitation is, therefore, a definition of

> an existential act of self-affirmation, a decision to affirm and take pride in those things for which the Negro has been despised . . . principally and symbolically, in his black skin, but also in his uninventiveness, his failure to dominate, his irresponsible gaiety before life.[4]

Aimé Césaire has eulogized this new pride thus:

> Heia for those who have never invented anything
> those who never explained anything
> those who never tamed anything
> those who give themselves up to the essence of all things
> ignorant of surfaces but struck by the movement of all things
> free of the desire to tame but familiar with the play of the world[5]

Let us make sure that we take the idea of otherness in the strong sense of belonging to a different race. To account for the African lack of technological orientation in terms that are not demeaning, it is necessary to go beyond the mere subjective understanding of negritude, the very one confining it to a mere attitude imparted by the revolt against racist discourses and practices. To be sure, the subjectivist position does not rule out the existence of differences between the African and the European. It admits that the historical determinations of slavery and colonial hegemony and the subsequent association of black skin with an inferior, undeveloped human essence have pushed blacks and whites on divergent courses.

This divergence brought about disparate subjective outlooks pertaining to human experience inasmuch as the references of those who dominate cannot tally in terms of values and conditions of liberation with those who go through the bitter experience of oppression and discrimination. Still, the idea of race confined to social relationships distorted by racism and fraught with pending revolts falls short of denoting an objective determination. The notion simply defines the tension between those who exclude and those who contest that exclusion, and so only carries a socio-historical meaning. If we are to believe Appiah, this meaning relates to W. E. B. Du Bois's trajectory. Following his failure to come up with a scientific definition of race based on objective, biological determinations, Du Bois moved to "substitute for the biological conception of race a socio-historical one. And that . . . is simply to bury the biological conception below the surface, not to transcend it."[6]

Lucius Outlaw provides another interesting limitation of the idea of race to a socio-historical notion when he maintains "that race or ethnicity are without scientific bases in biological terms does *not* mean, thereby, that they are without any social value whatsoever, racism notwithstanding."[7] However sharply social divides separate groups of people and however inevitably the separation develops idiosyncratic views and aspirations, once the biological supports are removed, the concept of race can hardly signify anything more than cultural particularity. Even if Outlaw does not totally exclude biological characteristics, he expressly refrains from correlating the physical and the mental in the causal sense of physical features impacting on the orientation of the thinking activity. Outlaw says:

> the term *race* is thus a vehicle for beliefs and values deployed in the organization of our life-worlds and to structure our encounters and relations with persons who are significantly different from us in terms of physical features (skin color and other anatomical characteristics) and, combined with these, differences in language, behavior, ideas, and other cultural matters.[8]

The noted differences in thinking and behavior are not the emanations of biological prods; they are instead constructs reflecting the association of physical features with definite social positions as a result of conflictual encounters with other peoples.

The negritude thinkers fully agree with Appiah's assessment: anything less than a biological underpinning entails the dissolution of races, as is the case each time physical features are associated with the thinking externally and accidentally. This defense of a causal connection between the physical and the mental is consistent with Du Bois's primary position ascribing to races deeper differences than mere physical ones. Du Bois deduced "the deeper differences" from "spiritual, psychical, differences—undoubtedly based on the physical, but infinitely transcending them."[9] The rooting of the mental in the biological makes up races, their particularity, their distinct way of thinking and behaving, in a word, their unique aptitudes. The negritude thinkers do not discount the subjective meaning, even if they are convinced that restriction to subjectivism only encourages a unilateral and skewed assimilation. Only when the idea of race remains encrusted with objective determinations does it offer a better reason to plead for the conservation of races.

To make plain that the idea of race cannot be reduced to a mere existential choice, a construct, Senghor correlates the physical traits and the mental orientation of the black essence with environmental influences on the grounds that the environment "causes those physical and psychic mutations which become hereditary."[10] According to him, the influence of the "warm and humid" tropical climate on the nerves of black peoples sets off the mutation that leads to the upgrading of sensitivity among black peoples.[11] Thanks to the hereditary process, the mutation is subsequently shaped into "the gift of emotion."[12] The high sensitivity implicated in emotion characteristically weakens the desire of black peoples to fix and objectify objects, thereby inducing an epistemological orientation that explores the world more through the eyes of affectivity than scrutiny. The hereditary dimension becomes most striking when we recall how remarkably the black diaspora in America preserves the same sensitivity despite the environmental change.

On the other hand, the aptitude of the European white to fix and keep the object at distance so as to dissect it "with a ruthless analysis" is attributed to the rigor of Europe's extremely variable climatic conditions.[13] The rigor of the environment reduces sensitivity in favor of inspection, and so activates an analytic turn of mind. As Césaire points out, whereas the affective approach of Africans ushers in the desire to play with the world, the composedness of the analytic attitude fosters the desire to tame it.

The role accorded to environmental factors argues for the derivation of racial groups from a common descent. Since for Senghor the protracted impact of a specific environment results in the emergence of specific traits, which then become hereditary, race is an acquired determination. If Westerners were to live for an appreciable biological time in the African environment, they too would develop African characteristics. The inherent and original particularity of the common descent does not explain the racial group; the permanence and particularity of the environment shapes the mutations of the group. Races are transmitters of acquired characteristics, not original donors. This means that all human races originate from a common source, the products of which became diverse by the addition of mutations stemming from the impact of different environments. Even understood in the strong sense of hereditary attributes, the discrepancies between blacks and whites are for Senghor more a matter of accentuation than of original endowments. While Africans put the emphasis on emotion, Westerners give primacy to the analytic approach.

One important conclusion follows: Europeans are not alien to emotion, any more than Africans are deprived of rationality. Even though Africans have a different temperament and a different turn of mind, "the reasoning faculty" is "the same in all men. . . . I am no believer in 'prelogical' mentality," says Senghor.[14] The statement does not invite contradiction if the accentuation of aptitudes is exclusively ascribed to the intervention of the environment. The notion of race does not, therefore, signify a drastic disparity among peoples, but the fact that some dispositions that are taken from a common stock of endowments become more accentuated in some peoples than in others as a result of the protracted impact of the environment. The influence of the milieu leads to a specialization, in the case of the African, to the gift of emotion, "and Senghor postulates just such a nature, such a genius, for the Negro race."[15] Neither the African gift nor the Western aptitude represents a higher moment of an evolutionary process; both are crystallizations of tendencies inherent in the human species.

The notion of gift reiterates that otherness is not a mere subjective moment in the struggle for recognition. The gift was already there as an objective characteristic long before the arrival of Europeans on the black continent. To back down from an objective determination of the idea of race is to give up making sense of Africans as Africans. Despite all the reproaches, often acrimonious, made against his position, Senghor maintains that, unless an objective determination is brought into play, he does not see "how one can account otherwise for our characteristics."[16] Since the issue is to explain the undeniable indifference of Africans to technological progress to the satisfaction of Africans, the defense of a different mental orientation alone avoids turning Africans into misfired Europeans.

Discard the explanation by otherness, and the European ascends to the position of a prototype with the major consequence that the African failure to rise to the level of the prototype irresistibly evokes evolutionary concepts. The terms used to uphold the characteristic retardation of black peoples, such as, "primitive," "backward," and "savage," indicate a blockage of evolution. What Africans have realized while being in this arrested position has no intrinsic value, being but the outcome of a dragging mind rather than an original and *sui generis* inspiration. For Senghor, what is most offensive and diminishing is not so much the discrepancy between races as the evolutionary ranking that paints the one race as retarded expression of another. The notion of advanced race takes away all meaning from the "lagging" race, which is then simply a remnant, a living human fossil.

According to Césaire, the rejection of otherness is typical of the "good-nigger," who says to the white man: "I am different from you in nothing; pay no attention to my black skin; it's the sun that has burnt it."[17] The statement reveals the position of the universalist and assimilationist African thinker who rejects the idea of race, arguing that the black skin is only a superficial and accidental characteristic against the background of an overwhelming inner sameness. Such a position does no more than promote "the white man" to the level of prototype of the human, the outcome of which is the stigmatization of all those aspects of the black life that do not fall under the category of the same. To the extent that these black traits become unwanted deviations from the prototype, assimilationist blacks are caught in the paradox of defining the human essence in terms excluding their own specificities.

Let there be no talk of an exclusion confined to the superficial and meaningless color of the skin when the association of blackness with lack of great achievements is the issue. No other way exists to disengage from these demeaning associations than to move the idea of blackness from deficiency to racial particularity. This defines negritude as "affirmation," that is, as "rooting oneself in oneself, and self confirmation: confirmation of one's *being*."[18] The definition asserts the original and distinct nature of African mode of life in terms of social and religious values, themselves resulting from a *sui generis* epistemological orientation. The gift of emotion, the notion of vital force, and African communalism state in unison the originality of the black essence.

Besides restoring pride, the sense of uniqueness and originality imparts a calling, a mission to each race and culture. Because distinctiveness prevents the elevation of one particular civilization to a model, no race stoops to the level of copying another race. The conception assigns a particular contribution to each race, with the invitation to remain original. Accordingly, in not being like the West, Africans are in no way failing in their humanity.

The conviction of having a unique task invests people with a galvanizing sense of mission as a result of which they become creative and daring. "Every people who [do] not believe they bear a unique message which only they can proclaim, Dostoievsky the Russian tells us, are already a museum piece," warns Senghor.[19] The idea of mission explains the emphasis on the originality of the African mind and its unique contributions, such as, emotion, communalism, and the metaphysical notion of vital force. The unique value of negritude lies in this attempt to give meaning by acknowledging Africa as the initiator of a different civilization. Africa is no more the continent that failed to be like Europe; it is the siege of a *sui generis* civilization, which came under the barbaric assault of colonialism.

So contrived, otherness, even the one which surrenders rationality, has the conspicuous effect of downplaying the African deficiency in technological prowess. Moreover, the Senghorian epistemological opposition between blacks and whites reveals that the Western type of knowledge exhibits an inner and deleterious aggressiveness. Senghor likens the European turn of mind to "a warrior, a bird of prey" in that it treats the natural environment in the same way as warriors treat enemies or the bird of prey pounces on its victims.[20] Césaire too, as we saw, endorses the disparity by describing the African approach as "free of the desire to tame but familiar with the play of world."[21] All this amounts to saying that the European aggressive and dismantling approach to nature is spurred on by an intention replete with greed and the lust for domination. The greed explains why the Western social system is entangled in class distinctions and conflicts, a clear outcome of the unbridled desire to dominate and possess.

In direct opposition to Western individualism and class divisions, Senghor finds that the African is held in "a tight network of vertical and horizontal communities, which bind and at the same time support him."[22] The village, the tribe, and the kingdom are mutually dependent enlargements of the family, which therefore constitutes the first cell of an expanding system. All these concentric circles in which the individual is encompassed gives a good idea of social life perceived as the expression of human solidarity, of individuals sustaining themselves through exchange and cooperation with larger forces. Transcending the present, the cooperation extends to the past so as to include the dead as well, and still beyond the founding fathers of tribes—what came to be known as the cult of ancestors. No less expressive of social solidarity is the fact that in Africa "there is no 'right of property' over the soil and its wealth, nor even a 'right of possession'."[23] In addition to preventing the rise of propertyless workers, this absence of private property reveals a conception opposed to the idea of considering nature as a thing, an object of manipulation and personal enrichment.

Let us insist on the epistemological disparity between Africa and the West. When Senghor stipulates that "classical European reason is analytical and makes use of the object, African reason is intuitive and participates in the object," his strategy is to argue that practical success, mastery of the world, is not tantamount to reaching the truth, the inner reality.[24] The price for controlling and manipulating things, that is, the gift of technicalness, is metaphysical superficiality. By contrast, the resolution to know things in their depth and inner reality requires the giving up of the conquering impulse.

Only when things are approached from a perspective free of all manipulative intent do they allow access to their intimate secrets. Their outward manifestations, as they appear through the superficial order of deterministic connections, hide the real world, which is magic in the sense of being indeterminate. The African way constitutes, says Senghor, "an interruption of the mystical or magical world into the world of determinism. The African is moved not so much by the outward appearance of the object as by its profound reality, less by the *sign* than by its *sense*."[25]

This opposition between the outward and the inward, to the extent that it reveals two different ways of being in the world, draws the main line of demarcation between black Africa and the West. The evolutionary approach cannot but define the African way as a developmental lag: Africanness is a negative characteristic, a flaw resulting from the blockage of a progression, not a divergence, a specialization. In being devoid of any positive meaning, the African way accomplishes nothing except errors and confusions. For the negritude thinker, what defines the demarcation is less a developmental lag than the opposition between the inward and the outward, which opposition reveals an original disparity pertaining to intentions. While the confinement to the outward reveals and actualizes a manipulative intent, the concern for the inward points to an approach that substitutes participation for subjugation.

Once things permit proximity the knower becomes a partner, an accomplice, not a trapper, "a bird of prey." Since the inward knowledge upgrades Africans to the level of participants, it invites them to cooperate with things, to reciprocate by according their movements to the movements of things like in a dancing engagement. Instead of subduing nature by dislocating or provoking its deployment—a method otherwise known as experiment—Africans satisfy their desires by accomplishing nature, that is, by partaking in its course in such a way that the objects of their desires come to fruition and are offered to them as entitlements to partnership.

In light of the detestable inspiration of greed and domination pervading the Western type of knowledge, the highly adulated Western rationality loses much of its magnetism. As Jean-Paul Sartre comments, the "proud claim of non-technicalness reverses the situation; that which might appear to be deficiency becomes a positive source of riches. A technical rapport with Nature reveals it as a quantity pure, inert, foreign; it dies."[26] What is more, from the conviction that the communal spirit prevented the rise of classes, there follows the conclusion that the alleged African backwardness is an outcome of the ethical thrust of African societies.

Karl Marx gave a pertinent confirmation when he explained European social evolution by the concept of class struggle. By singling out the motivation of greed and domination as the secret of the Western advance, the Marxist explanation insinuates that "lagging" societies are those that are not impelled by similar vices. In view of the West owing its material superiority to an unethical turn of mind, the African indifference to material power, ascribable as it is to the absence of acquisitiveness and conquering ethos, becomes a source of comfort.

For negritude thinkers, the conclusion is obvious: the moral superiority of blacks, not their alleged mental inferiority, explains their technological lag. Consequently, the theory of African socialism best expresses the contrast between the African alterity with its communal values and the acquisitiveness and competitive values of the West. That "Negro-African civilization is a *collectivist and communal* civilization and therefore socialist" means that the gift of emotion gives primacy to the social nature of the human person, to a civilization pursuing the social integration of individuals above all else.[27] The choice of social integration compensates for the African loss of control over nature; it deserts the evolutionary and ranking concept of stages of development for the much more promising view of human diversity.

To the question whether such a thing as an African philosophy exists, the answer is an unrestricted "yes." This answer is all the more confident as it points to a philosophy whose originality is imparted by a unique racial inspiration. By contrasting the deeper penetrating power of emotion with the dismantling technique of Western *episteme*, negritude promises a vision of the world emphasizing cohesion and integration. Because it grasps the world as a living reality, it thinks of being as vital force and individuals as communal beings. Being neither premodern nor antirational, it proposes, in line with the inspiration of a different epistemology, an alternative conception of things and of being in the world that pursues integration and harmony in place of conquest and domination.

B. The Modernity of Negritude

A strategy of rehabilitation founded on the renunciation of reason inevitably arouses an array of hostile reactions. Rationality being the major criterion that Europe used to classify peoples as advanced or backward, the reduction of African thinking to emotion could not but incite critics to point out "the correspondence of certain aspects of Senghor's ideas of the basic African personality with Western racist theories and with the 'primitive mentality' of Lévy-Bruhl," which correspondence "seems to them to leave intact in any case the racial hierarchy established by the colonial ideology."[28] The endorsement of non-rationality puts Africans at variance with scientific thinking, with the drastic consequence that they become unable to catch up with modernity. The first condition to get out of their marginal existence being the mastery of science and technology, the surrender of the rational faculty is a sure way of remaining in that situation.

As Senghor is perfectly aware of the danger of permanent marginalization, what else can we conclude but that he uses the notion of race to justify his submission to the hierarchical order of the West? In defining the particularity of black peoples by an emotional cognition and the West by the practice of rationality, Senghor substantiates the reality of different and unequal aptitudes. The inevitable outcome of this inequality is the assignment of a subordinate role to black peoples in a world shaped and dominated by Western rationality. Far from signifying emancipation and autonomy, the notion of otherness is thus consenting to the idea of blacks playing a minor role in a world admittedly built against them. As one author explains:

> negritude envisioned humanity as a single orchestra composed of different sections. The fact that European powers control the universe—conduct the orchestra—is taken for granted. Modernity is European modernity, from which Africa has been excluded; Présence Africaine will work to change this absence into a presence.[29]

The renunciation of science and technology reduces the alleged African contribution to a decorative input. The contribution can barely venture outside the artistic field, alone commensurate with the African originality in dance and music. To make this contribution, the black must learn some attributes of the West, for instance, the French language. Still, the purpose of acculturation is to assume a subaltern role, and this reveals the position of a philosophy that, Senghor admits, "no longer expresses itself as opposition to European values, but as a *complement* to them."[30] Western hegemony is quietly accepted in exchange for a role that is scarcely enough to change the absence into a presence. In thus militating for the presence of Africa in a hierarchical world rather than fighting for the advent of a decentered world, negritude lamentably fails to relativize the West. The notion of race consecrates the hierarchy among unequal partners; it does not seek the dethronement of the hierarchy.

According to opponents, nothing confirms better the acquiescence of the negritude movement to a subordinate position than its defense of a particularism drawn from the past. What else can result from this return to the past but the indefinite postponement of the modernization of Africa? Abiola Irele warns: "we cannot meet the challenges of the scientific and industrial civilization of today by draping ourselves with our particularisms."[31] The objection characterizes negritude as a useless, barren narcissism: the goal of rehabilitation can never become real for the simple reason that the philosophy of negritude is not an appropriate response to the challenge of the West. The cult of peculiarities steers Africans away from what they must do, namely, the construction of those machines that the West used to marginalize Africa. Unable to rescue Africa, the glorification of the black essence by the negritude philosopher thus leads to nothing.

However pertinent these criticisms may appear to be, we must not lose sight of their one-sidedness. A strategy of rehabilitation is judged by its final and general result, not by a partial view of its approach. This much is certain: the depletion of Africa is not unilateral. The African surrender of rationality immediately entails the relativization of the Western world. Senghor argues in no uncertain terms:

> The Europeans claimed that they were the only ones who had thought out a Civilization to the level and the dimension of Universality. From this to maintaining that European civilization was to be identified with the *Civilization of the Universal* is only a step and one which was taken many years ago. It was not difficult for us to show that every "exotic civilization" had also thought on a universal scale and that the only merit of Europe on this point was that through its conquests and its technology, it had diffused its own civilization throughout the world.[32]

The charge of consenting to a petty role in a world shaped by the hegemonic West is a misreading in view of the conviction of the negritude thinker that the human essence has burst into diverse and particularized trends. The African ceases to be a failure by the very fact that the European is dethroned from the position of prototype. The virtue of the explanation by otherness is that it champions self-acceptance by relativizing civilizations, however glorious they may pretend to be. In being different, particular, each civilization actually excels more in some aspects than in others so that arguments in favor of hierarchical conceptions appear fake. Relativization perfectly meets the pursuit of African rehabilitation, a stepping-stone to the decolonization of the African mind. It promotes self-acceptance, and so restores pride and confidence.

As to the accusation that the return to the source is a backward looking device that hinders modernization, critics press the charge under pain of flagrant inconsistency. For one thing, "there is no question of renouncing the industrial world," insists Senghor.[33] For another, those who accuse negritude of rejecting modernity also deplore that Senghor is not sufficiently anti-Western. Yet they do not explain how their own anti-Westernism does not stand in the way of modernization. When Senghor writes, "we must live a life that is original, African and French at the same time," he may be accused of reconciling with the previous colonizer, not of refusing modern values and life.[34] To deride the return to the past of the negritude movement, Ezekiel Mphahlele says that he has seen "too much that is good in western culture— for example, its music, literature and theater—to want to repudiate it."[35] The objection is little pertinent in view of Senghor's numerous appeals to a resolute mating with the Western world.

The revolutionary Césaire supports Senghor's overtures to the West. Césaire too rejects the choice between the African tradition, judged backward and inadequate, and European civilization, hailed as advanced and universal. The confinement of Africans to their particularity so as to refuse Western civilization, Césaire maintains, is just as unrealistic and puerile as the desertion of their legacy for an alien culture is foolish and detrimental. The choice between "fidelity and backwardness, or progress and renunciation . . . is not a valid one," for "in the African culture yet to be born . . . there will be many new elements, modern elements, elements, let us face it, borrowed from Europe. But we also believe that many traditional elements will persist in these cultures."[36] These words of Césaire echo those of Senghor who writes: "there is no question of reviving the past, of living in a Negro-African museum; the question is to inspire this world, *here and now*, with the values of our past."[37]

Where do critics read the cult of particularism and the rejection of modernity? What Senghor and Césaire say is that modernization does not amount to a total assimilation following the complete evacuation of African legacy. Modernization is an adaptation of a living culture to a different condition, mostly caused by the expansion and technological advances of the West. "When we have made this analysis," Senghor pursues, "the problem is to determine the present value of the institutions and style of life born of these [Negro-African] realities and how to adapt them to the requirements of the contemporary world."[38] Africans cannot go back to the past, nay, such a return is not a good thing, now that they have tasted the Western way. What Africans must do is to avoid the servile imitation of the West, for by passively importing Western ideas, institutions, and social structure, "all that can happen is that we [Africans] become pale copies of Frenchmen, consumers not producers of culture."[39] Africans avoid imitativeness when they retain their tradition: the revival and adaptation of their tradition make them creative and original.

All the more reason for advocating the return is that some of the important values of the past concur with modern life. A close study reveals that African tradition, so vehemently decried by the colonizer, exhibits traits that are at the forefront of advanced humanism. This position of forerunner shifts the return to the African legacy from the unearthing of outdated and useless values to a modernizing venture. The paradox of a precocious past is easily removed if we agree to accept that

> negritude, by its ontology (that is, its philosophy of being), its moral law and its aesthetic, is a response to the modern humanism that European philosophers and scientists have been preparing since the end of the nineteenth century.[40]

Modernity sides with African traits in many respects. Such is the case of the African ontology of vital force. The African emphasis on force and energy is more in tune with the assumptions of modern science than with Aristotle's static conception of being or René Descartes's mechanical view of matter. Such notions as relativity, wave mechanics, electron and neutron, unveil a dynamic inner world behind the static appearance. Another important case is the artistic domain: the most vanguard schools of contemporary art with their abstract style saw the light of day under the direct influence of African art. The error is to confine the influence to a stylistic change when in reality the change is deeper, as it pertains to the conception of art and hence of life itself.

Prior to their encounter with African art, Western artists had perceived art as a reproduction of the given, thereby according primacy to the object over the act of creation. African art teaches them that the purpose of art should be not so much the imitation of the object as the capture of what is behind, of the sub-reality. In the words of Senghor, thanks to African art, "a world of life forces that have to be *tamed* is substituted for a closed world of permanent and continuous substances that have to be *reproduced*."[41] The lesson is that life connects us, beyond the visible and the tangible, with deeper realities that we can tap to strengthen our life.

The aspiration to a socialist life coming from the capitalist world itself evinces the modernity of African traditional life more than anything else. The contradictions of capitalism, the rise of powerful socialist movements in the West, and the impact of Marxist doctrine salute the African mode of life as the future of the world. All these occurrences condemn in unison the individualistic and class-divided society of the West and propose the communal values of African tradition as a remedy for the evils of capitalism. Besides the communal values, Senghor mentions democracy as a traditional practice flowing from the communal structure of social life. He also illustrates the modernity of African values through the suggestion that, under the influence of the African spirit of dialogue and cooperation, the abandonment of confrontation in international relationships became institutionalized with the creation of the United Nations, just as

> it is through these virtues of negritude that decolonization has been accomplished without too much bloodshed or hatred and that a positive form of cooperation based on "dialogue and reciprocity" has been established between former colonizers and colonized.[42]

Senghor presents his attitude during the Algerian war as an example of the African contribution to peace. He notes that, in refusing to take the side of France or the FLN, he was unjustly criticized even though he was merely implementing the African sense of dialogue. "In this matter," he writes, "the reaction has been all too much in the Manichean spirit of Europe, the spirit of right or wrong, the spirit of passion."[43] Thanks to the curative effect of the African tradition on the drawbacks of capitalism, the modern world is at a crossroads: the dualist, either-or, and conquest-driven mentality of Europeans is tempted by the African virtues of dialogue, peace, and pluralism.

The discovery of the modernity of African values confirms that African modernization cannot mean Westernization. Since Westerners themselves appeal to African values to get out of their crises, to throw away values even as they prove to be so supportive of modernity would be inconsistent and self-damaging on the part of Africans. To pose the problem of modernization in terms of modernity versus tradition is to fall prey to a malicious paradigm.

This understanding credits negritude with an original theory of African modernization which supplants the dichotomy between tradition and modernity by the assurance that the major impediment is the colonization of the mind, as evinced by the propensity of African ruling elite to "importing just as they stand the political and social institutions of Europe, and even their cultural institutions."[44] This advanced character of African values shifts the direction of the civilizing mission: instead of going from Europe to Africa, civilization now goes from Africa to Europe. This allows Senghor to define negritude as a new humanism, valid in its own right as well as a solution to the crisis of modernity. The act by which the negritude movement takes root in the past is thus the act by which it opens up the future: retrogression changes into a forward movement.

As Senghor explains, the problem is less to reject Western institutions and values than "to determine what should be retained and how what is retained is to be implanted in Negro-African realities."[45] The great contradiction is to reject the colonial discourse while defining modernization in terms of exporting Western institutions and ideas, for to import everything from the West is obviously to endorse the notion of African primitiveness. African scholars cannot say that colonialism is unjust and colonial discourse false and demeaning if at the same time they define modernity as a full fledged Westernization. Taking root in Africa's legacy while reaching out to the West remains the only promising road to modernization.

C. The Production of the Universal

The modernity of African values confirms that neither Senghor nor Césaire understands race in the Western sense of hierarchy and unequal aptitudes. Given that they have the right to give words the meaning they want, provided they define them properly, the charge of endorsement of the colonial discourse is irrelevant. What both mean by human races is instead complementarity resulting from the impact of different environments. Environmental disparities lead to separate developments, with the understanding that the different trends are products of emphasis on attributes drawn from a common essence. They shape up different gifts from a common stock of physical and mental aptitudes that remain inherently human, universal. The athlete achieves more than the non-athlete, though the non-athlete too can become athlete thanks to exercises. This progress shows that the skills of the athlete grow from a common reserve of abilities, that talent is a matter of exercise, application, or orientation, not of original endowment.

This diverging process explains why Senghor prefers the idea of race to the softer notion of cultural differences. Granted that cultural differences signify pluralism, the fact remains that they do not go far enough. They flinch before the idea of complementarity to which Senghor assigns the rise of the civilization of the universal transcending African as well as Western particularities. Unlike cultural pluralism, racial determinations do not juxtapose differences; they internally connect them as aspects of the same essence that has split into different trends due to environmental influences. As internal splits, races call for reunification similar to gender split and coupling. The different directions resulting from the bifurcation of the same reality remain complementary, and hence are in need of each other. The reality of human races thus turns the universal into a future event, a coming synthesis.

Whereas the involvement of racial inheritances preserves both the universality and the particularity of the original seed, the concept of cultural pluralism either maintains the same universal essence, preferring to consider cultural disparities as superficial, or diversifies without a common theme, thereby losing sight of the original unity. In both cases, the issue of complementarity is downplayed. Accordingly, the view that "while accepting the objective reality of race as indicative of a specific, inner identity and aptitude, Senghor rejects the idea that the black man is inferior in his human quality to the white man" is not enough.[46] It must add that, unlike E. W. Blyden's notion of "*distinct* but equal" races in lieu of the racist "*identical . . .* but *unequal*" races, Senghor's formula is: distinct but complementary.[47] Equality is no longer a relevant concept, as the comparison between races, which are all partial and therefore deficient in some characters and accomplished in others, is an inherently flawed exercise. Instead, what must be stressed is that the full blossom of the human essence awaits the coming together of these partial realizations of the human being.

Senghor owes this idea of complementarity to Henri Bergson, who studied evolution more as divergence than as a cumulative and gradual progression. Specifically, speaking of intelligence and instinct, Bergson writes: "the two activities, which had begun by mutual interpenetration, had to part company in order to grow; but something of the one has remained attached to the other."[48] Not only does the concept of evolution as a divergent process posit the original unity between intelligence and instinct—rather than intelligence growing out of instinct—but also it establishes their unilaterality each time the one functions without the other. Now substitute emotion for instinct—a move all the more encouraged by Bergson's view that the original instinct became intuition and mystic ability as a result of being "disinterested and conscious"—and the elements of Senghorian epistemology fall into place.[49] Senghor's dichotomy between the West and Africa resumes the Bergsonian divergence between intelligence and intuition, with the difference that for Senghor races complement one another rather than different faculties.

Herein lies the deep meaning of the Senghorian notion of human races. In opposition to the hierarchical conception, Senghor proposes that the different races have generated civilizations, which, though original, are nevertheless one-sided and incomplete. The one-sidedness reflects the contradictory nature of human faculties: all of them could not develop within a single civilization. Nature has thus recourse to a division of labor by devolving on different races the task of developing separately these faculties until such time when the reunification, more exactly, the synthesis of these particular contributions, gathers the conditions of the civilization of the universal. As one commentator writes:

> the races of the world are necessarily complementary. . . . Europe and Africa are complementary, and together they can fashion a civilization more perfect than that which lies within the power of either world alone. Europe can contribute her scientific knowledge and her socialism; Africa her own ancient communism, her spiritual strength and her realization that in art is found the meaning of life.[50]

The secret of the disparity between Africa and the West is thus the generation of the civilization of the universal as a synthesis of particularized trends. If so, there is no greater crime than to abandon the African originality. That is why Senghor says "no" to assimilation, more accurately, pleads for *"an assimilation that leaves room for association."*[51] In addition to failing to institute the universal, assimilation ends in a drastic impoverishment of the particularized cultures. Different is the inclusion of pluralism: as association, pluralism specifies and enriches the universal, which then evolves from an abstract, static, and one-dimensional notion into a historically differentiated outcome.

A notion of the human person that has no room for the black essence is not universal, much less appropriate for black peoples. Those African scholars who extol universalism think that the best way to counter racism is to shake off particularism. Senghor disagrees: the commitment to African particularity alone can get over racism. No better way exists to soften Western contempt for Africa than to publicize its unique achievements to a public often misled by false information about Africa. Senghor writes:

> If white America conceded the claims of the Negroes it will be because writers and artists, by showing the true visage of the race, have restored its dignity; if Europe is beginning to reckon with Africa, it is because her traditional sculpture, music, dancing, literature and philosophy are henceforth forced upon an astonished world.[52]

Rejection of particularism means assimilation, and assimilation does not overcome racism. The attempt to conform to the white definition of the human being only lowers Africans to the level of a flawed version. So long as blackness and whiteness are not recognized as the two halves of the same human essence, contempt and racism cannot be removed. That is why black peoples must not strive to whiten themselves; instead, they must gain the respect of the West through the affirmation of their difference.

Senghor is not alone in pleading for the association of the discursive logic of West with Africa's gift of emotion. Césaire too wants a "rejuvenated world with its balance restored" by the cooperation of all peoples, who will then say we "have helped to found the universal humanism."[53] According to Césaire, because it feeds on abstractions and stereotypes, racism turns human beings into things.

A characteristic result of this dehumanization is the complete obstruction of communication and dialogue. For Césaire, humanism is not genuine without dialogue, that is, without the acceptance of diversity. The deep meaning of diversity is the transcendence of the human essence in that the recognition of particularism advises against the reduction of the human to particular standards. As an invitation to overcome provincialism, diversity rightly posits the universal as a product of dialogue, of reciprocal revelation. Racism proceeds otherwise: it stifles dialogue in favor of imposition. "We reject, as we are right to do, all idea of a period of apprenticeship," says Césaire.[54]

The universal, thus made of the contributions of each race, can only be an outcome of a changed world. In particular, the introduction of the values of Africa into the hierarchical dualism of the West will cause so radical a change that it will inaugurate a new humanism. Place, then, Africans and Europeans "at the extreme of objectivity and subjectivity, of discursive reason and intuitive reason, of the concept and the image, of arithmetic and emotion," and you understand that "the symbiosis of these different but complementary elements" is bound to revolutionize the existing world.[55] Recall that the best expression of modernity is contemporary art, a singular product of the influence of Africa on European conception. If the interbreeding gives birth to the bold creativity of contemporary art, then how much more so an unrestricted operation may revolutionize all the domains of life. What a peasant leader is reported to have said corresponds well to Senghor's view. Likening the synthesis of different civilizations to the improvement of fruits resulting from grafting, the leader said:

> In biology, the grafted mango is tastier than the original mango. Let me take an image borrowed from the writer Victor Hugo to explain what I mean. Hugo was writing about the marriage of a racially mixed couple, whom he compared to the night and day uniting to give birth to dawn and sunset, which are both more beautiful than either the day or the night alone.[56]

Let no one object that in view of the growing Westernization of the world, said mixture of civilizations is anything but real. Contrary to a superficial view, alongside Westernization a counter process of Africanization is taking place. The case of music in America gives a good illustration of Africanization. As a result of being exposed to the European style, African slaves did not merely abandon their traditional musical patterns. They "altered these patterns" and "developed forms," such as jazz, calypso, and rumba, in which traditional and European patterns are synthesized.[57] Another example is the emergence of separatist churches from the very attempt to mingle the teachings of the Christian missionary with traditional African beliefs. These glaring syncretic patterns "give us striking instances of continuity in the psychological resilience of African peoples."[58] Outside Africa, Japan provides a good example of a successful synthesis in which "traditional elements with those borrowed from Europe" gave birth to "a new culture that nevertheless remains Japanese."[59]

The great synthesis is yet to come. The marriage of capitalism and African communalism, though deferred many times, is not permanently excluded, as witnessed by the persistence of socialist ideas in the West. What makes socialism a powerful force is that it corrects the one-sidedness of capitalism: accumulation of power and wealth necessarily entails the issue of how they should be distributed. Only the dialectics is not evolutionary here inasmuch as the resolution of the contradictions of capitalism solicits the assistance of Africa. The West contributes its science and technology; Africa brings many of the characters associated with socialism. What Marx expects to happen as a result of socialist revolutions is none other than the intervention and contribution of Africa.

This plea for fusion appears to support Sartre's statement according to which "Negritude is dedicated to its own destruction."[60] The more negritude urges for synthesis and the production of the universal, the less it finds a place for its preservation. Since both whites and blacks go through a process of change and transformation as a result of the interbreeding, the dissolution of negritude into the reformed universal seems inevitable. As a mere moment of a dialectical process of integration, negritude ceases to be an end in itself. If so, what is to become of the racial determinations so forcefully defended by negritude? But more yet: given the racialization of differences, how is the synthesis expected to occur if hereditary disparities isolate each race? Either the negritude movement must back down from biological determinations by conceding the social meaning of race or must face the impossibility of transmutation as well as of synthesis if each race is immobilized by hereditary characteristics.

One thing is sure: when thinkers of negritude speak of synthesis, they mean not so much the abolition of races as of racism. Nor do they forget that the sense of particularity is a source of creativity. Where sameness prevails, uniformity and conformity become the rule. Fortunately, the concept of the universal as a synthesis averts the dissolution of particularity into the universal. The condition of synthesis is that the universal remains a human creation and race a natural determination. As such, the universal is unable to eliminate nature; what it can do is to get round natural determinations. It does so by means of acquisitions. To speak like Bergson, "there is such a thing as a fundamental nature, and there are acquisitions which . . . are superadded to nature."[61] The giving up of race determinations is, therefore, impossible; nor is it desirable. The acquisitions constitute the field of the cultural, which is accordingly equally open to all the races. However, you make the most of the acquired if you affix the cultural to what is permanent and forceful in you. In this way, you do the same thing as everybody else, though you do it differently and distinctively.

Natural determinations outline our limitations only to commit us to culture as a way of getting round these limitations. The error is to forget that this culture, this *"certain way, proper to each people, of feeling and thinking, of expressing itself and of acting . . .* is the symbiosis of the geography and history, of race and ethnic group."[62] As a result of a symbiosis by which it is particularized, culture becomes a most powerful weapon of assimilating, of Africanizing what is borrowed as well as what is invented. This certain way at which Africans excel is never to be traded, unseasonable though it may appear to be. The way represents a trump card that Africans must always use in their dealings with the world. It opens the modern world to them with the guarantee that they will be constructing their own house.

In providing the belief in the permanence of a special gift, the idea of race adds the flavor of authenticity to what is accomplished. While the reduction of human pluralism to mere cultural disparities, due to social exclusion or historical encounters, refuses to cross the threshold of subjective determinations, the idea of race provides a natural basis to a way, perceived as particular and advantageous, of constructing the world. It connects nature and human thinking in a manner justifying the belief that "each people possesses a mental constitution as fixed as its anatomical characteristics," thereby prompting the strong sentiments of vocation and mission.[63]

How does the notion of the universal as a synthesis of all civilizations both maintain and overcome racial divergences? From Senghor's viewpoint, Africans owe their emotional, intuitive ability to the impact of the environment, just as Europeans derive their analytic tendency from the characteristics of geography. To assume that they can dissolve their biological traits is not realistic; nor is the assumption advantageous considering that each culture has a special gift. Nevertheless, given that humans can learn, Africans can assimilate the rational method of the West without ceasing to be themselves.

For a difference exists between assimilation and being assimilated. The assimilated goes through Westernization, which is a dead end for Africans, as it implies that they will be doing nothing more than imitating, copying Westerners, who then will be the only creators. Different is assimilation, since it implies that Africans "will use European values to arouse the slumbering values of Negritude, which they will bring as their contribution to the Civilization of the Universal."[64] Assimilation advocates association, that is, the use of rationality to further intensify the intuitive power. The process does not eliminate the distinct orientation of each culture; it simply corrects their respective weaknesses by making the complementary function available. Thus, because rationality focuses on the need to conquer, it forsakes the sense of community as well as of inward knowledge, both emphasized by the

African orientation. In being impregnated by African values, rationality corrects its one-sidedness without thereby losing its specificity. The techno-logical achievements of the West, in turn, provide the African sense of community and inner knowledge with new powers that further intensity the original gift.

We can now resume and expand the comparison between Outlaw's posi-tion and the persistent loyalty of the thinkers of negritude to the concept of race. Refusing to relinquish the idea of race, Outlaw substitutes a new liber-alism that he termed *"cosmopolitan"* for the traditional notion of *"universalist liberalism."*[65] Even the complete dissolution of racism and social inequalities, so the new liberalism says, does not entail the withering away of the notion of race. The expectation of a society without racial distinctions overlooks that "elimination is both unlikely and unnecessary."[66] People remain attached to their identities, even though the causes that shaped them are no longer in operation. The preservation of these identities is a source of constant progress through the universal being kept under the pressure of recurring differences. Given these reasons, let us see whether the notion of the civilization of the universal of negritude converges on a cosmopolitan meaning. Unlike the Eurocentric universal, the cosmopolitan integrates pluralism. The whole question is to know how the integration is achieved. Admitting the difficulty, Outlaw says: "I can provide you no detailed scenario of what our social life would look like were this project completed."[67]

The failure to take the concepts of race and symbiosis seriously displays again its drawbacks. We have two choices: either the cosmopolitan is the result of an addition of disparate elements to the Eurocentric universality or it is a new conception. In the first case, the idea of race is not necessary: cultural differences can do the job of appending diversity to the Western universalism, henceforth considered as basically acceptable. In the second case, which is the proposition of the negritude thinker, there is need for a new humanism defined by a change such that the Western notion of the human is declared one-sided. As evinced by the origination of contemporary art, the new humanism must result from an act of creation synthesizing the major defining features of the different races. This means the tempering of rationality with emotion on the part of the white man and the infusion of analytic rationality into emotion on the part of the Negro. This new synthesis between nature and culture is called modern socialism. In other words, the new humanism is socialism, defined as the marriage of modern technology and African communalism.

What the concept of race provides is the commitment to a radical change of the world. Racialization is how the negritude thinker rejects the operation of merely annexing the differences of other peoples to the Eurocentric view so as to compose the universal. Just as a river grows as a result of lesser streams flowing into it, so is the new universal, made of the contribution of all races, transcending all racial limitations. No race can identity with this universal; as such, the new universal is the advent of the "super human being" or the "complete human being" thanks to the contribution of each race. The maintenance of particularities is essential, not only because the convergence of differences yields a masterpiece against which no race can match, but also because the recurrence of particularity feeds on the transcendence of the universal, which then becomes a continuous flow of creation. The conservation of races makes sense when, instead of being already made, the character of being-made defines the universal.

The "human being" that is thus created by combining the idiosyncrasies of nature is more a cultural than a physical reality. The creation is how human beings snatch the spiritual from the material by expanding the work of nature. Put otherwise, the human person is a product of the synthesis of nature and culture, of given determinations and acquired inventions. This malleability opens the possibility of a reciprocal complementarity of nature and culture so that what so far was one-sided achieves a balance. Hence the flexibility yields the universal humanism, no more as the negation of races, but as their integration. No compelling force directs the movement, however: the direction springs from a choice, the choice between socialism and capitalism, between assimilation and association.

The involvement of choice, it must be admitted, puts the notion of race in jeopardy by pulling its meaning in the direction of invention and construction. The coming chapters show that the best in the negritude movement is not so much the defense of race as the discovery of freedom in the very act of inverting the colonial insult. But we have yet to study a different version of African otherness.

2. Past-Oriented Temporality and Otherness: The Case of Mbiti

Though not so famous as negritude, another intriguing view of African otherness is developed by the African theologian, John S. Mbiti. Depicting the African difference in terms consonant with what he believes to be the original message of Christianity, Mbiti portrays the African as the genuine subject of the discourse of the Bible and, by extension, the authentic heir to Christianity. Hence arises the need to defend African religions, following his conviction that the West abandoned or betrayed the authentic path. This defense of African religions agrees with Tempels's view on the original monotheism of Africans and their closeness to the Bible. Yet in alluding to a different mental orientation, Mbiti sides with Senghor.

A. Religion and Philosophy

Mbiti puts emphasis on the philosophical content of African religions by treating "religion as an ontological phenomenon."[68] The explanation is that, unlike revealed religions, African religions stem from genuine philosophical reflections, given that they have "evolved slowly through many centuries, as people responded to the situations of their life and reflected upon their experiences."[69] This reflective and experimental origin of African religions is enough to prove that such a thing as an African philosophy exists. What seems an unreasoned or spontaneous belief stemmed from a reflective stance, so that, as Mbiti writes:

> philosophy of one kind or another is behind the thinking and acting of every people, and a study of traditional religions brings us into those areas of African life where, through word and action, we may be able to discern the philosophy behind.[70]

The spatial notion of "behind" suggests that the philosophical dimension has ceased to be part of the conscious process, even though it is presupposed as the initial foundation of present beliefs and actions. If anything, this defense of an unconscious philosophy seems utterly contradictory: How can the same viewpoint be reflective and unconscious at the same time? One answer is that the contradiction is merely apparent: as the original reflective attitude progressively solidifies into a religious belief, conscious awareness recedes and gives way to automatic responses. If the philosophical dimension is thus buried in the unconscious, retrieval obviously requires a work of interpretation. How then will Mbiti be able to differentiate his findings from his personal views?

Mbiti admits the difficulty: interpretation is necessary to separate philosophical notions from non-philosophical elements, and the work runs the risk of being subjective. Nonetheless, his answer is to say that even though "'African philosophy' may not amount to more than simply my own process of philosophizing the items under consideration . . . this cannot be helped, and in any case I am by birth an African."[71] The involvement of subjectivity does not entail that interpretation is always arbitrary, especially when interpreters deal with their native culture. Being himself an African, what Mbiti discovers subjectively is likely to correspond to what other Africans think and thus has an objective reach. This objectivism refutes those opponents of ethnophilosophy who think that, in the absence of written documents, the so-called African philosophy is simply the philosophy of an individual philosopher fraudulently baptized as African. For Mbiti, an interpretation, however subjective it may be, is not condemned to drift away from what the culture postulates if the interpretation is given by a native born into an African culture and using an African language.

About the philosophy which is found in the religions, proverbs, oral traditions, and morals of African societies, Mbiti says: it "refers to the understanding, attitude of mind, logic and perception behind the manner in which African peoples think, act or speak in different situations of life."[72] It springs to mind that this definition markedly differs from that of negritude, which he accuses of being an ideology prompted by an elitist and foreign-inspired attitude. "Nobody in the villages understands or subscribes to its philosophical expressions," he says.[73] The criticism forsakes the African speciality in emotion for the more common belief associating philosophy with logical reasoning. For Mbiti, where philosophy appears, perforce logic and logical reasoning also appear. Recall that Tempels too calls Bantu philosophy the corpus of logical thinking behind Bantu beliefs and values.

The presence of a logical substratum refutes the colonial thesis of African primitiveness by showing that African beliefs and customs are not arbitrary or irrational. Such beliefs do not emerge from fear, superstition, or ignorance, but from a mental process governed by consistency and deductive reasoning. The ultimate explanation for the distorted and demeaning representations of Africa remains the neglect or the rejection of African philosophy. A deeper knowledge of Africa is impossible while ignoring African philosophy. The affirmation of African philosophy is both the refutation of the colonial discourse and the redemption of Africa. Only through the recognition of the philosophical foundation of African culture do Africans become profound, serious, and intelligible to themselves as well as to others peoples.

This encounter between Tempels and Mbiti gives rise to the question why scholars coming from clerical circles are more inclined to defend the existence of an African philosophy than secular thinkers. Is it not because the presence of philosophy constitutes a defense of religious faith in general? For religion not to appear a mere product of superstition and fear in the age of science with its materialistic presuppositions, the best method is to lay out the philosophical references of religious beliefs. To say that all religious thoughts, even those unfamiliar with Christianity, have a philosophical foundation is to intimate that a set of logical principles justifies them. The procedure is no different from the case of St. Thomas Aquinas entering into dialogue with Aristotle. The dialogue displayed the rational content of Christianity by revealing the extent to which reason accompanies faith. Even if faith transcends reason, the separation occurs after they have gone a long way together. The clerical leaning for African philosophy is derived from the same resolution to keep faith and reason together by showing that philosophy, that is, reason and logic, is present even in the so-called primitive religions.

Like Tempels, Mbiti thinks that the understanding of African philosophy is crucial for the success of missionary work. One reason for the sensitivity of clerical circles to African philosophy is the need to adapt the Christian message to the local culture. The belief is that conversion cannot be successful if the Christian message does not take into account and satisfy local needs. For Christianity to replace or overcome local religions, it must be in a position to respond better to their expectations. As Mbiti writes:

> Since traditional religions occupy the whole person and the whole of his life, conversion to new religions like Christianity and Islam must embrace his language, thought patterns, fears, social relationships, attitudes, and philosophical disposition, if that conversion is to make a lasting impact upon the individual and his community.[74]

Conversion is likely to fail or remain superficial if it does not reach out to the traditional expectations, just as it risks being misunderstood if it does not acclimatize itself to the philosophical views and manner of thinking of the receiving cultures. Otherwise, discarded and suppressed, traditional cultures enter into conflict with the new religion, generating an intricate situation little conducive to a lasting conversion.

That "Africans have their own ontology . . . and to understand their religions we must penetrate that ontology" is best illustrated by the extent to which the neglect of the philosophy led to false and superficial understandings of African cultures.[75] Such neglect entails the refusal to go beyond appearances so as to grasp deeper meanings. Thus, from the observation of certain rituals and customs, Europeans falsely concluded that Africans are animist. The statement overlooks that African religions include all the elements of religion, and that "God, spirits and divinities are part of the traditional body of beliefs."[76] What is more, Africans never disregarded the issue of God's transcendence: for them, God is transcendent while being also near, as shown by the fact that "practically all African peoples associate God with the sky, in one way or another."[77]

The error has been to take this association literally, as though Africans meant that the sun were a divine spirit. The sun is not God; still less are the objects of sacrifice thrown in the direction of the rising sun causing the actual rise of sun. The offering is more accurately a celebration. The sun is simply a visible symbol for God's presence and transcendence. As D. A. Masolo elucidates:

> Witchcraft and magic in African religion, or the significance of the attributes of God in relation to natural objects and phenomena, are based on the simple criterion of analogical symbolism. Thus God is called the sun because He, like the celestial body, is powerful despite the great distance between Him and humans on earth. In this way, believes Mbiti, Africans try to explain the nature of the invisible spiritual world by

means of ordinary language and with reference to objects and phenomena of ordinary experience.[78]

Just as a word is a symbol, a sign of the thing and not the thing itself, so too animist expressions and magical practices exclude any real identification, being but mere designations. While this correction refutes the widely held allegation that Africans give more importance to other spirits because they believe in a remote God, Mbiti does not rule out that such spirits exist and that they can act as intermediaries. Such is notably the case of the "living-dead and other departed" who "convey human requests, needs, prayers, sacrifices and offerings to God, and sometimes relay His response back to human beings." [79]

All this reiterates the conviction that the very notion of primitive Africa originates from a superficial and misleading reading of African traditional cultures. To rise to a genuine understanding, we must go beyond appearances, and this means the recognition of African ontology. Because ontology commands the understanding of African religions and cultures, Mbiti undertakes a reflection on the African concept of time. He thinks that the work of Tempels went astray, for, unlike the notion of time, "the theory of 'vital force' cannot be applied to other African peoples with whose life and ideas I am familiar."[80] In thus mistaking a notion specific to the Bantu for a basic concept of African thinking, Tempels missed the deep originality of African ontology.

B. African Time

For Mbiti, "the concept of time may help to explain beliefs, attitudes, practices and general way of life of African peoples not only in the traditional set up but also in the modern situation (whether of political, economic, educational or Church life)."[81] According to Tempels, the African difference consists in a particular understanding of being; Senghor goes further by originating the difference from the way the African mind thinks. Mbiti's characterization of the concept of time as a key to African thinking and practice is not philosophically less sound. Major Western philosophers from Immanuel Kant and Hegel to Martin Heidegger and Bergson have pointed out time as a central concept on which the conception of being itself depends. Does this reference to a particular conception of time mean that Mbiti follows in Senghor's footsteps of racializing differences? Not at all: his reduction of negritude to a foreign ideology provides evidence of his little sympathy for all those scholars "who pin it [the African personality] down to biological roots."[82]

Compared to Senghor's denial of rationality, Mbiti's definition of otherness does not look demeaning for Africans. Unlike negritude, the African difference is not conceived of as a divergent trend; it is viewed as an expression of fidelity to the original intent of the Creator, without any opening for racial interpretation. Whereas Westerners wander away from that intention, Africans remain close to it. Mbiti defends traditional African religions on account of their closeness to the original, non-hellenized message of the Bible. What the West stigmatizes as primitive is the innocent human being, the one that remains loyal to the original wish of the Creator.

This defense of the African recalls the positive description of "the noble savage" in Europe, which is based on the argument that scientific and technological advances have only steered the Western mind away from the right path. As Masolo states, "for Mbiti, it would seem, Africans need no conversion to Christianity. They already live the Christian message."[83] Through the display of the fidelity of African religions to Christian life, Mbiti targets the rehabilitation of Africa: what the West despises and brutalizes as primitive is only its own ideal and aspiration.

What, then, is this notion of time thanks to which Africans gained a prior knowledge of the teachings of the Bible? It is the one proclaiming that "time is a two-dimensional phenomenon, with a long *past*, a *present* and virtually *no future*."[84] The statement is paradoxical, to say the least: What is time if it does not involve the future? Is not the future the distinguishing mark of time, specifically when compared to space, which only points to what is given as present? Clearly, the focus on the past instead of the future singles out the African conception of time in direct contrast with the strongly futuristic conception of the West. This means that, although future events occur, as the inevitable rhythm of nature testifies, time deploys its essence in a reverse way, and so "moves 'backward' rather than 'forward.'"[85] Future events do not make up time, that is, they are not yet time; they "at best constitute only *potential time*, not *actual time*."[86] Only as past or present do they become time.

This importance of the past reminds us of Bergson's insistence on the continuity of time and the subsequent primacy of the past. Discarding the discontinuous representation of time, Bergson calls duration the movement that makes up continuity by rolling on itself, as though it were moving backward. Such a rapprochement, though no doubt tempting, would be a complete misunderstanding, since the Bergsonian continuity is a swelling movement that inaugurates a new future by generating indetermination. "Duration," Bergson writes, "is the continuous progress of the past which gnaws into the future and which swells as it advances."[87] Such is not what Mbiti means: for him, the African conception of time moves into the past without ever bouncing into the future so that "people set their minds not on future things, but chiefly on what has taken place."[88]

In support of his analysis, Mbiti calls upon the fact that "in the east African languages . . . there are no concrete words or expressions to convey the idea of a distant future."[89] He also reminds the reader that the African reckoning of time is more event-oriented than mathematical. Because "Africans reckon time . . . in connection with events but not just for the sake of mathematics," the idea of time without any event filling it, that is, the idea of empty yet coming time, is repugnant to them.[90] Thus, the rising of the sun constitutes the event that announces the beginning of the day, whether the sun rises at five or seven o'clock in the morning.

Westerners misunderstand the African behavior when they accuse Africans of wasting their time by sitting idle while precious times pass them by. In light of the African conception of time, "those who are seen sitting down, are actually *not wasting* time, but either waiting for time or in the process of 'producing' time."[91] Had time been for Africans a mathematical notion, "to do nothing" would amount to a waste of time. But since time connects always with the occurrence of events, to say that time passes when nothing actually occurs is not intelligible. "To do nothing" is to wait, which is part of time since waiting participates in the occurrence of the event.

The identification of the reality of time with passing time means that for Africans "history moves backwards and, therefore, cannot head towards a goal, a climax, or a termination" so that African concepts "lack a telos; they are eschatological, but not teleological."[92] This lack of a final goal, of future destination seems to contradict the affinity that Mbiti detects between Christianity and African religions. The contradiction somewhat peters out if we take into account his contention that the original Christianity has been spoiled by a futuristic reading of time. In his eyes, on top of being "based on biblical or metaphysical exaggerations about the 'next' world, the world 'to come,' and the events that lead thereto," the teaching of Christianity conveys "a wrong interpretation of the central theological point of Christic intervention in history" by turning salvation into a future event.[93] The notion of salvation as a future occurrence stems from a hellenized reading of the Bible, that is, from a conception of history staging the unfolding and progressive realization of a divine plan.

This estrangement from futurism does not entail that traditional African religions disbelieve in life after death. It only means that the "belief does not constitute a hope for a future and better life. To live here and now is the most important concern of African religious activities and beliefs."[94] In light of this absence of a future hope, can we still say that the African system of belief corresponds to the usual meaning of religion? The answer is a definite "yes," provided Western dualism is replaced by the understanding that for the African "no line is drawn between the spiritual and the physical. Even life in the hereafter is conceived in materialistic and physical terms."[95]

The continuity of life is such that death must not be viewed as a break, a cessation to the point that life is expected to resurrect in the future. Once the secular and the spiritual are fused together, no ontological fence separates the

here and the hereafter. The hereafter is not where you go after a radical transformation; it is how you continue life in the past. Death is continuation of life;
death is life as past or in the past, and the future has nothing in store. Death is
not the transition to another world; it is simply how a person ceases to be in
the present. This cessation is the past itself, the mode of spiritual existence.
Given this conception of death, no need arises for a "messianic hope or
apocalyptic vision with God stepping in at some future moment to bring about
a radical reversal of man's normal life."[96] Accordingly, God is not conceived
of as intervening, that is, as rewarding or punishing individuals, and Africans
deal with divine omnipotence more in utilitarian than in ethical and spiritual
terms.

Like many other peoples, Africans thought that God was originally very
close to human beings until a separation occurred as a result of an incident.
Though Africans usually attribute trivial reasons for the cessation of God's
nearness, ranging from accidental causes to God's sheer discomfort at human
beings' petty requests, they admit that the separation brought the highest
tragedy on human beings. And Mbiti finds remarkable that

> out of [the] many myths concerning the primeval man and the loss of his
> original state, there is not a single myth . . . which even attempts to
> suggest a solution or reversal of this great loss. Man accepted the
> separation between him and God.[97]

Because Africans possessed no myth promising the reversal of the
separation, their relationship with the divine took a merely utilitarian turn.
They had to fall back on the intervention of lesser spirits: "the patriarchs,
living/dead, elders, priests, or even divinities and spirits" became "the daily
guardians or police of human morality."[98] The irreversibility of the separation
led to the withdrawal of God to the great advantage of lesser spirits: ancestors,
elders, and other spirits stepped in to provide protection and care as well as to
punish when rules are broken. Most of all, the permanent character of the loss
of reconciliation took away all mystical, otherworldly orientation from
religious fervor, leaving only secular pursuits. Besides confirming the lack of
futuristic notions, the African resignation reveals the great weakness of
African religions *vis-à-vis* other traditional religions, such as, Christianity,
Judaism, and Islam. In failing to "offer for mankind at large, a way of
'escape,' a message of 'redemption,'" African religions became powerless
against the message of hope emanating from other religions.[99]

One important issue remains. Given that African religions do not
promise the recovery of the lost paradise, in what terms do they visualize the
afterlife? The notion that death is how life continues as past entails the
conception of the dead as "the living-dead," that is, as the departed, as those
whose personality is still living with the people, even though they have lost

their physical presence. Relatives and friends, who continue to remember them, confer actuality on them. But when the time comes no living relative remembers dead persons, the latter become spirits and "enter into the state of *collective immortality*."[100] The admission signifies that the living-dead, being now truly dead, cease to be human beings.

The belief that remembrance keeps the dead alive may be considered as irrational. Yet it is no more irrational than the Christian idea of spiritual survival outside the body. Above all, the act of remembrance does not keep alive the dead in a causal fashion, but directs their attention or concern toward the present and the living. In so doing, remembrance preserves the dead by safeguarding their personality from oblivion. Forgotten spirits have no concern for the living, and so lose their personality. Hence the importance of such practices—wrongly called the worship of ancestors—as the gift of bits of food and drink to the departed. Rather than a worship of ancestors, these are rituals of remembrance designed to focus the attention of the dead on their living relatives. Naturally, the importance of the dead is proportional to their remoteness in time and culminates in the authority of the founding fathers of the tribe.

The assumption that the deceased survive as long as relatives and friends remember them explains the strong concern of the African that "at least some of his children survive to perform the necessary ceremonies and sacrifices to preserve this well-being in the after-life."[101] This concern, in turn, assigns a great value to having many children and explains the African infatuation for the extended family. If the family ensures the endurance of the personality of the dead, the aspiration to have as many children as possible becomes compelling. A large family becomes a religious duty, a way of prolonging a person's individuality, even through the practice of polygamy. Far from being a primitive or barbaric practice, polygamy thus flows from a philosophy of time that connects personal survival with the reminiscence of offspring.

The emphasis on African difference has made Mbiti quite aware of its implications for the modernization of Africa. That is why he insists on the conflicts arising from the encounter of Western and African cultural norms. Because of rapid change, he says:

> within one family or household may be found two totally different worlds coexisting: the children may be attending university studies, while the parents are illiterate and concerned mainly with cultivating their fields with wooden sticks.[102]

The disparity indicates the extent to which Africans exposed to Western education are cut off from their society, but even more so the bare fact that, having no firm roots in any of the two worlds, educated Africans are in a state of cultural errantry. Mbiti describes the uprootedness of the educated African thus:

> He becomes an alien both to traditional life and to the new life brought about by modern change. He is posed between two positions: the traditional solidarity which supplied for him land, customs, ethics, rites of passage, customary law, religious participation and a historical depth; and a modern way of life which for him has not yet acquired any solidarity.[103]

The clear outcome of rapid and imposed modernization is the multiplication of conflicts. Because a process of transition, of evolution from the past to the modern was not devised, the inevitable result is a mentality torn between Western and African norms. The problem is that this floating mentality, on top of being very influential on account of the prestige of modern education, is prone to erratic behaviors, being in harmony neither with the modern nor the traditional. Mbiti insists, Westernization, that is, the introduction of the future in the African mode of life "is not a smooth one and may well be at the root of, among other things, the political instability of our nations."[104]

Nothing shows better the drawbacks of this floating mentality than the proliferation of ethnic conflicts in Africa. While "nationhood scratches on the surface . . . the subconscious of tribal life is only dormant, not dead. These two levels do not always harmonize, and may even clash in an open conflict to the detriment of both sides."[105] Some African leaders have attempted to overcome the conflict by proposing a modern version of the traditional solidarity through such doctrines as the one-party system and African socialism. Both doctrines failed because, among other things, Africans were unable to adopt the traditional system to the modern world in a creative and progressist fashion.

The solution is not to get rid of the past. The traditional cannot be simply pushed away; to think so is an illusion, which only succeeds in turning the traditional into a subconscious force, all the more resentful because it is ignored. Instead of ignoring the past or pretending that it is no longer active, the best approach is to try to satisfy it by means of modern expressions. This harmonization of the traditional with the modern is called creative synthesis. Such a synthesis avoids the mere borrowing of Western institutions and ideas by placing modernity in continuity with the past. In this way, the synthesis counters the rise of a bastard culture, which is the main impediment to Africa's advances, there being no doubt that the dualism of norms explains the gap between theory and practice, solidarity and individualistic pursuits, modern methods and traditional references. What else could flow from a spurious culture but all out duplicity and inconsistency?

To sum up, what characterizes beyond their disagreement the main thinkers of the two schools of ethnophilosophy that we have studied, namely, Senghor's racial classification of human beings and Mbiti's notion of backward going temporality, is the attempt to rehabilitate Africa by refuting the disparaging colonial view of African traditional culture and society. The promotion of otherness alone, the two approaches maintain, is liable to snatch Africans from the state of sub-humanness. As a result, great worth is assigned to the African past, especially as the return to a rehabilitated past supposedly conditions the rise of Africa from marginalization and poverty. The next chapter discusses philosophical positions countering this apology of otherness.

Four

SAMENESS VERSUS OTHERNESS

Previous chapters disclose that the choice between otherness and sameness, itself a reaction to the colonial discourse, is the main theme of African philosophy. A philosophical debate is developing insofar as African scholars try to positively substantiate or oppose the idea of otherness. This chapter focuses on the position of those African scholars who radically reject ethno-philosophy by arguing that the defense of otherness is a sure way of perpetuating the marginalization of Africa.

1. Myth and Reality in African Philosophy

Remember that the debate over otherness is inextricably blended with the issue of the existence or nonexistence of a traditional African philosophy. Ethnophilosophers come out strongly in favor of the existence of African philosophy because they find the colonial denial of African philosophy highly insulting and degrading. They also assume that African philosophy must exist in a form commensurate with the particularity of Africans. Those who reject ethnophilosophy have two questions: (1) What is the price for the recognition of an African philosophy? (2) What kind of philosophy is recognized as being African? Since the price for having a philosophy is paid by the acceptance of otherness, Africa, they say, is better off without ethnophilosophy. On top of endorsing the colonial discourse, the acceptance of otherness alienates Africans from rationality and science, the crowning evidence being the definition of negritude thinkers of the black essence by emotion. The best way to counter this detrimental outcome is to repudiate the very notion of precolonial African philosophy.

A. The Universality of Philosophy

To give an idea of the complexity of this denial of philosophy, no better way exists than to study the position of the African thinker who has initiated the crusade against ethnophilosophy, namely, Paulin J. Hountondji. Let there be no misunderstanding: Hountondji does not deny the existence of African philosophy. As suggested by the title of his main book, *African Philosophy: Myth and Reality*, African philosophy is both myth and reality; it is not only a myth. The question of knowing what is myth and what is reality in African philosophy amounts to asking why those who talk about and practice African philosophy, instead of assuming full responsibility for their discourse, "believe that they are merely reproducing a pre-existing thought through it."[1] Individual thinkers claim philosophical systems because they produce them. Most abnormal, therefore, is the case of the thinker who refers to

> an implicit "philosophy" conceived as an unthinking, spontaneous, collective system of thought, common to all Africans or at least to all members severally, past, present, and future, of such-and-such an African ethnic group.[2]

As the expressions "Bantu philosophy," "African philosophy," and "black philosophy," imply, the problem with ethnophilosophy is its assumption that collective and spontaneous systems of philosophy exist.

Let no one claim that such expressions as "American philosophy," "European philosophy," or "German philosophy" denote the same collectiveness. Neither of these expressions refers to the contents of a philosophy believed to be characteristic of a particular ethnic group or nationality. They indicate "the geographical origin of the authors rather than an alleged specificity of content," as verified by the recognition of diverse, even contradictory philosophical views.[3] Such is not the case when ethnophilosophers speak of Bantu or African philosophy. Instead of the designation of the geographical whereabouts of individual thinkers, without the attachment of a collective meaning, what ethnophilosophers signify when they append a racial or ethnic attribute to philosophy is a metaphysical entity, a collective thinking particular to a group of individuals. They have in mind an individually undifferentiated thinking.

This notion of a collective and unconscious philosophy is clearly a contradiction in terms. Philosophy is an individual, critical, and systematic reflection; as such, it swears against the very idea of collectiveness. Are not religions, mythologies, and worldviews particularly distinguished from philosophy because they do not appeal to the critical awareness of the individual? In opposition to philosophy, they all solicit the spontaneous adherence of individuals to a common and transmitted credo of beliefs that is expressly protected against critical inquiry. So that, having none of the attributes by which a philosophical discourse is usually defined, what is identified as Bantu or African philosophy presents all the characters of a religious system or worldview, not of philosophy. Marcien Towa, another formidable opponent of ethnophilosophy, speaks of a "dilation of the concept of philosophy to such a point that this concept becomes coextensive with the concept of culture."[4] This stretching of the meaning of philosophy to culture shows the extent to which the claim of ethnophilosophers to have established the universality of philosophy is based on the fraudulent identification of philosophy with culture.

Hountondji goes further than the necessity of individual and critical thinking by adding the requirement of science on the grounds that "philosophical revolutions are functions of scientific revolutions."[5] The correlation establishes the appearance of a scientific discipline as a prerequisite to philosophy whose essential function is then to become a theory of science, that is, an investigation into the nature and possibility of scientific knowledge. Philosophy is thus unthinkable without science, while religions and mythologies can develop independently of science. Since no African scholar argues in favor of the existence of a scientific form of knowledge in traditional Africa, this dependence of philosophy on science takes philosophy as far away as possible from Africa.

All these arguments are supposed to uncover the fact that the ethnophilosopher is "arbitrarily projecting a *philosophical discourse* on to products of language which expressly offer themselves as something other than philosophy."[6] The detection of an illegitimate projection is enough to exhibit the flawed and deceptive nature of the very attempt to convert ethnophilosophy into a revival of a precolonial or traditional philosophy. While this vigorous denial allows Hountondji to argue that the revival of what has never existed is impossible, it also enables him to discriminate between what is real and what is fake in African philosophy.

A first step toward establishing the distinction is to pinpoint that the assumption feeding on the ethnophilosophical discourse is also "one of the founding acts of the 'science' (or rather the pseudo-science) called ethnology, namely, the generally tacit thesis that non-Western societies are absolutely specific."[7] In other words, the thesis of African otherness is the common source that inspires anthropological and ethnophilosophical discourses. The idea of a collective and unconscious philosophy is how the alleged otherness of Africans finds a philosophical corroboration. Those who have a different nature cannot philosophize as Westerners; they need a philosophy commensurate with their specificity. Hence the charge that ethnophilosophy does no more than endorse the colonial discourse. Hountondji calls the acceptance of otherness "'folklorism', a sort of collective exhibitionism which compels the 'Third World' intellectual to 'defend and illustrate' the peculiarities of his tradition for the benefit of a Western public."[8]

The conformity to Western stereotypes is illustrated by the similarity between the ethnophilosophical portrait of the African essence and Lucien Lévy-Bruhl's notion of "primitive mentality." What else is Placide Tempels's conceptualization of the Bantu comprehension of being as vital force but a philosophical translation of the assumption that Africans are unable to perceive being as given and manipulable? Léopold Sédar Senghor's specification of emotion as an African speciality promotes the same idea of African irrationality with even greater strength. Likewise, John Mbiti's exclusion of the future from the African notion of time portrays a mentality acting counter to rationality.

For Hountondji, the crucial question is to know why ethnophilosophers fall back on the past, that is, why they think they are reproducing a past philosophy when to all appearances they produce said philosophy. The question targets nothing less than the function, the purpose of ethnophilosophy. To find the answer, Hountondji uses the method of reduction characteristic of Marxism: he assimilates ethnophilosophy to a false consciousness, to a disguised way of promoting social projects, in his words, to "a self-deluding invention that hides behind its own products."[9] Accordingly, what impels ethnophilosophers to revert to the past is none other than a deeply conservative social project that would like to pass off as a revolutionary discourse. This conservative project becomes obvious as soon as we understand that

> behind this [implicit and collective worldview] usage . . . there is a myth at work, the myth of primitive unanimity, with its suggestion that in "primitive" societies—that is to say, non-Western societies—everybody always agrees with everybody else. It follows that in such societies there can never be individual beliefs or philosophies but only collective systems of belief.[10]

Grant that the philosophy supposedly belonging to an ethnic group is in reality the philosophy of the individual philosopher who is thinking and expressing it, and it becomes clear that the renunciation of individual responsibility is how said system of thought is metamorphosed into an African trait. In thus portraying their individual thinking as a derivative of African alterity, ethnophilosophers hope to obtain a collective sanction without going through the ordeal of providing rational arguments. They place themselves above examinations and criticisms and demand unanimous approval in the name of African authenticity and the authority of tradition. By calling philosophy an ensemble of uncritical beliefs, they reaffirm its permanence and indispensable character, and so valorize and consecrate its proposals. Even retrograde and pernicious beliefs are revalorized, and what is but the exclusive view of some ruling circles is extended to all Africans.

To say that what is presented as the philosophy of the Bantu or the Africans is neither more nor less than the philosophy of Tempels, Mbiti, or Senghor is to reveal the extent to which, in the happy expression of Hountondji, "ethnophilosophy is always a constructed knowledge that would like to be taken as a knowledge of restitution."[11] The obvious aim of the conjuration of the past is to stigmatize individual and critical thinking to the great delight of the totalitarian ideologies that govern African countries, such as, African socialism, pseudo-Marxism, the one-party system, and the return to authenticity. Besides branding democratic practices as un-African, the resurgence of the past retards the development and spread of rational thinking whose precondition is the rise and recognition of individual critical thinking. This retardation, in turn, blocks the process of modernization. That is why Hountondji reverses the trend of finding philosophy in the past and insists that "we must begin at the beginning; we must restore the right to criticism and free expression which are so seriously threatened by our regimes of terror and ideological confusion."[12]

Such insistence establishes that African philosophy begins when the traditional and collective thoughts of Africans are critically assessed by others, when African philosophers study them "outside of all apologetic perspectives," as philosophers normally do.[13] When this happens, there follows the resolution to claim only those aspects of the traditional culture that stand the test of critical examination because they are found to be either progressist or useful for modernization. Put otherwise, the attitude of African scholars to the past should reflect not so much rejection as the resolution to be critical. Hountondji is against ethnophilosophy because it advocates an indiscriminate consecration, not because it wants to reappropriate traditional knowledge. The task of the philosopher is to examine everything critically; the critical appraisal of the past necessarily leads, unlike the unanimist reading of ethnophilosophers, to a pluralist interpretation of the traditional thinking.

For Hountondji, the reappropriation of past knowledge failing to be the restitution of a past philosophy, African philosophy is yet to come; "it is before us, not behind us, and must be created today by decisive action."[14] While African philosophy "will not be effected *ex nihilo*, that it will necessarily embrace the heritage of the past," it will also "be a recreation," given that the submission of the past to a critical assessment will bring about change by turning the past into a philosophical material.[15] Hountondji notes that this goal of African philosophy, that is, the critical reflections on African legacy, is pushing ahead in the form of literature displaying a reconstruction of traditional systems of thought by means of critical evaluation. To underline its divergence from the naïve ethnophilosophy of the pioneers, Hountondji calls this reconstruction "learned ethnophilosophy."[16]

How does Hountondji's enlightened, critical ethnophilosophy proceed? It basically attempts to elucidate the genesis of traditional African beliefs and practices by connecting them with the then prevailing conditions of life. In conceiving traditional beliefs as products of given socioeconomic conditions, the critical approach goes beyond the frozen appearance of beliefs and thought structures. The exposure of the correspondence of the form and contents of the thinking with the conditions of life confirms the limitations of the thinking to specific times and places. Contrary to Tempels's method, this learned approach does not mystify by calling philosophy what is not, but shows how real and changing conditions of material existence impact on the thinking. It reveals the historical and transient nature of these thoughts, and hence avoids changing them into eternal African categories. We recognize the basic credo of the method of historical materialism, to wit, the derivativeness of the thought process from the conditions of material life.

One basic question springs to mind: Does such a method refute the colonial discourse? The belief is that it does, mainly by disproving the assumption that Africans have by nature a different way of thinking or a different mind. In short, it repudiates African otherness in favor of historicity. It also demonstrates the rationality of the thought process by displaying the relevance of the thinking to the mode of life. African thoughts and beliefs are no longer the mere products of magic; they are reflections, albeit idealized, of real conditions of life. Whereas otherness petrifies the African retardation, the correspondence between the mode of life and the mode of thinking proposes the notion of delay in development. The correspondence shows that the disparity between the West and Africa is "merely in the *evolutionary stage* attained, with regard to particular types of achievement . . . merely in quantity or *scale.*"[17] In the face of the undeniable technological backwardness of Africa, Hountondji admits the existence of difference with the understanding that said difference is wrongly ascribed to a difference in nature when the disparity is merely a gap in social evolution, in the stage attained.

This stage disparity puts Africa in the same unilinear process as the West so that the failure of Africans to reach the same level of evolution at the same time is attributed to the conditions of life, not to their mental unfitness. The conception of a difference in kind makes the African appropriation of Western methods and rationality problematic, not to say unlikely. Not so the difference in quantity: a quantitative gap promises a rapid attainment, given that it views Western achievements as an expansion of universal qualities equally shared by Africans as well.

A parenthesis is in order. Though fully agreeing with the dismissal of ethnophilosophy, Towa does not follow Hountondji on the issue of the existence of traditional philosophy and the recovery of past knowledge. For Towa, a traditional African philosophy had existed, but it need not be recovered for the simple reason that it was utterly worthless. "The reduction of philosophy to epistemology" explains Hountondji's mistaken rejection of traditional African philosophy.[18] The point is not so much to deny its existence as to get over it by exhibiting its complete irrelevance to the present needs of Africa. If the liberation of Africa is the goal, then Africans, Towa argues, must avoid the restoration of the ancient world in any form and shape. The preservation of the past is not justified when the imputation of Africa's defeat and dependent status to its traditional features is so widely accepted.

The lesson is clear: to affirm itself, the African self must deny its essence and its past so as to acquire Western qualities, thereby becoming uncolonizable. As Abiola Irele states, Towa's "renunciation of the self as constituted by the African past . . . is given direct expression in his advocacy of Western philosophy as the only intellectual method capable of leading to the transformation of Africa."[19]

B. Echoing Eurocentrism

Critics have emphasized the contrast between Hountondji's and Towa's severe and uncompromising criticisms of ethnophilosophy and their total surrender of all critical attitude toward Western philosophy. To say that both are mesmerized by Western philosophy to the point of endorsing the anthropological discourse by characterizing African thinking as collective, spontaneous, and irrational is hardly an exaggeration. Nowhere do we see them developing the slightest doubt about the accuracy of the terms used to describe African traditional thinking.

Against the charge of collective, uncritical, nonindividual thinking, Kwame Gyekye finds:

> there is, strictly speaking, no such thing as "collective" thought, if this means that ideas result from the intellectual production of a whole collectivity. What has come to be described as "collective" is nothing but the ideas of individual wise people.[20]

The riposte suggests that the various communal beliefs, first born of the critical thinking of individuals, become collective because the community considers them as useful. Gyekye adds that in all the researches and interviews that he has conducted in Africa, he always runs into diverse opinions on the most important questions so that the alleged monolithic nature of African traditional thought is a fiction.

Gyekye pursues, "we obviously cannot divorce the philosophy of an individual thinker from the ideas current among the people, for the philosophy of the individual thinker is rooted in the beliefs and assumptions of the culture."[21] Each time a philosophical system is termed Greek, French, or British, the classification is not merely geographical, but refers to patterns of thought indicating the extent to which individual thinkers are influenced by their cultural environment. For instance, the persistence of idealistic thinking in the West cannot be explained otherwise than by the influence of the religious allegiances of Western philosophers.

This objection becomes particularly serious when the reference is to Marxist philosophy from which both Hountondji and Towa draw their major inspiration. If anything, the defense of the individual thinker appears discordant, given that, for Marxism, philosophy is itself an ideological discourse. As such, the content of philosophy is collective in the sense of reflecting class interests, and the individual philosopher is simply the transmitter of the interest of a given group. Hountondji and Towa would have been consistent disciples of Marxism if they had in fact criticized the notion of individual philosophy as ideological by showing that all philosophy is in the final analysis collective.

This major oversight indicates the degree to which Towa and Hountondji are stupefied by the notion of philosophy. Instead of demystifying philosophy, as Karl Marx does, they view philosophy as the ultimate incarnation of rationality. Closing their eyes to the considerable part that mysticism and irrationality play in philosophical systems, they identify philosophy with critical thinking, if not with science, even though what is paraded as scientific is merely an exploitation of sciences for ideological purposes. Because their veneration conceals this deceptive method of philosophy from them, both accept the idea of Western philosophy as a universal yardstick, thereby overlooking the grave distortions imparted by Eurocentrism. Speaking of Hountondji, one critic notes: he "fails to do that preliminary work of questioning the Eurocentric structures as he appropriates European notions of philosophy."[22] On account of this failure to challenge Western philosophy, Africa appears to Hountondji as the land of myths and irrational beliefs.

Hountondji's criticism of the anthropological discourse and his denunciation of the unanimist reading of African tradition should have brought him around to the idea that tradition is misrepresented by Western concepts. What fails him is that his criticisms of the West, no doubt pertinent, are not radical enough, being but a repetition of what Marx says about capitalism. A Marxist critique of the West does not really question Western hegemony; it only advocates assimilation to the European culture defined as the universal and most progressive culture. Real and radical criticism starts when the West is no longer viewed as a model, when its Eurocentrism is denounced and its model of philosophy questioned. Once the Western paradigm is denounced as Eurocentric, the quest for otherness becomes legitimate. The need to reject the colonial definition of Africans must not suppress the idea of African difference. The problem is not so much the African difference as its formulation in terms free of Eurocentric stereotypes.

Hountondji fails to appreciate ethnophilosophers' disrespect for the Western canons of philosophy and their subsequent rejection of the exclusion of philosophy from non-Western cultures. Correctly understood, the defense of African philosophy means that "there is no timeless *essence* or 'essential unity' that characterizes all philosophizing, certainly no *single* style of inquiry, as Hountondji would have it."[23] The claim to otherness denounces the illegitimacy of reducing the human essence to the Western model, and so pleads in favor of diversity by allowing peoples the right to define themselves as they think appropriate. The charge that ethnophilosophy is devoid of critical approach is thus not receivable. The attempt to rehabilitate Africa contains a radical criticism of the Western view of Africa. Ethnophilosophy goes against the basic premises of Eurocentrism and denounces the error of acknowledging the West as a universal model both in philosophy and the definition of the human essence.

2. Philosophic Sagacity

The major objection of Hountondji and Towa is that ethnophilosophy conflates culture and collective beliefs with philosophy. The denial of the existence of a traditional philosophy in its authentic form can be refuted if the proof is given that individuals with a critical mind existed in traditional Africa. The Kenyan philosopher Henry Odera Oruka initiates this approach, which is an attempt to steer the middle course between ethnophilosophy and professional philosophy. Let us first indicate in what sense his approach refuses ethnophilosophy.

A. The Critical Individual

Odera Oruka supports Hountondji's and Towa's stipulation that the appearance of individuals who are critical of traditional beliefs is a necessary condition of philosophy. For him too, ethnophilosophy is unacceptable because "it identifies with the totality of customs and common beliefs of a people," and so "forms a sharp contrast with philosophy developed by reason and logic."[24] Instead of deriving African philosophy from the traditional cultures, as ethnophilosophy does, Odera Oruka attempts to identify individuals who, although otherwise immersed in the traditional life, are nevertheless critical of it. The method avoids the mistaken identification of philosophy with culture or collective thoughts: it looks for native individuals who adopt a critical position *vis-à-vis* the collective thinking. The discovery of a critical attitude among Africans not yet Westernized disproves the colonial allegation that Africans are incapable of critical mind. Odera Oruka coined the term "philosophic sagacity" to differentiate from ethnophilosophy the authentic nature of this practice of philosophy in a traditional setup.

The expression "philosophic sagacity" refers to the existence of sages who, in contradistinction to traditional sages, are also thinkers. Though folk sages are experts in the wisdoms and traditions of their people, they are deficient in critical thinking, and so are not philosophers. They become so only if they are also thinkers, for "as thinkers, they are rationally critical and they opt for or recommend only those aspects of the beliefs and wisdoms which satisfy their rational scrutiny."[25] This distinction between the sage and the sage philosopher means that people with deep knowledge of traditional beliefs and practices are not yet philosophers if they lack the critical attitude. More often than not, such people are harsh defenders of the traditional system and differ from the common member of the group only by the depth of their knowledge. By contrast, in addition to having a first hand knowledge of the traditional culture, sage philosophers exhibit the rare attribute of being skeptical about many aspects of the traditional culture, especially as regards its mythological contents. As one scholar writes, "the result of Sagacity is critical effort, which is the property of individuals rather than the community at large. It is that feature that Odera Oruka takes to distinguish what he calls Sagacity from ethnophilosophy."[26]

This need for a critical approach does not, however, entail the endorsement of the other requirements of professional philosophers. Notably, Odera Oruka resents "the claim that authentic African philosophy can and must only be a scientific (i.e., systematic) and/or written philosophy," for such a claim "rules out philosophic sagacity as a part of African philosophy, since this trend is largely unwritten and apparently 'pre-scientific.'"[27] He finds the claim totally unjustified in view of the fact that neither writing nor scientific knowledge is a precondition of philosophical thought. Witness: "Socrates . . . never wrote any of the doctrines 'attributed' to him as his philosophy. And among the pile of written philosophical literature there is no single methodology identifiable as belonging specifically to philosophy."[28]

While the emphasis on the critical individual places Odera Oruka among the professional philosophers, his rejection of science and script as prerequisites for philosophical thinking sets him apart. As he says, philosophic sagacity "is the only trend that . . . can give an all-acceptable decisive blow to the position of ethnophilosophy," while avoiding the weakness of the professional school.[29] Ethnophilosophy continues to appeal to Africans so long as they are offered no other alternative than the view of professional philosophers. Since the issue of African philosophy pertains to dignity, Africans will accept whatever is proposed to them as philosophy rather than acquiesce to the denial of African philosophy. The best refutation of the colonial allegation is to show that philosophers in the true sense of the world have existed in precolonial Africa. Against the view of Lévy-Bruhl and others, philosophic sagacity proves:

> the problem in traditional African is not lack of logic, reason, or scientific curiosity, since we can find many sages there with a system of thought employing a rigorous use of these mental gifts. It shows that communal consensus, a fact typical of most traditional societies, should not be seen as a hindrance for individual critical reflection.[30]

Besides disproving the alleged irrationality of Africans, philosophic sagacity assigns to modern African philosophy the task of collecting and recording the thoughts of traditional thinkers. The purpose of this work is not to repeat the past, but to provide a basis for the emergence of a modern

African thinking. The collection of traditional philosophical thoughts by trained African philosophers supplies the necessary materials for the inauguration of a properly African and modern philosophical discourse. As D. A. Masolo explains, "the traditional discourse which must be retrieved from the sages and sage philosophers must be the runway from which [contemporary African philosophy discourse] ought to take place."[31]

B. The Individual and the Collective

Critics are quick to point out the elusive nature of the notion of sage philosophy by arguing that Odera Oruka proves not so much the real existence of African philosophers as their abstract possibility or potentiality. To begin with, the method of interview and questionnaire used to ascertain the existence of sage philosophers is dubious. Its outcome so heavily involves the interpretative work of the interviewer, namely, of the modern African philosopher, that the concepts and ideas properly belonging to the interviewee are difficult to determine. Peter O. Bodunrin speaks of "the product of the joint enquiry of the traditional sage and the trained philosopher" as being itself "a new phenomenon," a mixture of traditional notions and Western views belonging to the interviewer.[32] Indeed, the interviews and questionnaires are arranged according to Western concepts and lines of thinking. Whether this alien transcription of the traditional thought does not reproduce the very defect of ethnophilosophy, to wit, the arbitrary projection of philosophical concepts on to beliefs originally foreign to philosophy, is a legitimate question.

Odera Oruka's use of Socrates, which is an important piece of his argument, hardly proves the point he is trying to make. True, Socrates did not write, though he definitely knew how to write in addition to belonging to a tradition of script. His membership in a culture of script creates a situation quite different from a purely oral tradition. Furthermore, "writing is an important vehicle for the systematization and growth of knowledge."[33] Without skeptical thoughts being communicated across time and space by means of script, a critical tradition can scarcely exist. Still less can these thoughts accumulate and grow if they are constantly undone by the lack of systematic recording. Stated otherwise, the absence of script may have in fact prevented sages from becoming really philosophers, that is, from developing a systematic critical thinking. What the thesis of sage philosopher really proves is then the abstract potentiality of philosophers in traditional Africa, which potentiality never became real simply because the lack of writing thwarted the evolution of sages into real philosophers.

The emergence of such philosophers is rendered all the more difficult by Odera Oruka's persistent portrayal of philosophic sages as exceptional individuals entirely at odds with their culture. Socrates did not appear out of nothing: he is the product of the sophist tradition and Greek democracy. If a favorable social environment is thus necessary for the blooming of philosophers, then on top of repeating the colonial allegation of primitive Africa, the way Odera Oruka isolates the African thinker makes the appearance of philosophic sagacity extremely unlikely. Just as the antagonism between the individual thinker and the prevailing culture rules out the emergence of the sage philosopher from the traditional culture, neither does it allow the derivation of traditional beliefs from the critical thinking of individuals. The supposition of a culture totally alien to critical attitudes completely blocks the very possibility of philosophic sagacity, to say nothing of the difficulty in explaining the protracted survival of societies without their beliefs being constantly refined and adapted to the various challenges of life.

If societies cannot survive without a minimum of critical aptitude, then the radical antagonism between sage philosophy and its cultural milieu is an overstatement. Consequently,

> the thesis put forward by Oruka that philosophic sagacity differs from ethnophilosophy (culture philosophy) on the grounds that philosophic sagacity entails critical and personal thought, while ethnophilosophy does not, cannot be sustained.[34]

Instead, the conviction should be that the so-called collective and uncritical beliefs owe their existence to critical inquiries, however scanty and faulty they may have been, for the simple reason that individual thinkers first initiated them.

The net result of this criticism is to show the untenability of the antinomy between sage philosophers and their society. The truth is that the opposition ends up by endorsing the colonial discourse on the primitive character of African thinking. The best way is still to assign the authorship of the collective thoughts to individual thinkers with the understanding that their actual dogmatic form is typical of a frozen tradition. The tactic of sacrificing the whole as irrational, in order to save some individuals, backfires. The scheme admits that, in the main, African cultures were established without any critical spirit, and that critical views, if any, were so marginal and isolated that they have no part in the formulation of African cultures.

3. Fanon and the Rehabilitation through Violence

Among the critics of ethnophilosophy, Frantz Fanon occupies a distinct place by the argument that only a philosophy of violence consummates the rejection of both otherness and the restoration of the past. As Hountondji, Fanon sympathizes with the goal of rehabilitation and perfectly understands the meaning of the strategy of otherness and the passionate attempt to revive the past. Ethnophilosophy aims at persuading Africans that they have no reason to put up with the degrading interpretation of their past, that they can and must reinterpret their past in a way consonant with their pride and interests. In countering the disabilities induced by colonial rule, ethnophilosophy thinks of preparing Africans for a promising future. The purpose of the return to the source, Fanon writes, is to show:

> there was nothing to be ashamed of in the past, but rather dignity, glory, and solemnity. The claim to a national culture in the past does not only rehabilitate that nation and serve as a justification for the hope of a future national culture. In the sphere of psycho-affective equilibrium it is responsible for an important change in the native.[35]

Neither the racialization of Africans nor the return to the source can bring about the promised bright future. Instead of understanding black identity as an outcome forged by the process of the actual struggle, the negritude movement resorts to a fixed and ahistorical race attribute, even at the expense of endorsing colonial descriptions of the black entity. The result is the definition of African identity in terms antagonistic to modern requirements. The gap between Africa and Europe further enlarges to the detriment of Africans. Fanon depicts the effects of the African endorsement of racialization as follows:

> He [the Negro] congratulates himself on this, and enlarging the difference, the incomprehension, the disharmony, he finds in them the meaning of his real humanity. . . . And it is with rage in his mouth and abandon in his heart that he buries himself in the vast black abyss. We shall see that this attitude, so heroically absolute, renounces the present and the future in the name of a mystical past.[36]

Since all African attempts to differ from the West backfire by further enlarging the gap, the only choice left for Africans is to settle the issue by means of confrontation.

A. Violence as Self-Creation

To understand the role of violence in Fanon's philosophy, we begin by indicating why for Fanon the relationship between the colonized and the colonizer cannot be translated in terms of Hegelian dialectics. Georg Wilhelm Friedrich Hegel's dialectics between master and slave relates a situation in which the need for recognition sets one human being against another human being. Recognition refers to the desire of each individual to be accepted as a free being, that is, as a being beyond the mere act of existing. At the initial stage of human history, the demonstration that human dignity "is not tied up with life" is the only way by which one individual can gain recognition from another individual.[37] The extent of the readiness of individuals to sacrifice their life is a manifestation of freedom, and the proof that they are indeed beyond mere existence. To use Hegel's words:

> it is solely by risking life that freedom is obtained; only thus is it tried and proved that the essential nature of self-consciousness is not bare existence, is not merely immediate form in which it at first makes its appearance, is not its mere absorption in the expanse of life.[38]

The struggle for recognition turns into a fight for life and death. Those individuals who back down from staking their life accept defeat and become slaves. Because slaves accept to work in exchange for the preservation of their life, their masters are relieved of the necessity of working. In thus placing between themselves and nature human tools, slave owners fully assert and enjoy their freedom. This is not, however, the end of the story. Through toiling and the subsequent mastery of nature, slaves reappropriate the sense of dignity and freedom. In shaping nature, the toiling consciousness "only becomes aware of its own proper negativity, its existence on its own account, as an object, through the fact that it cancels the actual form confronting it."[39] By contrast, the master is in a precarious situation. For one reason, the freedom that the master enjoys is recognized by an unfree human being. For another, the choice of a mode of life reduced to the mere consumption of nature accelerates the dependence of the master on the slave, thereby turning the autonomy of the master into "a dependent consciousness."[40]

This dialectical reversal is headed for the rehabilitation of the slave even as it knocks the master off the pedestal. The reversal opens up an historical process progressively leading to the dissolution of bondage and lordship in favor of the universal recognition of equality and freedom. What Hegel establishes is, then, that violence is a necessary moment in the history of the recognition of human freedom. This history initiates a contradictory outcome: it asserts freedom through the negation of freedom. However, slavery generates the conditions of its emancipation so that the process moves toward the mutual cancellation of servitude and domination.

According to Fanon, the colonial situation cannot deliver this outcome of mutual recognition, blocked as it is by the assumption of the inferiority of the colonized peoples. The Hegelian situation describes the loss of freedom as a result of defeat between two contending individuals; it does not portray a situation where the one partner is considered as subhuman. In the colonial situation, defeat itself is construed as an expression of that inferiority and not, as Hegel describes, as a lack of courage. In the dialectics of struggle for recognition, the humanity of the contenders is never in question; the fight is about knowing who is ready to defend freedom to the point of accepting to sacrifice life. Radically different is the colonial situation. Though the situation exhibits a similar desire for recognition, it does not fall under the same dialectical rules. Because bondage is more a loss of freedom than an attribute of inferiority, Hegelian slaves can recover their freedom from defeat. Not so the colonized, who are slaves by nature, so to speak. Toiling can never remove their sub-humanity. Here servitude is a dialectics without possible synthesis, that is, mutual recognition.

This awareness of colonialism as an obstructed dialectics explains Fanon's philosophy of violence. The colonial situation is not expressive of a struggle for recognition similar to what Hegel had in mind. Unlike the Hegelian slave who "withdraws into the object and submission, Fanon's Negro aspires to be like the master, he aspires toward freedom."[41] Why? Because colonial servitude has no positive, human outcome for the colonized: this kind of servitude is a deadlock. The demonstration of the desire for freedom and recognition by risking one's life remains the only option. Since colonial racism deprives the colonized self of any hope of obtaining recognition, some such absence of positive outcome brings dialectics back to the initial stage of confrontation where the willingness to die decides the fate of one's freedom. Showing that the African is beyond life becomes the only assertive expression of freedom and dignity.

Violence begins its dissolving impact by subjecting the colonial master to fear. This fear suspends the assurance of the colonial lords; it also inculcates in them the respect of those individuals who prefer death to continued servitude. This violence becomes decisive, as the colonized, fully identifying with their wretchedness, understand that they have nothing to lose. Hegelian slaves have a stake in the world that their labor shaped, and hence aspire to become full members. Such is not the case of the colonized, who have nothing to gain as a result of racial exclusion. Dispossessed of attributes and belongings, their essence is their wretchedness. To assume this wretchedness is for them to acquire the experience of pure subjectivity as absolute negativity.

This level of identification defines the colonized by the readiness to risk their life. No identity drawn from the past can reach this new self. Such a self has no other definition than this readiness: it is pure freedom because it values freedom more than life. In relating themselves to freedom through the readiness to die, the colonized clearly indicate what is at stake. They no longer consent to be defined by fixed attributes, for instance, as belonging to a race or having this or that glorious past. All these attempts have failed, and the colonized must show their humanity, not in an incarnated form, but in a pure, transcendent, universal form, as ready to die for freedom, in short, as untamable. "No," says Fanon, in the colonial situation, "I do not have the right to be a Negro . . . I have one right alone: That of demanding human behavior from the other."[42] What comes first is the humanity of the colonized, the struggle for recognition as human beings, not the recognition of particularity. The struggle is for human rights, not for the recognition of difference or sameness.

Violence expresses this disincarnate, ethereal freedom. It is how freedom exists less as an attribute than as the very subject exacting recognition through the risking of life. The rehabilitating value of violence lies in the unequivocal assertion that the colonized are ready to risk the only and most precious thing they have, to wit, their life, for their dignity and equality. Violence brings the whole issue of the emancipation of the colonized to a final showdown: the awe-inspiring act of violence cleans the disabilities inflicted by colonial rule off the soul of the colonized. It forces respect on the colonizer, but more importantly, it brings the colonized round to the idea of their own self-respect. Completely disavowing the method of ethnophilosophy, which expects the rise of pride and dare from cultural revival, Fanon maintains that "violence alone, violence committed by the people, violence organized and educated by its leaders, makes it possible for the masses to understand social truths and gives the key to them."[43]

Violence alone can succeed in undoing the drawbacks of colonial rule. In particular, it dissolves the inferiority complex from which the colonized suffer. Contrary to native thinkers who internalize the feeling of inferiority by endorsing otherness, the revolutionary thinker does not demand the equality of races without ever explaining how equality tallies with the notion of racial differences. Fanon finds the whole attempt to find an untarnished definition of the black essence useless and self-defeating. Clearly differentiating his project from that of ethnophilosophy, he writes:

> it would be easy to prove, or to win the admission, that the black is the equal of the white. But my purpose is quite different: What I want to do is help the black man to free himself of the arsenal of complexes that has been developed by the colonial environment.[44]

Discourses on the equality of races are far removed from the right solution for the simple reason that they do not attack the inferiority complex with which the notion of race is saddled.

Fanon's position concerning the issue of race and racism best accounts for his choice of violence as the only efficient form of rehabilitation. For him, the concept of race is debilitating; it offers no escape. The belief in race coming from the colonized can only be the product of an internalized colonial mentality. When Blacks speak of race, even to demand equality, a white internalized voice is speaking through them. Race is therefore an invented concept: "the Negro is not. Any more than the white man."[45] Accordingly, there is no way by which the notion of race can be brought to signify equality, given that it was originally designed to negate equality and express hierarchy.

Fanon finds stupid and naive the attempt to salvage the notion of race. The racialization of human beings was an insult and remains so. You do not rehabilitate an insult.

The best way to remove the insult is first to specify its exact meaning so as to avoid fighting against phantoms. This means the deconstruction of the notion of race. The result of the deconstruction is that inferiority complex "is the outcome of a double process:—primarily, economic—; subsequently, the internalization—or better, the epidermalization—of this inferiority."[46] If racial distinctions are the manner economic inequalities are justified, then the internalization of those distinctions by the colonized turns into an endorsement of inferiority. Negritude and other philosophies calling for the recognition of the equality of races forget that races are originally designed to justify inequality. Nor do they understand that the acceptance of racial classification is an admission of inferiority. The disguise of the social meaning of race as a natural determinant induces these theories to believe wrongly that the parade of diverse inheritances strongly militates in favor of equal status. The exposure of the initial dispersion of the human essence is never tantamount to dissolving the hierarchical conception of race.

For Fanon, the primary task of native scholars should have been to avoid falling into the trap of racialist discourses. They should have begun attacking the very notion of race by exposing the practices to which the notion leads. Most of all, the unadulterated affirmation of the human, in lieu of the equalization of races, should have been their dominant theme. If they had taken such a resolute stand against the notion of race, violence would have appeared to them as the only nonracist, unqualified affirmation of the human person.

As soon as people exclusively connect themselves with the defense of their dignity as human beings, their subsequent response is less to convince than to remove oppressors. For Fanon, the promised renaissance of black people cannot come through a mere cultural redefinition. Insofar as race signifies economic exclusion, the only remedy is social revolution, the complete transformation of the economic order. Fanon thus joins the Marxist analysis: violence is necessary to destroy an unjust socioeconomic system. The merit of the social analysis of the notion of race is that everybody is put in the same socioeconomic system and races are conceptualized as expressions of unequal distribution of rights and power. The social approach grasps the notion of race as a social construct and reduces its meaning to discrimination. In this way, the fight targets the equal affirmation of human rights through the extirpation of the notion of race.

This breakdown of race classification into human and socioeconomic contents forcefully vindicates the regenerating impact of violence. The irreplaceable value of violence originates from the unique power to dissipate the deference inculcated in the natives. The colonized cannot free themselves from this deference unless they learn to become daring and disrespectful.

Violence is the way to such learning: it smashes what the natives have been taught to respect and revere. Only when the natives develop such an irreverent attitude can they rise above all oppressive forces. By subjecting the colonial world to the dissolving impact of violence, they commit the crime of *lese-majesty* that unleashes their autonomy. "Violence is a cleansing force. It frees the native from his inferiority complex and from his despair and inaction; it makes him fearless and restores his self-respect," says Fanon.[47]

Violence cannot extract the colonized from the arsenal of complexes without at the same time inaugurating their historicity. The act by which the colonized become defiant is also how they begin to exist for themselves, and so become real subjects. Violence thus attains self-creation. It is transition to historicity, since "it is only when the colonized appropriates the violence of the colonizer and puts forth his own concrete counterviolence that he reenters the realm of history and human historical becoming."[48] Resistance against the colonial army requires a new and higher form of organization, just as it institutes new forms of relationship among the participants. Such a struggle promotes a whole process of culture change in which people develop new ideas and forms of struggle to defeat a more powerful army. On the basis of their fighting organization, they also imagine a new social order. As Irele remarks:

> In the general mobilization of the physical and psychic energies of an entire people, old values inappropriate to the situation were swept away, new values created, presaging a new social order. The revolution thus took on the significance of an immense process of collective metamorphosis.[49]

To recapitulate, Fanon goes beyond the Marxist characterization of violence as the "midwife of history." He reads into the aggressive resistance against colonialism the gestation, the birth of a historical subject. Through the violence directed at their oppressors, the colonized peoples reconstitute their human self in an autonomous and unrestricted way. They emancipate from colonial neurosis by chasing out the settler through force of arms. During the struggle, they also develop efficient and more humane social relationships that can readily serve as a foundation for a new and just social order. Jean-Paul Sartre summarizes the whole outcome when he writes that, for Fanon, "violence is neither sound and fury, nor the resurrection of savage instincts, nor even the effect of resentment: it is man recreating himself."[50]

B. Impotent Violence

The evaluation of Fanon's stand against ethnophilosophy must bear in mind that Fanon does not raise the issue of violence only as a means of expelling the rule of an outsider. He attributes to violence a therapeutic and creative value: violence liberates the colonized from inferiority complex and turns them into active makers of history. My purpose is to question the alleged therapeutic and creative value of violence.

Let me begin by saying that Fanon's rejection of the rehabilitation of the past sounds excessive. His position would have been correct if, instead of characterizing the rehabilitation of the past as a useless and detrimental attempt, he had implied that it was not enough to obtain liberation. What makes his argument against the rehabilitation of the past even less receivable is that, more than anybody else, Fanon has studied the profound and devastating effects of inferiority complex on the colonized peoples. His study suggests that this sense of inferiority has been inculcated by a deliberately disparaging discourse on the history of these peoples. If so, the reason why the attempt to refute the colonial discourse would be without effect is not clear. The discredit of the legacy of the colonized peoples having induced the inferiority complex, the rehabilitation of the legacy should act as an antidote.

Fanon's resolution to convince the colonized that they have no other option than recourse to violence is at best exaggerated and highly restrictive. The method of ethnophilosophy, notably the claim to otherness and the subsequent endorsement of the notion of race, can be debilitating. Still, other ways than racial classifications exist to defend pluralism. Such is the case, for instance, of cultural pluralism, which draws diversity from cultural rather than biological inheritances. This position is all the more consistent the more identities are ascribed to inventions, a case in point being Fanon himself. To say that "the nigger" does not exist any more than the white man is to hold that what distinguishes people is less their biological determinants than the way they choose to define themselves. This fact of identities being constructs allows the cultural approach to pluralism.

Fanon's opposition to cultural rehabilitation does not yet indicate why violence should take the lead. His argument that the rehabilitation drawn from the past is an illusory wealth, which distracts the colonized from fully identifying with their wretchedness and hence from growing into a real revolutionary force, can be seriously contested. The question whether violence is an efficient and relevant response to the challenge posed by Western hegemony must be posed against the background of economic power being the major driving force of the modern world. No response is really defiant of the West if it does not pave the way to economic power.

This issue of economic power is how Hegel takes his revenge on Fanon. Does not Hegel's analysis point out that the mastery of nature is the only dialectical, progressive way to liberation? Contrary to the dialectics of Hegel in which the slave submits and turns his attention to work, Fanon wants the colonized to rebel. Without the episode of violent confrontation, Fanon maintains, the colonized will never gain freedom and self-respect. Freedom remains a mere grant of the colonizers so long as it is not wrenched from them. Galvanizing and fulfilling though the snatching of freedom may appear to be, in the context of colonial and neocolonial domination, Fanon's view overlooks one crucial aspect of the question: the colonized are yet to understand the real reason for their subordination. They will understand the real reason if they ascribe their inferiority to their inability to dominate nature.

But then, the issue is not so much the violent expulsion of the colonizer as the resolution to rise to the economic challenge. So long as the economic handicap persists, independence remains illusory. Fanon is right when he states that independence is not enough, but wrong when he stipulates that regeneration cannot occur without the moment of violent confrontation.

Without economic and technological power, the violence that the colonized brandish against the West is anything but frightening. The violence of arrows and spears against missiles and jet fighters is unable to achieve any positive outcome. So long as violence is not backed by science and technology, the whole idea of considering the third world as a rising revolutionary force intent on toppling the developed world is nothing but laughable. Insofar as the poor world is granted a power of violence that it does not yet possess, Fanon can be justifiably accused of putting the cart before the horse. In being technologically insignificant, the violence of the third world will be countered by real violence, to paraphrase Fanon. If violence thus resolves nothing because it cannot even be real violence without the power of technology, the narrowing of the technological gap emerges as the only antidote to Western hegemony, and hence the only dissolvent of the inferiority complex. Let alone curing the disease, the prescription of bravado retards the administration of the real remedy.

As to Fanon's equation of negritude and ethnophilosophy to an internalization of the colonial world, the whole question is to know whether the valorization of violence and the vision of human relationships in terms of violent confrontations are not an internalization of the violent colonial world. The question makes sense in view of the fact that Fanon endows violence with a curative mission. If violence is an outcome of colonial rule, how can it possess curative virtues? The attempt to decontaminate one's soul from such a perversion would be the right attitude.

Fanon rightly takes note of the accumulated anger of the colonized people, but never shows how this immense anger could be transformed into a creative work. His proposal is not to sublimate anger; it is instead to let anger explode. Yet is capitulation to anger likely to have a positive outcome when it is merely providing an outlet to destructive impulses? What the third world needs is less to surrender to its anger than to channel it into constructive works. The sublimation of violence, and that alone, would be the right therapy. Alluding to the curative and creative role of sublimation, the apostle of nonviolence Mohandas K. Gandhi gives us the following lesson:

I have learned by bitter experience, through a period of close upon thirty years, the one supreme lesson, namely, to conserve my anger, to control it, and just as heat conserved is transmuted into energy, so also our anger, conserved and controlled, can result in a power that becomes irresistible throughout the world.[51]

Nonviolent resistance has the clear impact of denouncing the barbarism of the colonizer, thereby drawing a clear demarcation line between the values of the oppressor and the ideals of liberation. In demystifying and rejecting violence, nonviolence graciously prepares a bright and democratic future, the very one where force will have no say. Whereas the myth of violence ends up by valorizing violence as a legitimate resource, Gandhi's nonviolent option banishes forever the use of force from human society. Not even against the colonizer was violence used: such is the norm that nonviolence establishes.

When anger is given full vent, instead of being conserved and controlled, the outcome is rarely positive. History has repeatedly confirmed the sticking mania of violence. Guerilla movements interiorize violence so deeply that, despite their often generous goal, they end up by instituting violent regimes for the simple reason that they have lost the sense of true human relationships. In this regard, the Algerian case is instructive. As an active participant in the Algerian war of liberation, Fanon believed that the ideals of the war would preside over the emergence of a modern and peaceful Algerian society. The fact that independent Algeria is still torn by violent conflicts and little engaged in a resolute process of modernization invalidates the alleged creative role of violence.

Once violence is internalized, it will sully all the behavior of the colonized, who would then behave in the same violent way *vis-à-vis* each other. This violent disposition has a hand in the failure of most third-world countries to institute democratic societies. Grant violence with the power to provide solutions, and no reason exists to assume that the problems of postcolonial societies do not fall under the same treatment. Viewed from this necessity of cleansing the colonized soul of the accumulated anger, the appeal of negritude thinkers to the particular essence of the black soul appears as a protection against colonial contaminations, as an attempt to preserve a measure of human countenance in a world disfigured by violence. In terms of learning disrespect and shaking off inferiority complex, Fanon and many African scholars fail to appreciate the insolence inscribed in the aloofness from Western rationality that the philosophy of negritude glorifies.

Five

PARTICULARISM VERSUS OTHERNESS

The previous chapter has studied the arguments of those thinkers who reject ethnophilosophy as a result of their commitment to human sameness. This chapter deals with African thinkers who earmark a place for particularism while rejecting ethnophilosophy. They decline otherness because it defines Africans as antithetical to Westerners, though they also resent the normativeness of the West through the universalist interpretation of Western history. Between opposition and assimilation, there is place, they say, for a diversity that avoids both the negative polarization of ethnophilosophy and the reductionist direction of professional philosophers. Most controversial among such African thinkers is Cheikh Anta Diop's non-othering racialization.

1. Diop and the Stolen Legacy

Diop agrees with the professional philosophers: no matter the point of originality that Léopold Sédar Senghor tries to make, the very attempt to dissociate blackness from the rational type of knowledge comes up against the goal of rehabilitation. In Diop's eyes, the valorization of the emotional aptitude indicates the degree to which "the Negro intellectual" has lost "confidence in his own potential and that of his race."[1] However, the professional philosophers too wander when they attribute the paternity of rational knowledge to the West; in reality, the black race is the original inventor of rationality.

A. Migrating Rationality

To refute the colonialist argument that the black race has produced no great civilization, Diop settles down to the job of demonstrating the African origin and character of ancient Egyptian civilization. For him, Egypt was essentially an African civilization in the sense that "its founders and sustainers were of the same racial groups that are currently dominant in sub-Saharan Africa, i.e., they were Black."[2] Since Egypt is admittedly the cradle of many great headways of world civilization, the thesis of black Egypt refutes the Hegelian denial of any contribution of the black continent. Above all, the thesis turns Europe into an eternal debtor of Africa by suggesting that the Greeks owe their scientific as well as philosophical inspiration to black Egyptians. As Diop writes, "Greece borrowed from Egypt all the elements of her civilization, even the cult of the gods, and that Egypt was the cradle of civilization."[3] Far from endorsing the non-technicalness of the black race, Diop operates an inversion that restores the merit of technical civilization to the rightful

African initiator. An inversion of such proportion has a formidable redemptive power. To quote Diop:

> to his great surprise and satisfaction, he [the African] will discover that most of the ideas used today to domesticate, atrophy, dissolve, or steal his "soul," were conceived by his own ancestors. To become conscious of that fact is perhaps the first step toward a genuine retrieval of himself; without it, intellectual sterility is the general rule, or else the creations bear I know not what imprint of the subhuman.[4]

For Diop, the clear defect of negritude is that the return to the source is not a return to a glorious past; instead, it is a return to insignificance. He corrects the mistake by conceiving the return as a retrieval of a high position previously held.

How does Diop establish the racial identity between black Africa and ancient Egyptians? (1) He begins by contesting the validity of Eurocentric writings on Africa. Because these writings are rigged by racist prejudices, they are not a dependable source of knowledge. (2) He appeals to testimonies of ancient as well as more recent historians who had visited Egypt: "eyewitnesses . . . formally affirm that the Egyptians were Blacks. On several occasions Herodotus insists on the Negro character of the Egyptians and even uses this for indirect demonstrations," he writes.[5] (3) He finds many sociocultural affinities between ancient Egyptians and black Africa, such as, totemism, circumcision, matriarchy, and cosmogonical beliefs, including the vitalist conception of reality and the ancestor cult.

To the question whether or not a traditional African philosophy existed, the answer is therefore a straight "yes," all the more confidently as the traditional thinking was a philosophy in the strict sense of the word. Going against the assumption of ethnophilosophy, Diop argues that for a thought to be called philosophical the thinking must be conscious of its existence as thought and must realize the separation between myth and concept to a sufficient degree. He maintains that this kind of thought was perfectly achieved by the Egyptians before everybody else, including the Greeks, who have but copied it from the Egyptians.[6] This suggests that the conscious and reflective source of what now exists in Africa as a collective and unconscious thought is ancient Egyptian philosophy. In view of the fact that these collective beliefs are frozen to the point of becoming unconscious, "it would be excessive to consider them as philosophical systems today."[7]

The revival of African philosophy on the strength of existing customs and beliefs, as practiced by ethnophilosophy, is not the correct method. There is no such a thing as an implicit and collective philosophy. The authentic African philosophy where all these beliefs and customs have their conscious and reasoned origin is ancient Egyptian philosophy. Africans must go to the direct source. For instance, the original inspiration of Bantu thinking, as studied by Placide Tempels, is to be found in ancient Egyptian philosophy, since the thinking "reveals, at the basis of every activity of being, vitalist conceptions that have grown semi-conscious."[8] This Egyptian connection removes another major objection against African philosophy by providing the proof of written documents.

As concerns the issue of otherness, Diop's position is somewhat complex. One thing is sure: as we saw, he rejects the Senghorian idea of an epistemological disparity between the West and Africa by ascribing the paternity of reason to Africa. The so-called Greek miracle is just a fraud: the miracle was African. The only originality that Diop recognizes to the Greeks is to have developed the materialist component of Egyptian cosmology: "materialist atheism is a purely Greek creation," he writes.[9]

That said, Diop is convinced that Africans belong to a different race on account of which they exhibit a deep and compelling cultural unity. He speaks of his attempt to "bring out the profound cultural unity still alive beneath the deceptive appearance of cultural heterogeneity."[10] For a substrate of cultural unity supposedly derived from ancient Egypt to thus persist beneath the superficial cultural diversity of Africans today, there must be something more than the mere geographical neighborliness of African societies, something as deep and stubborn as the racial oneness of Africans. "In this respect," Irele Abiola writes, "Diop comes closest to Senghor, both in his vision of the African world as a unified whole and in his acquiescence with the theory of Tempels as regards the vitalist conception of the world."[11]

Another essential confirmation of the racialization of Africans is the concurrence of Senghor's idea of different civilizations with Diop's thesis of the two cradles of civilization. Through a comparative study, Diop finds, as the thinkers of negritude, striking differences between "the southern cradle of mankind" and "the northern cradle" that pertain to their "conceptions of domestic life, statecraft, philosophy, and morals."[12] Again agreeing with the thinkers of negritude, Diop proposes the operation of divergent forces, thereby suggesting that there was no evolution from the one cradle to the other. Instead, the two systems had coexisted until the European invasion of Africa.

One question comes to mind. Diop speaks of the two cradles of civilization while maintaining that the Negro is the real father of Western civilization: Are not these two statements contradictory? The African essence is either different from or similar to the Western form. In the first case, Africa cannot be the originator of the Western type of civilization; in the second, the African technical retardation becomes a mystery. Diop's theory is seemingly subtle enough to reconcile the two positions. That black Africa remains the sole inventor of the technical and scientific orientation is a direct product of racial endowments and the type of civilization the endowments have promoted in Egypt. The European spirit, defined by patriarchy, the war spirit, and nomadic life, which are all symptomatic of a backward mode of life, was congenitally unable to generate the cultural premises of rational thinking.

The only explanation left to the unexpected migration of rationality from Africa to Europe is that Europeans stole rationality from Africans and developed it in the direction of gratifying their conquering impulse, a development that proved extremely detrimental to African civilization. In brief, the racial excellence of Africans, and that alone, explains the emergence of rationality at a time when Europe was wallowing in savagery.

The aggressive march of the northern cradle against the southern cradle was facilitated by the progressive desertification of the Sahara, which cut off the northern part from the rest of Africa, while Egypt itself became the victim of successive invasions as a result of which the impact of the black race was progressively diminished. From then onward, Diop writes,

> separated from the mother country [Egypt] which was invaded by the foreigner, and withdrawn in a geographical setting [south of the Sahara] requiring a minimum of effort of adjustment, the Blacks were oriented toward the development of their social, political, and moral organization, rather than toward speculative scientific research that their circumstances failed to justify, and even rendered impossible.[13]

The sharp opposition between Africans and Westerners is not true, not because there are no differences between them, but because Europeans stole and adopted a rationality that the black essence had invented. Europeans Africanized their culture and thanks to their military conquest and technological supremacy they were able to erase the African paternity of their changed culture.

Besides the misfortune of ecological change, Diop attributes the technological stagnation of Africa to the communalism of its social life. Though African communalism represents a morally higher social system that protects individuals from abusive expropriation and exploitation, some such protective system has "a tendency to become petrified."[14] By contrast, the barbaric system of the north was quick to develop into class divisions, fraught with permanent conflicts as well as with social mobility and technological advances. We owe to Karl Marx the complete elucidation of the revolutionary potential of class struggle both in terms of social change and technological progress. The Marxist idea of class struggle as the motive force of history suggests a connection between the hindrance of the development of classes by the African egalitarian and collective system and the lack of progress of material life. Collective ownership of the means of production and egalitarian distribution discourage the accumulation of economic surplus by banning labor exploitation. Though morally commendable, such a social system becomes a fetter to material progress. As one scholar comments:

> Africa was spared revolutions because all social classes enjoyed a tolerable existence, including even the least fortunate, such as the slaves. This very stability led to stagnation and explains African technological backwardness.[15]

As the retarding effect of the social system is a ransom for moral superiority, Africans must no longer be embarrassed about technological backwardness. Nevertheless, Africans paid dearly for their moral superiority. Though they had a civilization superior to that of Europe in many ways, the technological advantage of Europe, soon stepped up by the production of firearms, made them powerlessness to withstand colonialism. In the words of Diop, "the Negro, although he was the first to discover iron, had cast no canons."[16] But let it never be forgotten that Africa owes its defeat not so much to its alleged primitiveness as to a cultural choice vulnerable to the more aggressive drive of the northern peoples. The peaceful orientation made Africa defenseless even as the orientation generated the kind of philosophy that made possible the Western technological advance. The West divorced the stolen African rationality from the original sociocultural premises of peaceful orientation and used it for the purpose of conquest and hegemony.

The relation between Diop and negritude can therefore be characterized as a disagreement that evolves into an agreement. There is disagreement on the African paternity of reason and agreement as to the distinct cultural orientations of Africans and Westerners. Stated otherwise, Diop drifts away from negritude by a conception of racial identity that refrains from othering Africans: while the notion of the two cradles of civilization accommodates the specificity of black peoples, the African paternity of reason dissolves all binary opposition between the West and Africa.

B. Reverse Racism

Many critics locate the main weakness of Diop in his inability to raise the thesis of black Egypt to the level of a credible theory. The idea of the Negro origin of Egyptian civilization sounds so far-fetched that many speak of an eagerness to prove a point in lieu of a thorough presentation of facts. Others pinpoint exaggerations, as for instance the French historian, Jean Suret-Canale, who writes:

> If Sheikh Anta Diop jeers with reason at such European "scholars" who, through unadmitted racial prejudice, have tried to "whiten" ancient Egypt at all costs, then he himself falls into the same trap in seeking to

"blacken" at all costs, and to give a "Negro" origin to the civilizations of the Sumerians, Carthaginians . . . and Bretons.[17]

For this historian, the racial composition of the Egyptian population in antiquity was

> no different from what it is today; thousands of perfectly preserved mummies as well as skeletons, leave no doubt at all on this point!. . . . The truth is that in the past, as today, there was more or less pronounced miscegenation with the back population of the Upper Nile (such interbreeding also takes place in the opposite direction via the infiltration of white elements into Nubia). There are, and there always have been, Negro elements in Egypt, and even possibly Negro dynasties ruling over a white population.[18]

The abrupt manner Diop falls into the trap of the racist paradigm is indeed what many critics denounce. They say that Diop inverts the Hegelian formula, but he does the inversion "in the manner of Western scholars before him," since "he identifies with his own culture as the originator of world civilization."[19] The idea that other races owe everything to the black race, the sole creator of civilization, is simply an inverted racism. This way of denying the contributions of other races repeats the mistakes of Eurocentric racism when the attempt to go out of the racist paradigm altogether by refusing to establish any hierarchy between races should have been the right answer.

Palpable also are the internal tensions of Diop's theory. Thus, the explanation according to which Africans gave up rationality as a result of altered conditions of life is little convincing: the stipulation that sub-Saharan geographical conditions were not stringent enough to require the mobilization of rationality is hard to accept. Neither is consistent the recourse to the Marxist notion of class struggle to explain the African stagnation when class distinction is not evoked to account for the rise of Egyptian civilization in the first place. What is more, the use of the Marxist theory brings back evolutionary notions describing the classless social life of Africa as a backward stage. The theory of the two cradles of civilization suffers great damages as a result of these tensions. The idea of different civilizations had appeared plausible with negritude because the thinkers of negritude understood the two orientations as original dispositions. The plausibility vanishes with Diop who speaks of a rationality that begins in Africa only to desert for Europe. In addition to emptying the notion of the two cradles of all pugnacity, the idea of a migrant rationality introduces an element of surprise that suffuses the whole theory with unlikeliness.

These theoretical frictions together with the lack of factual supports assimilate Diop's work to a mythical enterprise. The assimilation is so true that some critics, reiterating the need for a radical questioning of the whole work, speak of "the sumptuous philosophy of history that has paralyzed the critical mind of generations of Africans."[20] According to such critics, just as was the case with negritude, the racist idealization of Africa has had a tremendously retarding effect on Africa. The glorification has blocked the development of critical thinking, while supporting the racist and nationalist ideologies of undemocratic and totalitarian regimes. Instead of concrete and scientific studies of African societies, the racialization of Africans has inspired the glorification of an illusory black unity and solidarity.

In thus deterring and castigating critical studies, the theory contributed to the blockage of the modernization of Africa. For such critics, then, the main question is not so much the credibility of Diop's theory as the detrimental effects of the theory on African societies. V. Y. Mudimbe expresses a similar skepticism about the positive effects of the myth making Africa into a cradle of civilization by asking whether "these potentially mobilizing myths provide, as Diop hoped, the possibility of a new political order in Africa."[21]

My position says the following: since we cannot imagine the rise of powerful African states without some mythical appeal, the issue is indeed less the necessity of a mythical conception than the efficiency, the empowering impact of the myth. In this regard, the reversal of Eurocentric racism seems little conducive to the liberation and empowerment of Africans. Diop is right when he believes that a glorious legacy feeds on the great ambitions of today; he is wrong when he infers that the canons of said greatness must be those of Europe. We saw how the negritude movement imagined a new greatness by particularizing the Western criterion of rationality. The aim is to decolonize the African mind to the point where Africans take pride of their characteristics regardless of whether or not they agree with Western canons. In this respect, by claiming the paternity of reason, Diop only exhibits his allegiance to Western norms.

The other belief that mars Diop's intellectual trajectory is his conviction that a theory cannot be acceptable and influential unless it is scientific. In his eyes, the attempt "to delude the masses engaged in a struggle for national independence by taking liberties with scientific truth, by unveiling a mythical, embellished past" is futile.[22] The need to give his theory a scientific appearance draws him into the thesis of black Egypt to begin with. This commitment to the scientific criterion holds him back from admitting the inventive, mythical character of his own thought, all the more regrettably that he detects the presence of human choice in the shift of African civilization from rationality to communal life. Predictably enough, nothing really good comes out of his scientific effort: the attempt provokes various objections whose outcome is the assimilation of his ideas to a controversial theory, not to mention the discomfort implicated in the claim to the glory of Egyptians when they themselves do not as yet identify with the claimers. As Kwame Anthony Appiah says mildly, Diop

> makes no argument that the Egyptian problematic is that of the contemporary African, and allows for a hovering, if inexplicit, suggestion that the Egyptians are important because the originators of the Pharaonic dynasties were black.[23]

A theory arouses belief because it supports present efforts, not because it is scientific. The best way to accomplish this empowering function is precisely to be inventive. In so being, the theory finds the opportunity of reflecting the deep aspirations of the people. The theory becomes true, credible because it invents the people as they themselves aspire to be, because it becomes the mirror of their imagination. Such a work is different from mere fancy insofar as it produces a consistent, coherent view that structures the perception of reality itself. The work connects the past with the present in such a way that present ambitions flow from past heritage, which is therefore reinvented. The secret of the operation lies in the interpretative power making reality itself into an accomplice of the mythical vision.

The next chapter will reflect on the operation of the mythical thinking. We have still to deal with chief African philosophers who pursue the cause of pluralism as the best alternative between ethnophilosophy and professional philosophers. One such author is the Ghanaian philosopher Kwasi Wiredu.

2. Traditionality in lieu of Otherness

For Wiredu, rationality has not reached in Africa a level of growth comparable to the West. Even so, African thinking is not totally unphilosophical. To have a sober assessment of the issue, it is essential to remember that rationality grows out from irrationality, that it is the outcome of a progressive and difficult conquest and not a fixed attribute given once and for all.

A. The Universal and the Particular

Wiredu approves Henry Odera Oruka's distinction between the sage and the sage philosopher, with the proviso that the collective thinking is considered as a philosophy in its own right. The reason for taking it as a philosophy is that collective beliefs originate in the brain of specific individuals before being adopted by the community. In short, they stem from critical reflections. As these reflections spread across the community, they solidify into more dogmatic and truncated forms that sages acting as keepers of tradition transmit. Accordingly,

there are two types of exponents of traditional philosophy. There are the
traditionalist reporters of the communal philosophy, and there are the
indigenous thinkers of philosophic originality. The former are, as a rule,
content with, or even insistent on, the transmission of the heritage
through quotation, paraphrase or, at best, exegetical flourishes, and do
not take too kindly to the idea of criticism and reconstruction. The
latter—a rare species in any society—are usually appreciative of the
tradition and cognizant of its rationale, but are not hide-bound to it. They
can reject or amend aspects of received conceptions and innovate with
their own contributions.[24]

The distinction should always be made between the thinking of those who
preserve the transmitted knowledge and the thinking of those who develop
critical views. Not that the one is philosophical while the other is not, but
because the transmitted one no longer refers to its individual and critical
origins as a result of being institutionalized.

Grant the philosophical origin of the folk thinking, and the interesting
question becomes that of knowing whether the thinking has any relevance to
contemporary Africans. In this regard Wiredu is categorical: the greater part
of the folk thinking is an obstacle to the major goal of modernization. If so,
traditionality in the precise sense of premodernity best defines the nature of
the collective thinking. Though philosophical, the precolonial thinking was
based on traditional concepts and assumptions. Because of this allegiance to
tradition, the thinking did not fully exhibit norms congruent with modern
rationality. This incongruence, however, did not signify otherness, but simply
the lower stage of evolution characteristic of traditional societies. Wiredu
explains the problem as follows:

> instead of seeing the basic non-scientific characteristics of African
> traditional thought as typifying traditional thought in general, Western
> anthropologists and others besides have tended to take them as defining
> a peculiarly African way of thinking.[25]

Western anthropologists had compelling reasons not to jump to the
conclusion that Africans are different. The smallest consideration of their own
history was enough to persuade them that what they take to be particular of
Africans was also overwhelmingly present in the recent history of Europe.
"Witchcraft in African," Wiredu reminds us, has never "attained the heights
to which it reached in Europe in the 16th and 17th centuries."[26] Even today
spiritistic beliefs are not just quite common among ordinary people; they "are,
in fact, deeply embedded in the philosophical thought of many contemporary
westerners—philosophers and even scientists."[27] An honest parallel between

Western history and African societies simply shows that the African of the anthropologists greatly resembles the premodern European.

From the fact that past Europeans differed from contemporary ones, nobody suggested that their disparity should be expressed in terms of otherness. The concept of modernity versus tradition is enough to account for the difference. Arrogance and racism alone, therefore, explain why the same disjunction between modernity and tradition is not applied to African societies when obviously "rational knowledge is not the preserve of the modern West nor is superstition a peculiarity of the African peoples."[28]

After a protracted tendency to self-aggrandizement, movements of thought appeared in the West, especially under the influence of postmodernism,

> displaying extreme abstemiousness with respect to claims of universality. At the same time, peoples previously marginalized (by reason of colonialism and related adversities) find the need, in seeking to redefine their self-identity, to insist on particulars—their own previously unrespected or neglected particularities—rather than universals.[29]

The coincidence of the abdication of universalism by a sector of Western thinking with the glorification of particularism by marginalized peoples is easy to understand. The increasing tendency of postmodernism to consider the West as a civilization among others, with its strengths and weaknesses, has a liberating effect. Postmodernism encourages peoples marginalized by colonial conquests to single out the particularity of their traditions. Sadly, this understandable assertion of dignity was soon disfigured by the cult of difference. Such a cult brought about a disastrous trend that Appiah, referring to Wiredu, characterized as "the evaluative assumption that the recovery of this tradition is worthwhile."[30] Given that traditionality is what Europe has already abandoned, the famous defense of African difference turns out to be the celebration of an anachronistic mode of thought. Not only is there nothing original, authentically African about the thinking, but also the revival of a premodern, folk philosophy is detrimental to the modernization of Africa. Since some such revival makes Africans impervious to science and technology and perpetuates their marginality, "ethnophilosophy is essentially a system of prescientific or preindustrial folk philosophies that have no direct relevance for the modern African who has adopted modern patterns of living."[31]

Most essential for Wiredu is that Africans cease to set particularity against universality by having a correct understanding of their connections. He finds that the alleged "incompatibility between the perspectives of universalism and particularism . . . is illusory," for the simple reason that "without . . . universals intercultural communication must be impossible."[32] Had the thesis of otherness and universal relativism been true, communication and exchange between cultures would have been impossible. Having nothing in common, cultures would simply fail to communicate. Yet communication between cultures is a reality, and the explanation cannot be other than "the possibility of cultural universals [being] predicated on our common biological identity as a species of bipeds."[33] Meanings cannot be confined to cultural peculiarities, any more than they can be reducible to individuals. Their transcendence overcomes all forms of human contingency. Such is the case of the principles of non-contradiction and induction as well as of the categorical imperative, considered by Wiredu as "the three supreme laws of thought and conduct." [34]

In light of this radical rejection of all forms of relativism, is there a place for particularism? Inasmuch as there are traits that are particular to Africans, particularism is a fact. The presence of cultural universals refutes the notion of human races without excluding the existence of particularities. Particular traits are the products of geography and history; they are acquired and contingent, and are simply added to the innate stock of universals.

Thus, the faculty of speech is instinctive, biological, while the use of a particular language is acquired and contingent. Religiosity is universal, yet different religions are particular. For instance, the determination of God as a "supra-human Supreme Being" is not African but particular to the West.[35] Resisting the temptation to humanize, Africans did not worship God, even though they consider Him to be powerful in the highest. Missionaries wrongly assigned this particularity to the primitiveness of Africans, to their inability to transcend the crude notion of an absentee God. The same can be said about morality: though moral customs are contingent, particular, there is a universal principle without which no action can be called moral in any culture of the world, as evinced by the fact that all moral values, such as "truthfulness, honesty, justice, chastity, etc., are simply aspects of sympathetic impartiality and do not differentiate morality from culture to culture"[36]

Unless the defenders of otherness get out of their either/or fixation and admit the impregnation of universals with particulars, they will not understand the extent to which the modernization of Africa is bound to be a synthesis of borrowed elements and particular traits. That is why African philosophy must not be reduced to African traditional philosophy. Even though African traditional philosophy was a philosophy in its own right, the task of contemporary African philosophers is not to exhume and extol the past. Instead, they should develop a critical approach to determine the relevance of the traditional philosophy for the modern world with the view of integrating those elements that support the effort of modernization.

In the agenda for contemporary African philosophy, Wiredu includes "the critical and reconstructive treatment of the oral tradition and the exploitation of the literary and scientific resources of the modern world in pursuit of a synthesis."[37] Of course, Wiredu thinks that European modernity too results from a synthesis of traditional beliefs and scientific notions, as shown by the survival of spiritualist beliefs. Why should modernization be otherwise for Africans?

To modernize in a serious way, Africans must break up with traditional habits of thought. The clear discrimination between what they must preserve from what they must not preserve is crucial to modernization. Those traits of the traditional life which are contingent, such as, customs, language, and styles, must be preserved because they relate to issues of identity while having no hindering effect on modernization. However, when the traits are such that they have bearing on issues of truth and falsehood, good and evil, then they must be extirpated and replaced by rationally acceptable criteria.

The truth is that "a culture can shed off many of its traits and gather foreign accretions without sacrificing its identity, provided that it does not lose its contingent features."[38] Every time a belief unknown or rejected by a traditional culture is proven to be true according to acceptable standards, the right attitude is to appropriate the belief. Any attempt "to ignore the proof in the name of cultural self-identity would demonstrate nothing more glorious than a collective pigheadedness."[39] Hence the crucial role of African philosophy inasmuch as philosophical assessment establishes the relevance of traditional beliefs in terms of what is true and right.

Wiredu suggests a smart middle course between Westernization and Africanness. African cultures can be profoundly westernized without loss of uniqueness so long as they preserve their native contingent traits. The preservation of these traits is enough to maintain the sense of distinct identities. But where fundamental issues are at stake, change in the sense of Westernization is inevitable under pain of stagnation. For Wiredu, Westernization is welcome, for the simple reason that it is the outcome of scientific rationality, which is universal. We have universal criteria of truth by which we can analyze all beliefs, be they African or Western, and reject those that are not rational. Turning his back to postmodernism, Wiredu maintains that the world is going toward universalism, not pluralism. Hence his statement that "the time might come when only humanly contingent features will individuate cultures."[40]

B. The Need to Limit Science

Wiredu's analysis of tradition and modernity is interesting if only because it downplays their alleged antagonism. The recognition of the traditional thinking as a philosophy, and not merely as a collection of irrational beliefs, tempers the antagonism. Even so, there is no denying that his criticism of tradition is harsh enough to resurrect incompatibility. At times the condemnation of tradition is total as when he writes:

It was a certain pervasive trait of this same culture that enabled sparse groups of Europeans to subjugate large masses of African populations and keep them in colonial subjection for many long years and which even now makes them a prey to neo-colonialism.[41]

The refusal of otherness obviously brings Wiredu round to the idea of turning tradition into a culprit, just as it deters him from asking whether the blame for the oppression of Africans should not be put on the intrinsic aggressivity of Western culture. Given this strong inclination to blame tradition, the extent to which his position differs from Paulin Hountondji's assessment is not clear. Also, calling the traditional thinking philosophy while complaining about its deficiency in rationality seems contradictory.

Some such position reimmerses Wiredu in the evolutionary approach, which weakens his criticisms of the West and prevents him from attempting an understanding of Africa free from Eurocentric biases. His belief in the universality and unquestionable value of scientific rationality and his assertion that cultures should differ only by contingent aspects rather than by deep alternative worldviews do not give much chance to Africa. Instead of blaming tradition, Wiredu should have asked how the universal rationality of science got involved in such activities as colonialism and slavery. Is not the involvement devious enough to challenge the absolute value and truth invested in scientific rationality? In addition to showing that the Cartesian project to become master and possessor of the world is not universally valid, one of the merits of the philosophy of negritude is the suggestion that there is a connection between the scientific advance of the West and its war-driven and racist ethos.

Because of his high regard for the scientific spirit, Wiredu does not raise the question of knowing whether his bias against tradition is not imparted by a Westernizing reading. Yet from a trend of thought that has inspired colonialism and racism, what else should be expected but an outright distortion of African beliefs and customs? Wiredu does not really delve into the distortion, being but content with the assertion that Westerners have forgotten how their own traditional thinking was full of irrational beliefs. His trust in the scientific method acts as a limitation preventing him from understanding the Western idea of Africa as a deliberate creation for the purpose of marginalizing African peoples and justifying their conquest. He analyzes the Western idea as an exaggerated description, not as a purposefully deceptive and demeaning view.

Wiredu's attempt to rehabilitate some African characteristics puts additional strain on his approach. Recall that for him, in contradistinction to Western traditional thought, "there is no bifurcation between nature and supernature" in the traditional African thought.[42] If Africans are thus more rational than Westerners, who have a greater inclination toward mysticism, the reason why they did not develop science and technology is unclear. May it be that Africans did not create science because they were not mystical enough? This would mean that the traditional worldliness of African thinking was not after all a positive factor: African beliefs were too down-to-earth to be able to rise to the level of science and technology. In effect, what if mysticism is a condition of modern rationality? Wiredu is so mesmerized by scientific rationality that he makes no attempt to understand the role of mysticism.

Yield for a moment to the temptation of giving mysticism a positive inspiration, and there grows the suspicion that what retards progress in Africa is less the persistence of traditional beliefs than the loss of the power to believe as a result of excessive criticism induced by the internalization of the colonial discourse. Wrongly hailed as a proof of modernity, the excessive valorization of criticism undermines Africa's power to believe, and hence its ability to generate galvanizing myths, so necessary to modernize. This is the place to reflect on the great merit of Immanuel Kant's project "to deny *knowledge*, in order to make room for *faith*."[43] Human beings must assign limits to science under pain of becoming victim of their creation. Though modern, Kant understands the need to protect human initiative from the absolute reign of scientific criteria, thereby reasserting the sovereignty of thought. Each time Africans, overwhelmed by the Western advances, call for the emptying of their unscientific beliefs, they undercut their own transcendence. Is it surprising if after this spiritual castration they lack the strength to cope with the exigencies of modernity?

3. From Otherness to Historicity: Hermeneutical School

Wiredu's dedication to the universalist framework does not give enough leverage for the emancipation of Africa. What is needed is a relativization such that Western philosophy, thus toppled from the universalist pedestal, enters into a free dialogue with African tradition. For the hermeneutical school, the revelation of the historicity of cultures is alone liable to liberate Africa from the suffocating tutorship of the West.

A. Historicity as Particularism

The African hermeneutical school rejects both the school of professional philosophers and ethnophilosophy. Against ethnophilosophy, it finds the identification of philosophy with culture and collective beliefs unacceptable. Instead, a collective and unconscious thought calls for philosophy, which is hermeneutics, interpretation intent on making the unconscious explicit. While taking culture as philosophy is a mistake, a philosophical reflection on culture is most relevant, the great difference being that, contrary to ethnophilosophy, hermeneutics remains distinct from the culture whose explication it is. In other words, "culture provides the horizon and the objection of life; philosophy is its hermeneutics or interpretation"; as such, hermeneutics is "an explicitation of what is already understood."[44]

Though hermeneutical thinkers refuse the identification of philosophy with culture, they do not endorse the position of professional philosophers. True, philosophy is different from culture; it is an individual, critical, and reflective mode of thought. Still, the African hermeneutical thinker maintains, the material for such a reflection stems from concrete cultures and traditions, not from abstract and universal premises. The hermeneutical philosopher takes seriously the historicity of human beings, arguing that philosophical reflection misses an essential dimension when it wanders away from the concrete conditions of life. Whether professional philosophers like it or not, the object of reflection is the concrete life of Africans with their legacy and the adverse forces that surround them, not "the universal man." As one scholar explains:

> Philosophers in the hermeneutical tradition have challenged both ethno-philosophical and universalist perspectives. These philosophers take African traditions as their starting point. Rooting themselves in what is traditional to Africa, they seek to escape an enslavement to the past by using that past to open up the future. Philosophy properly construed must move beyond a preoccupation with ethnological considerations and universalist abstraction and call into question the real relations of power in Africa.[45]

Tsenay Serequeberhan underlines the equal inability of ethnophilosophy and professional philosophers to get out of Eurocentrism. The mistake of professional philosophy is to remain "implicated in the 'prejudice that views Africa as primitive' by universalizing, as ontologically normative, the specific metaphysical singularity of European modernity."[46] Once the European experience is raised to the level of a universal norm, the particular experience of Africans turns into negative characteristics. Ethnophilosophy too echoes the same message of African primitiveness by "inadvertently valorizing essentialist stereotypical notions of Africa and Africans."[47] The error is that both schools uncritically endorse the Eurocentric descriptions of Africa. To correct the mistake, the hermeneutical orientation

> counters itself to the *particularistic antiquarianism* of Ethnophilosophy and to the *abstract universalism* of Professional Philosophy. It does so in an effort to think through the historicity of post-colonial "independent" Africa. In doing so, furthermore, it is fully cognizant of the fact that its

own hermeneutic efforts are part of the struggle to expand and properly consummate our presently unfulfilled and paradoxical "independence."[48]

Contrary to the position of professional philosophers, hermeneutical philosophers are open to and respectful of the cultural heritage of Africa, in addition to being careful not to endorse Western stereotypes about Africa. Nonetheless, they admit that the heritage is ossified to the point of being a hindrance to the modernization of Africa. This gives the proper scope of contemporary African philosophy: it "is constituted by its critical relation to the former [traditional thinking], in terms and in the context of contemporary problems and concerns."[49]

One strong point of the hermeneutical position is thus its commitments to engage fully in the reflection on the current crises of Africa. It speaks of a situation characterized by the non-fulfillment of the promises of independence, since neither real liberation nor economic prosperity became reality in a world dominated by neocolonialism. One specific result of neocolonial domination is that African elites, fashioned into "Europeanized Africans," act as agents of imperialism.[50] Talked into the idea of African primitiveness by their Westernized education, indigenous elites so internalize the colonial discourse and attitude that they unconsciously end up by applying the colonial policy to their own peoples. This secret adoption of colonial ideology and methods explains why African regimes are violent and non-democratic. Since they assume the task of continuing the civilizing mission of colonialism, such regimes have no respect for the peoples and are not accountable to them.

For Serequeberhan, this colossal failure is the challenge that invites philosophical thinking. In his words:

> the indisputable historical and violent diremption effected by colonialism and the continued 'misunderstanding' of our situation perpetuated by neocolonialism . . . calls forth and provokes thought in post-colonial Africa.[51]

Why does the failure provoke philosophical questions that are specifically African? For the obvious reason that it discloses the reconnection with the African past as a prerequisite to decolonization. The overlooking of cultural specificity leads to the policy of imposition of the Western model. The trouble is that the imposition calls for and justifies colonial methods: even indigenous elites give themselves over to such methods as a result of being Westernized. In light of this necessity to reconnect with the past, the task of African philosophy becomes the "critical and explorative engagement of one's cultural specificity and lived historicalness. It is a critically aware explorative appropriation of our cultural, political, and historical existence."[52] In being critical of the past, African philosophy is open to modernity; in being appropriation of cultural specificity, it contests the hegemony of the West, and so promotes self-affirmation.

B. The Persistence of Eurocentrism

A critical appraisal must begin by wondering whether the hermeneutical position does not dodge the issue by confining African philosophy to the contemporary world. We must not forget that the issue is about the legitimacy of identifying the traditional thought of Africa as philosophy. Nobody denies that an African philosophy exits today, but what about the past? Was the traditional thought also philosophy? The refutation of the colonial denigration of Africa depends on a clear answer to this question.

The hermeneutical philosopher sets one condition for the reappropriation of the past, namely, critical examination. The approach accepts the imperative to return to the past, under pain of perpetuating Western hegemony, but adds that the return to the past must be selective. As in the case of Wiredu, a harsh judgment is thus passed on tradition even before said tradition is saved from Western deformations. Unless the African intellectual first deconstructs Western concepts, the critical assessment of tradition is bound to remain prisoner of Eurocentric stereotypes. The tendency to find African tradition inadequate to modern life even before recovering the authentic features of Africa shows how hard the avoidance of the notion of primitive Africa is. In the name of what norms should tradition be criticized? If the criticism is done in the name of Western values, then we are back to Eurocentric views.

Recall how strongly ethnophilosophers contested this type of criticism of tradition. In their eyes, any submission of traditional thinking to alien norms cannot but stigmatize Africans for being different from Europeans. The capability of the European way to lead to greater material power does not change the issue. Africans must first assert their right to be different, for only when the West is no longer a model can the African difference cease to be a deviation or retardation. The hermeneutical approach does not enlighten us about the African difference itself. Though historicity is rightly emphasized, the emphasis does not go so far as to speak of Africa as the siege of a *sui generis* civilization. Particularities are more answerable to the circumstances of life than to deep splits in the conception of life itself.

4. The Primacy of Deconstruction

The difficulty of the hermeneutical approach to free itself from Eurocentrism illustrates the necessity of the prior deconstruction of Western concepts and methods. No view of African difference and philosophy can be authentic so long as the African mind remains entangled in Eurocentric distortions. The deconstructive standpoint relativizes the West while unraveling the hidden motives and mechanism of Western thinking and practice. It therefore provides the best possible tools both to critically analyze the colonial discourse on Africa and to approach Africa from a new perspective.

A. The Idiosyncrasy of the West

The African deconstructionist school, best represented by the works of Mudimbe, finds that what passes for African philosophy and knowledge of Africa is essentially a product of Western *episteme*. To quote Mudimbe:

> modern African thought seems somehow to be basically a product of the West. What is more, since most African leaders and thinkers have received a Western education, their thought is at the crossroads of Western epistemological filiation and African ethnocentrism. Moreover, many concepts and categories underpinning their ethnocentrism are inventions of the West.[53]

The dependence on Western concepts is most obvious in the way ethno-philosophy conceptualizes the African difference. What is unacceptable in the negritude movement is not so much the defense of difference as the formulation of otherness that fully maintains "the binary opposition between European and African, civilized and primitive, rational and emotional, religious and idolatrous."[54] On top of confirming its Western origin, the opposition simply reasserts the superiority of the West over Africa. What is intended to be a protest thus turns into an acceptance of hierarchy.

Those who oppose negritude do not escape the Western ascendancy either. Fully recognizing the main contribution of Hountondji, Mudimbe pays tribute to his position demanding the decolonization of human sciences through "a radical break in African anthropology, history, and ideology."[55] Still, Houtondji's criticisms of negritude reflect his uncritical allegiance to the Western model, especially to the universal validity of scientific practice. Because of this allegiance, he belongs to the same *episteme*. He finds negritude unacceptable because it does not conform to the Western idea of the human being, to wit, the primacy of rationality. Likewise, the idea of traditional African philosophy is refused because it amounts to a confusion of culture with philosophy, which is shocking to Western ears.

If the science of the West is capable of producing the gross misconception of anthropology, is it not because a fundamentally wrong orientation pervades the whole Western conceptual apparatus? Such should be Hountondji's question. The anthropological discourse is not an accident. Nor are the demeaning descriptions of Africans mere errors. As a product born of the epistemological specificity of the West, anthropology implicates idiosyncratic premises. Far from being a universal model, Western *episteme* is a reductionist conception alien to a positive idea of human diversity. To say that anthropology is a product of Western rationality is to underline the goal of domination as the initial project of anthropology. So that, anthropologists

> speak about neither Africa nor Africans, but rather justify the process of inventing and conquering a continent and naming its "primitiveness" or "disorder" as well as the subsequent means of its exploitation and methods for its "regeneration."[56]

The point is that both the schools of ethnophilosophy and professional philosophy fall victim to the ideology of objectivity. In endorsing the anthropological discourse, ethnophilosophers thought that they were dealing with an objective account of something given, namely, the African alterity.

Though professional philosophers denounce the errors of anthropology, their loyalty to Western *episteme* prevents them from ascribing said errors to its inherently reductionist trend. The purpose of anthropology is not to study other peoples; it is to construct their particularity in a way that sets them against the West. The opposition marginalizes these peoples, and so singles them out for domination. Both schools miss the basic orientation of the philosophy inspiring Western scientific practice. For Mudimbe, philosophy has to do with representations and explanations of history the crucial aspect of which is the involvement of epistemological values directed toward the centering of a given perspective. Commenting on Mudimbe's position D. A. Masolo writes: as a means of constructing and structuring the world, "no philosophical system can validly judge others. No one enjoys the privilege of being at the center while others remain peripheralized."[57]

This strong denunciation of Eurocentrism suggests that Mudimbe is quite open to the idea of African difference, provided that it does not rest on the anthropological opposition. Accordingly, to the important question whether there is such a thing as a traditional African philosophy, the answer must be, to paraphrase a scholar, "No! Not yet!"[58] The main problem is to find an approach free of Western premises and stereotypes before the attempt to reconnect with the past is made. While it may be true that ethnophilosophy confuses culture with philosophy, it does not follow that the Western type of philosophy should be taken as a model. Unlike the professional philosophers, Mudimbe refuses to deny the existence of African philosophy on the pretext that it does not agree with the Western definition of philosophy. But his refusal does not entail the endorsement of the ethnophilosophical definition.

The idea of difference leads to the same view. Mudimbe states:

> There are natural features, cultural characteristics, and, probably, values that contribute to the reality of Africa as a continent and its civilizations as constituting a totality different from those of, say, Asia and Europe.

On the other hand, any analysis would sort out the fact that Africa (as well as Asia and Europe) is represented in Western scholarship by "fantasies" and "constructs" made up by scholars and writers since the Greek times.[59]

The problem is not so much the particularity of Africans as the strong presence of Eurocentric concepts whose effect is to misconstrue the perception of particularity. We must not underestimate the impact of these Western concepts. Such concepts are no longer what Africans have borrowed; they have been internalized to the point of becoming their unconscious references. The necessity of a simultaneous critical analysis of Western concepts and their internalized versions renders the task of dissolving Western *episteme* all the more difficult. Mudimbe speaks of "an indefinite critical and autocritical enterprise."[60]

Most interesting is the clear correlation that Mudimbe establishes between the socioeconomic reality and the mental setup of Africa. To uphold economic exploitation, the colonial system instilled a subservient mentality or mental outlook into natives. The techniques of exploiting colonies presuppose a policy of domestication, which in turn calls for the production of intellectual representations and beliefs inducing mental dependency. The main tool of this mental shaping was the missionary's project of disseminating Christianity and civilization. "The outcome of these policies was the process of underdevelopment," which is neither poverty nor backwardness, but the product of dependency and marginality.[61] On account of the dependent mode of thinking and producing characteristic of the colonies, what exists in Africa is no longer the traditional society, but a peripherized society.

While this characterization of dependent societies as peculiar formations resulting from colonial and neocolonial satellizations draws Mudimbe closer to the position of the neo-Marxist school of dependency, defended by such scholars as André Gunter Frank and Samir Amin, his extension of dependency to the mental realm carries him further. In the eyes of the dependency school, what economic dependency imparts to the colonized is not so much mental submissiveness as the tendency to rebel. This explains why the school assimilated the third world to a huge reservoir of rebellion against imperialism. At times it even qualified the underdeveloped world as the new birth place of socialism, following the weakening of revolutionary spirit among the working class of the West as a result of the corrupting effect of imperialist expansions. In revealing the injection of dependency right into the self-representation of the third world, Mudimbe portrays a situation that singularly complicates, not to say falsifies, the alleged rebellious stand of underdeveloped peoples.

The internalization of the colonial world does no more than reiterate the absolute primacy of deconstruction. Mudimbe's approach places the whole issue of African philosophy at the center of Africa's problems of modernization. If the mental is so conditioned as to promote the Western dominance, even as Africans seem to contest that dominance, liberation is unthinkable without the radical dissipation of Western categories. What comes first is thus subjective liberation, the decolonization of the mind. The gateway to liberation is the prior and complete deconstruction of the mental setup, not the adoption of a revolutionary theory, as African Marxists believed wrongly. Some such dismantling alone is liable to initiate an authentic, unspoiled comprehension of African traditionality.

Talk about difference without hierarchy or opposition becomes possible only when Western concepts are deconstructed. Deconstruction inaugurates the authentic phase of relativism and pluralism by dismissing the antagonism between Europe and Africa. When the opposition is deconstructed, the outcome is the relativization of the West itself. In lieu of the Hegelian model of universal history painting the West as the driving engine toying backward cultures, relativization promotes the fragmentation of the world. In the words of Manthia Diawara:

> the concept of difference . . . seeks to undo hierarchies and create the possibilities for cultures and nations that are diverse in origin, customs, religion, and race to work together. The notion of difference is opposed to imperialist and colonialist structures created by universalist views of the world. The universalist discourse, whether it comes under a marxist, religious, or assimilationist guise, leaves unsaid contradictions between cultures and within societies. We must promote African difference within a condition of relativized desires (sexual, political, and religious) without making repression the norm.[62]

Universalist norms are imperialist, hierarchical because behind the claim to universalism looms a given particularity raised to the dignity of a norm. The outcome of this usurpation is the conceptualization of the particularity of other cultures as deficient and backward—a prelude to conquest and absorption. The deconstructionist school is not opposed to the idea of difference: what the school rejects is the slide into otherness whose unique virtue is the depiction of difference as lack, imperfection, and inferiority. The issue is not that the West is universal and Africans are different; instead, the West itself is particular, different, just as Africans are.

The deconstruction of Western paradigm implies, among other things, the rejection of the antinomy between modernity and tradition. Since the representation of the African past has been subjected to a systematic deformation, there is no reason to endorse the idea that modernity requires the ostracization of tradition. Nothing justifies "the static binary opposition between tradition and modernity, for tradition (*traditio*) means discontinuities through dynamic continuation and possible conversion of *tradita* (legacies)."[63] The role of tradition being to integrate discontinuities by fitting them into a dynamic continuity, the traditional diversity does not stand in the way of modernization.

B. The Limitation of Relativism

Critics point out two major drawbacks in the deconstructionist approach. (1) Mudimbe is unable to free himself from the vicious circle inherent in the deconstructive stand; (2) he gives a diagnosis of African malady, not yet the cure. To begin with the charge of inconsistency, Mudimbe establishes a sharp distinction between the facts of Africa and the Western representations of these facts. Since he characterizes the representations as constructs or inventions, critics wonder whether, given the premises of the deconstructive stance, the distinction between facts and representations can be made.

Such a distinction is hard to justify once knowledge is equated with construction. Mudimbe has no valid reason to believe that his descriptions of Africa are not also constructs. To speak of the possibility of grasping the authentic reality of Africa, the equation of knowledge with invention must cease. The renunciation of the idea of invention requires, in turn, the acknowledgment that some elements of truth are recognizable in the Western discourse. Because Mudimbe does not want to make this concession, he is caught in an ambiguous project: he promises the truth about Africa without however indicating how the discovered truth succeeds in overcoming the curse of invention.

Mudimbe is of the opinion that Western scholars, such as, E. E. Evans-Pritchard and French structuralists, have made serious attempts to study other cultures outside the framework of Eurocentrism. We know that the African deconstructionist school is indebted to Western scholars who have denounced Eurocentrism. The question is to know whether this deconstructive tendency in the West is not a hint of universalist potentials inherent in Western *episteme*. Unless Western categories possess elements that allow them to soar above particularism and the pursuit of hegemony, the emergence of postmodernism from the womb of Western philosophy remains a mystery.

While Mudimbe's deconstructive effort scores some undeniable successes, the same cannot be said about the promised new idea of Africa. Though he discredits ethnophilosophy in its present form and suggests that there is a need to recapture Africa by using proper epistemological categories, we still do not know what the categories of Africa are and in what sense they differ from those of the West. The alternative to Western rationality does not appear and does not seem to appear any time soon. The prevailing impression is that "he fails, in *The Invention of Africa* and elsewhere, to show clearly how the 'usable past' should be used by 'experts' to construct an 'authentic' African *episteme*."[64]

The promise of an authentic discourse on Africa seems unable to secure a vision superior or better to the one suggested by negritude. Since the best qualities (rationality, science) are already taken by the West, what is left for African particularity if not the lower attributes of non-rationality? Add that relativism encourages the debunking of positive values under the pretext of uncovering Western inventions. In so doing, it dampens the resolution to learn from the West, to steal the secret of its power. Relativism cripples the African determination to embark on a competitive course with the West. This negative effect on modernization is further intensified by the tendency of relativism to postpone self-criticism. Though Mudimbe encourages self-criticism, unless Africans cease to consider Western views on Africa as utter inventions and lies, the motive stimulating them to undertake a serious self-examination is imperceptible.

In terms of deconstruction and relativization, what Mudimbe has achieved does not seem to surpass negritude. When critics condemn the endorsement of colonial discourse by the philosophy of negritude, they all miss its deep meaning, to wit, the reevaluation, in the Nietzschean sense of the word, of Western values. To praise and claim what the West despises is so disrespectful and subversive of Western norms that the claim represents the summit of deconstruction. A deconstruction restricted to denouncing invention and projection does not go far enough. Such a deconstruction is too respectful of the West in that it refuses emotion, non-rationality. It complains about being misrepresented but refrains from claiming what the West despises, that is, the name of Negro. Jean-Paul Sartre underlined this revolutionary dimension of the reevaluative project of the thinkers of negritude when he wrote: "insulted, enslaved, he [the Negro] redresses himself; he accepts the word 'Negro' which is hurled at him as an epithet, and revendicates himself, in pride, as black in the face of white."[65]

The extent to which Mudimbe's project differs from ethnophilosophy is not clear, given his reliance on Claude Lévi-Strauss's idea of complementarity. According to Masolo:

> Mudimbe's new anthropology draws prominently from Lévi-Strauss's structuralism, which proposes not opposition but complementarity between history and anthropology, between the Same and the Other. Anthropology is the science of the concrete and it is illustrated in magic and mythical thought; it is the *bricolage*, as opposed to history, which is the engineered, the abstract, the invented, the construed or the constructed, the scientific.[66]

Since for Lévi-Strauss the two modes of knowledge must be seen less as different stages of the evolution of knowledge than as valid and complementary forms of knowledge, the structuralist position calls for a revisit of negritude, especially for the dismissal of the charge of a hierarchical opposition between the West and Africa as a misreading of negritude. Be it called *bricolage* or emotion, the truth remains that, beyond different characterizations, there is convergence on the notion of complementarity. My approach to negritude insists that Senghor's notion of the civilization of the universal posits less the opposition of European and African epistemological particularities than their complementarity.

Racialization by means of biological underpinnings undermines the revolutionary intent of the negritude movement. When instead of involving choice, the African mode of life is depicted as a biological orientation, the project of inventing a new notion of the human being through the reevaluation of Western values is thereby compromised. For the idea of new humanism to bear fruit, the inventive character of negritude must be maintained throughout. This is what Sartre suggests when he writes: "the words of Césaire do not describe negritude, they do not designate it, they do not copy it from outside as a painter does of a model; they *make* it, they compose it under our eyes."[67]

The involvement of choice and invention helps to overcome the debate over the reality or non-reality of the black essence as a racial entity. Choice refers to freedom, and so excludes objective determinations. The whole question is then to know whether such a choice is galvanizing and empowering, whether it can handle the crisis at hand. Taking note of the fact that African critics of ethnophilosophy have failed to develop some such approach, the coming chapters take up the issue.

Six

THE FUTURE AS FORWARD MOVEMENT INTO THE PAST: THE CONSTRUCTEDNESS OF IDENTITY

The African philosophical debate on sameness and otherness is about the universality of rationality. Though sameness grants the universality of reason, the African technological lag compels universalism to commit evolutionary slips by alluding to delayed or curtailed rationality. Otherness shuns evolutionary themes, only to concede the estrangement of Africans from rationality. To make sense of and to positively overcome this debate, the last chapter suggests that the discussion should be brought under the issue of empowerment through the following question: given the African marginalization, which of the two conceptions is promising a better future for Africa? So posited, the possibility of overcoming the conflict of interpretations through the revelation of their complementarity stands out on the horizon. The best way to do so is to reexamine the controversy over the revival of the African past.

1. The Return to the Past

The debate between ethnophilosophers and their opponents over the revival of the African past raises the whole issue of the function of the past in the process of change. While change is normally conceptualized as the process of going out of tradition, the African philosophical debate suggests that there is more to change than a resigned or earnest farewell to tradition. Ethnophilosophers argue that the act of opening the future is consecutive to a retrospective engagement whose result is the nurture of a goal-oriented thinking. Convinced that Africans cannot rise to the challenge of modernity unless they position themselves as inheritors of a legacy cleared of the degrading discourse of colonialism, they maintain that change and modernization pass through the restoration of the past. Chief in this restoration is the defense of a precolonial philosophy whose presumed absence had served to justify the demeaning views on Africa and the need to civilize African peoples.

The position of professional philosophers opposes the whole idea of the past as a forerunner of the future. For both Paulin Hountondji and Marcien Towa, ethnophilosophy is condemned to valorize tradition to make the past worthy of harboring an African philosophy. They understand the purpose of the restorationist thinking: as "a passionate search for the identity that was denied by the colonizer," ethnophilosophy seeks the rehabilitation of Africa through the refutation of the degrading colonial discourse.[1] Since the denial of the existence of a precolonial African philosophy was used to fashion the image of an irrational and primitive Africa, professional philosophers sympathize with the attempt to refute the denial. Nevertheless, however commendable the project of rehabilitation may be, the fact remains that the backward inspiration of ethnophilosophy backfires on African modernization. Hountondji and Towa accuse the whole project of being irrelevant, deceptive, and highly detrimental to African interests and liberation.

The attempt to revive what is already dead reveals the deceptive nature of the ethnophilosophical project. The regression subreptitiously carries elements of the modern world that it pastes onto the traditional culture. This unusual process of going from the present into the past instead of the present pushing back the past invites what Towa calls an "arbitrary interpretation."[2] So manipulated, the retrieved past has no scientific value. The retrieval remains a polemical undertaking that fails to justify the adherence of the philosopher. The easy discovery of socialist, Christian, Islamic, or existentialist echoes in traditional Africa evinces the fallacy of the ethnophilosophical approach.

Of what use will the revival of the past be? On top of none of the aspects of traditional life being able to solve the problems that Africa now faces, the inevitable outcome of such a revival can only be the obstruction of modernization by instances opposed to modern life. Since what Africa needs most is to get out of its impediments by a resolute commitment to change, the recourse to traditionalism, to the values of the past is at variance with the exigencies of the present, especially with the practical issues of socioeconomic and technological developments. When the overriding requirement is to acquire a new spirit by departing from what Africa used to be, strange is the way traditionalism claims to initiate its renaissance through a backward looking device. In the situation of Africa, "looking back means giving up the future," all the more drastically since the very obstacle that needs to be removed parades as a solution.[3]

Hountondji does not recommend the complete rejection of the past. Mere rejection is highly detrimental, as it passes over the need to evaluate critically the past. What perverts ethnophilosophy is less the resolution to deal with the past than the apologetic stand resulting in the consecration of the past. The correct attitude is to study critically the past so as to be able to distinguish between those elements of the past that are frankly inimical to modern life from those which deserve to be retained because they are usable. In this way, African philosophy bathes again in the true spirit of philosophy, which is to examine critically a given proposition before the decision to reject or accept is taken. In admitting that "the analysis of these [collectives] representations should consequently be pursued outside of all apologetic perspectives," African philosophy does nothing less than reverse the backward looking pattern into a progressist project.[4]

A word of caution: the selective revival of the past cannot be truly progressist unless the selection maintains the commitment to a complete rupture with the past. The backward looking ethos of ethnophilosophy insists on connecting African modernization with the traditional world under the pretext of restoring the continuity shattered by colonial intrusion. This attempt to strip change of disruptive meaning by integrating alterations into the continuity of African societies, laudable though it may seem, prevents Africa from entering the mainstream of modern nations. Its scheme downplays the gap existing between the traditional world and modernity, thereby diverting Africans from the need to effect a radical change if they mean to join modernity. Criticizing what he calls the "organic fallacy" of the conception of history, Abiola Irele writes: "the life of societies is likened to that of a tree, growing slowly and imperceptibly, and sending down firm and strong roots, producing with time the ripe fruits of a settled way of life."[5]

This vegetal metaphor, Irele continues, misses that

> the colonial experience was not an interlude in our history, a storm that broke upon us, causing damage here and there but leaving us the possibility, after its passing, to pick up the pieces. It marked a sea change of the historical process in Africa; it effected a qualitative reordering of life. It has rendered the traditional way of life no longer a viable option for our continued existence and apprehension of the world.[6]

The apologetic perception of the past precludes Africans from taking the full measure of the disruption introduced by the colonial experience. It creates the illusion that Africans can think of modernization in terms of continuity. Yet how could such a conclusion be legitimate when ethnophilosophers admit that the African traditional culture was wallowing in a direction of thought opposed to modern values?

The way out is a radical rupture with the past. Stating the exact terms of the rupture, Towa writes: "in order to affirm and assume oneself, the self must deny itself, it must deny its essence and therefore its past, it must expressly aim at becoming like the other, similar to him and hence uncolonizable by him."[7] This calls for the renunciation of the self raises discontinuity to a condition of African passage into modernity. The call openly advocates Westernization, convinced as it is that Westernization alone can beat Westerners at their own game. The choice is then between loyalty to or betrayal of African identity. While the former perpetuates the peripheral life, the latter promises the dethronement of the masters of Africa. Such payoff clearly changes the betrayal into greater fidelity.

2. Questioning the Conflict between Tradition and Modernity

The contrast between the resounding confidence of the opponents of ethnophilosophy and the fact of Africa slipping into greater marginalization agitates the question of knowing whether the future of Africa really bifurcates between denial and fidelity. Many reasons point to the fallacy of such a choice, the most commanding being the theoretical challenge flowing from the idea of progress itself. When we read the thinker who has given to the idea of progress a most advanced philosophical expression, namely, G. W. F. Hegel, the mind is gripped by the puzzle of progress being a movement into the past.

What basically characterizes Hegel's approach is the conviction that, change and transformation, far from occurring at random or being caused by fortuitous events, are internally impelled processes of betterment. He defines change as dialectical, that is, as resulting from an internal split leading a given reality to higher organization and functionality. The laws of dialectics indicate the manner the phenomenon, thrown into self-movement by the internal split, seeks a solution for the contradiction through the generation of higher forms. Since higher forms spring from lower ones, Hegel characterizes development as the process by which the implicit becomes explicit. He writes:

> Existence presents itself, not as an exclusively dependent one, subjected to external changes, but as one which expands itself in virtue of an internal unchangeable principle; a simple essence—whose existence, *i.e.*, as a germ, is primarily simple—but which subsequently develops a variety of parts, that become involved with other objects, and consequently live through a continuous process of changes.[8]

A major implication of the higher growing from the lower is that development does not bring fresh and undetermined novelties into existence. As an actualization of the past, the movement toward the future is exactly backward going.

A little reflection shows that for progress to make sense, to have a direction, the beginning and the end must coincide. A given reality is positively developed if the end of the process actualizes what was only potentially given. To think otherwise is to fall prey to mechanical or accidental notion of change. If the developed reality does not coincide with the potentially given, then the outcome has been subjected to alien and accidental detours. Stated otherwise, history turns out senseless or goalless if the future does not target the past. Unless history reverses change into preservation, the loss of the self, not its development, would define history. This imperative to make a circle turns the point of arrival into the point of departure realized. History has finality if forward movement implicates a backward movement, and thus brings about a totalizing outcome. Only this reversion can inaugurate a process such that differentiations as well as the actions of external things result in the continuous self-enrichment of the subject.

Hegel's definition of the point of departure as the Absolute further justifies his understanding of the future as a movement into the past. To assume that the departure can be something else than the Absolute is to fall into the entanglements of mechanical materialism. The latter draws movement from imperfection, not understanding that imperfection has no reason to move unless the nostalgia of perfection propels the imperfect. Since the Absolute is at the beginning, all movement starts from the Absolute and returns to it. As David Carney maintains, for Hegel, development is:

> the unfolding, or overt manifestation of (hidden) reality or perfection (Absolute Idea or Spirit) as it is; pre-existent to its manifestation. . . . time or history is the dynamic or progressive unfolding of an already existing static (eternity, eternal verities, Absolute Idea, Spirit or what have you) contained within a dynamic: eternity in and outside time, time within eternity.[9]

A parenthesis is in order. For all the radical alterations that Karl Marx introduced into the Hegelian system of thought, he has nevertheless preserved the idea of history as a pursuit of the past. The exigency of attributing continuity and sense to history landed Marx on the same assumption. Human history makes sense, the protracted antagonism that sets human beings against each other in class divided societies becomes intelligible, only when history results in the retrieval of a fundamental and initial state of fraternity. Because the initial fraternity was based on undeveloped human potentials at a time when human beings were far from controlling nature, human solidarity shifted to animosity and conflict over scarce material resources. However, a basic consequence of the intensification of class struggle being the development of production itself, the whole movement is determined to make "the existence of different classes of society . . . an anachronism" by progressively removing the scarcity which sets individuals against individuals.[10] Marxism calls communism this recreation of the primitive condition of human fraternity on a developed material basis.

Hegel draws the suppositions of his thinking from a deep-seated tradition that goes back to Plato. Though Plato is alien to the idea of progress, he construes movement and change as deficient expressions of the static that he identified with perfection. With Plato, movement is a search for a perfection that is already given. There was a fall from perfection, and movement is a clumsy attempt to retrieve perfection. On the basis of the anteriority of the immutable, Plato establishes the world of ideas, of perfect and unchanging forms, as models to finite and moving things. Visible things try to imitate the perfection of the model so that the best they can be or aspire to be is always behind them. Going forward is thus returning, inverting a fall. A good example is the theory of reminiscence.

Contrary to the received idea that the progression from ignorance to science fills an empty container, Plato maintains that knowledge is reminiscence, retrieval of what the mind had previously contemplated yet forgotten. Being but acts of finding a prior state of science, "seeking and learning are in fact nothing but recollection," says Plato.[11] The Cartesian defense of innate ideas and the Kantian notion of a priori knowledge, with their subsequent rejection of the theory of *tabula rasa*, are modifications of the same theory.

Equally significant is the affinity of Plato's theory with the Christian idea of the fall of humanity. Despite the use of a different terminology, the Christian suggestion that the human being lost everything as a result of a fall so that history is an expiation intent on recovering the lost paradise tallies with the Platonic vision. Interestingly, this preexistence of perfection, which compels movement to go backward, also recalls the ancient Greek idea of the golden age. Referring to the community of beliefs, Carney writes:

> All of this is similar to the "golden age" concept of the ancient Greek philosopher. Indeed, it is exactly the same as the ancient Greek concept of "eternity" or pre-existing, instantaneous perfection, and of time as the "moving image of eternity," with which is also associated the Greek concept of "entelechy" or the progressive structural unfolding of that which already existed from the beginning in complete and perfect form.[12]

African culture is no exception to the rule: the mythical past acts as a model to present realities. Alluding to the lack of the notion of the future in the African concept of time, Carney explains that the traditional society did not expect positive novelties because the "content and pattern [of the future] had been set in the mythic past of the tribe and its heroes, in the 'golden days,' the time of the best, containing all the best models that the tribe could only emulate but not surpass, or supersede."[13]

This universal belief in the priority of perfection mitigates the drastic opposition that John S. Mbiti detects between Western and African conceptions of time. The necessity to fasten the future to the past so as to make sense of history shows that time is not merely a forward movement even for Westerners. The same necessity explains why human beings tend to conceptualize crucial moments of change as renaissances. The term "renaissance" signifies that a return to the right path occurred after a period of decline and wandering. Consider the inauguration of European modernization. To highlight the end of medieval obscurantism, this period of crucial change defines itself as a renaissance, specifically as a rebirth of Greek philosophy. At the religious level, the movement conserves the idea of renaissance, given that

Protestantism advocates a return to the Bible as a remedy to the deviations and betrayals of the authentic Christian faith. As an exigency of purification, the movement imagines itself as a return to the original faith.

Nationalism too is inspired by this idea of a return to the source. In effect, in direct response to the need of nationalist movements to cultivate the sense of the past, most European countries entered the path to modernity under the banner of a return to the source. Reference to and systematic cultivation of the past were particularly manifest during the rise of nationalism in the nineteenth century. As Robert W. July explains, the nationalist content of European identities

> was marked by a vast production of historical literature dedicated to showing that this or that nation sprang from illustrious antecedents, and counted in its history at least one era of ascendant glory. Though the facts of the past were what they were, the need was of the present—to provide a sense of roots, of continuity, of cohesion, and of mission, and to dress all these in the language of heroes and epics, of great deeds and broad contributions to civilization.[14]

Take the case of Germany. Dismissing beforehand Hountondji's fear that indulgence in emotion and ethnic identity stand in the way of modern ideas, in the face of French and British advances, the German nationalist inspiration triggered the movement known as "German Romanticism." In the name of difference, the movement praises feeling and intuition, leading to a sense of uniqueness from which Germany draws its nationalist expression and much of its competitive spirit.

Let us reflect on this connection of nationalism with emotional expression. Admittedly, the nation is an essential component of modernity: the national state provides the framework by which impersonal rules replace the ascriptive order of traditional communities. Scholars are also impressed by the emotional power emanating from nationalism. This affective dimension inspires the most varied and extreme positions, supporting democracy, conservatism, revolution, and despotism.

Scholars can find no other explanation for this extremism than to link the revival of past loyalties with the emotional upsurge. This amounts to saying that the rationalization of modern life and the dehumanization of industrialism transfer the psychic and emotional components of traditional longings and religious beliefs to nationalism. Since commodity relations progressively weaken patriarchal and idyllic relationships, the old values of traditional societies, such as, localism, patriotism, shared culture, and solidarity, find refuge in the new national community. As one author states, nationalism "offered people living in the modern state a set of values that succeeded in capturing their primary loyalty. . . . It follows that a precondition of its success was the fact that it was built on the solid foundation of preexisting values."[15]

These formidable examples of relapses into the past refute Hountondji's and Towa's equation of ethnophilosophers' quest for the past with reactionary and detrimental trends of thought. In reality, "as modern African nations began to take shape and, more particularly, as they approached the prospect of national independence, like the people of Europe, they felt a growing need for a greater sense of their past."[16] Since the African return to the past is not so much an anomaly as a universal requirement of culture change, the question that needs to be asked is why so many African scholars rise against the return. Thus, Oyeka Owomoyela notes:

> Long before Africans were colonized the Hebrews suffered a similar fate. They always relied, however, on the survival of a faithful remnant that would in more auspicious times reconstruct the essentials of Hebrewness. . . . Africans are unique in their belief that their future lies in becoming, in thought, speech, and habit, like their erstwhile colonizers.[17]

The fact that, among all the dominated peoples, Africans show a peculiar tendency to reject their past requires a proper explanation.

The rejection indicates the extent of the African alienation, the depth of the internalization of the colonial discourse. Basically, most Africans believe that their past culture was primitive and worthless. Crucial, therefore, is the association of Africa's failure to modernize with the poisoned relationship of the elite with its own legacy. A major implication follows: rehabilitation requires the radical questioning of the alleged conflict between tradition and modernity, as belief in this conflict talks Africans into self-denial to the great delight of acculturation and Westernization.

What else could provide the best argument against such a denigration of tradition but a pluralistic understanding of history? Only in the framework of a unilinear time can the particularity of one civilization appear as a lag while another and equally particular civilization takes the lead. When civilizations are asked to cross over into the time of a civilization arbitrarily ranked as a model, they appear to be at different moments of the realization of the same goal. Without the presupposition of a single time, similar criteria cannot be used to evaluate and rank so that each civilization appears to be moving independently in its own time and according to its own criteria. This message of diversity is the very one that the African school of pluralism considers as a landmark achievement in the rehabilitation of the African self.

3. Postmodernist Approaches to African Identity

The rejection of the dichotomy between tradition and modernity and the subsequent denunciation of Eurocentrism land us on the shore of African relativism. Wondering "whether the Western imperium over the world was as clearly of universal *value* as it was certainly of universal *significance*," the school begins by questioning the scheme of evolutionary thinking by which both the centrality of Europe and the imposition of a unilinear process of history are justified.[18] To be sure, the West was universally significant by its expansion, influence, and power. Nonetheless, African postmodernism maintains, a hegemonic position of such nature is hardly a model with universal applicability. If so, the urgent task of the African intellectual is to expose the usurpation by a thorough deconstruction of Western categories and assumptions.

The last chapter discussed the manner the disclosure of Western categories as inventions designed to marginalize other cultures lays the ground for a positive understanding of pluralism. As soon as the mind is liberated from such a degrading categorization, the perception of other cultures changes. A non-Western culture is no longer the inferior other of the West; nor is such a culture destined to be assimilated into the superior culture. Such a culture is defined by a difference free from all hierarchical and ranking implications. Though the negritude thinkers spoke of African specificity, the difference was depicted as a lack, as witnessed by the Senghorian antinomy between Western reason and African emotion, and so missed the sense of real disparity. Real difference appears only in a fragmented world, that is, in a world that has no center, where there are no universal norms, where the particular is not conceived of as a moment of the universal.

Thus, for V. Y. Mudimbe, the return to the past must be condemned, not because the process is backward looking, but because it is unable to capture the authentic African self. Without the prior deconstruction of Western categories, Mudimbe warns, analyses by African scholars of African realities will "be basically a product of the West."[19] Witness the African return to the past has only resulted in the endorsement of the colonial discourse by establishing the African as the antithesis of the white, in agreement with the colonial assumption. The charge of endorsement of Eurocentric views equally applies to the critics of ethnophilosophy, for their dismissal of the return to the past is how they remain faithful to the Western idea of antithesis between African tradition and modernity.

Let us ask why African postmodernist thinkers refuse the dismissal of the past? An immediate answer is that for them the negative accounts of the past is an active cause of the present paralysis of Africans. Indeed, degrading descriptions of Africa's past have induced Africans to secretly accept their inferiority *vis-à-vis* the West. Some such withdrawal of self-confidence and sense of ambition has, in turn, persuaded Africans to admit that no other option exists for them than dependency and imitativeness. This analysis elevates the representation of the past to the rank of an essential ingredient of the notion that peoples have of themselves. Modernity and development are unthinkable if peoples are bogged down in a degrading account of their legacy.

The alleged role of the representation of the past reveals a strange process of causation. The representation of a dead reality is credited with influencing present thinking and behavior. One way of removing the strangeness is to prove that the function of the representation of the past is less to describe the past than to be supportive of the present. The error is to think that history should be a descriptive account when in reality it is "saga and myth," says Mudimbe quoting Janheinz Jahn.[20]

This enhancing role of history together with the noted deformation of the African past by Western categories put Mudimbe in the mood to reject the alleged conflict between tradition and modernity. Since the function of the Western representation of the African past is to diminish Africans in their present reality, no reason exists to endorse the opposition between tradition and modernity. On the contrary, we must insist that the advent of modernization requires the reinstatement of continuity. If the past draws its strengthening effect on the present from the competence of tradition to integrate discontinuities through the institution of a dynamic continuity, then the inclusion of a radical conflict between tradition and modernity robs African history of continuity. The loss of continuity decrees that Africans must come within the Western orbit if they aspire to modernize. This transference into another history guarantees the total assimilation of Africans by requiring the surrender of their creative forces in favor of passive imitativeness.

For Mudimbe, since the demeaning descriptions of the past pass as evidence of inferiority, no better way exists to liberate the inner creative forces of Africans from the fetters of colonial and postcolonial discourses than the dissolving power of deconstruction. By rejecting the universalist claim of the West, deconstruction authorizes the African difference more as a reality in its own right than as antithetical to the West, in the manner of negritude. In thus preparing the rediscovery of the true, authentic African self, deconstruction promises to unleash the process of African renaissance.

Another, but no less influential African postmodernist voice is Kwame Anthony Appiah. Like Mudimbe, he begins by questioning the validity of the opposition between tradition and modernity. He does so by showing how Max Weber's characterization of modernity as the triumph of rationalization finds little evidence in the modern world. He writes:

> For Weber, charismatic authority—the authority of Stalin, Hitler, Mao, Guevara, Nkrumah—is antirational, yet modernity has been dominated

by just such charisma. Secularization seems hardly to be proceeding: religions grow in all parts of the world . . . ; what we call "fundamentalism" is as alive in the West as it is in Africa and the Middle and Far East.[21]

Contrary to predictions, the expansion of the West did not lead to the mere dissolution of local identities in favor of Western standards. Instead, "the experience of colonization and extended interaction with the West has produced a culture in transition from tradition to modernity, a culture that, for want of a better word, I shall call nontraditional."[22] Such culture is not opposed to modernity; nor is it a revamped version of tradition. Being in transition to modernity, it combines traditional elements with modern experience.

This eclectic process strongly supports the idea that identities are constructions. The overlooking of this fact misled ethnophilosophy into a mistaken conception, to wit, the racial qualification of African identity. The price for this mistake was the presentation of the African as the antithesis of the Westerner in line with the colonial discourse. In light of the debilitating implications of this antinomy, "it is clear that a biologically rooted conceptions of race is both dangerous in practice and misleading in theory; African unity, African identity, need securer foundation than race."[23] If identities are constructions, their empowering impact matters much more than their descriptive elements or contents. The idea of construction thus calls for the adoption of a pragmatic criterion: the dismissal of the descriptive concern gives primacy to the question whether the identities that peoples claim empower them, whether they do the good things that they expect them to do. As Appiah explains:

> If an African identity is to empower us, so it seems to me, what is required is not so much that we throw out falsehood but that we acknowledge first of all that race and history and metaphysics do not enforce an identity: that we can choose, within broad limits set by ecological, political, and economic realities what it will mean to be African in the coming years.[24]

The involvement of choice fully confirms that the purpose of the representation of the past is to support present efforts. Choice activates a selective thinking that retains and organizes events of the past according to present choices. The movement is actually retrospective, going from the present into the past. Speaking of tradition, Appiah says: "history may have made us what we are, but the choice of a slice of the past in a period before your birth as your own history is always exactly that: a choice. The phrase the 'invention of tradition' is a pleonasm."[25] Take the representation of history as a process unfolding logically according to a sequential order. Neither the selected events, nor the temporal sequence they seem to follow, still less the logic that is supposed to pervade the whole process, really reproduces the past as it used to be. All these attributes are products of construction interpreting the past on the basis of present needs.

The constructedness of histories allows the free assumption of identities in combination with the rejection of the universalist claim of the West and of all essentialist determinations. Thanks to this decentered view of the world, differences of identity are no longer due to racial or cultural determinations, but to freely assumed existential choices. This freely assumed identity is perforce a flexible one: it gives and receives, and hence is ready to negotiate and cooperate in a pluralistic world. Some such flexible, open identity does not burden itself with the aspiration to retrieve the authentic past. It does not reject the African heritage, any more than it rejects the experiences of the encounter with the West. The chosen identity navigates in an atmosphere of crossbreeding of African and Western contributions and accepts the two references without opposing them. Unlike the essentialist discourse of negritude, the eclectic view that results from the mixture of cultures does not alienate Africans from modern views by hammering on the incompatibility of identities.

The relativization of the West relativizes modernity itself, and so encourages the search for agreed and creative solutions in place of the passive imitation of a model. When dialogue and exchange based on the interests of Africans replace the imposition of a model, the outcome is the liberation of creativity, the essential ingredient of modernity. What makes postmodernism crucial for Africa is that the theory rehabilitates Africa even as it suggests alternative ways of achieving modernity and development.

An assessment of Appiah begins by asking whether he does not constantly bump against what he wants to avoid. Granted that all identities are invented, how are we to reconcile this fancy nature of identities with the fact that their empowering impact depends on the extent to which people give credence to their descriptive content? Unless identities appear in realistic or descriptive terms, they have no grip on people. Appiah admits the dilemma when he writes:

> recognizing the constructedness of the history of identities has seemed to many incompatible with taking these new identities with the seriousness they have for those who invent—or, as they would no doubt rather say, discover—and possess them.[26]

His solution is that credibility is possible without recourse to the mystification of objectivism if the beliefs are clearly assessed according to the criterion of usefulness. If an idea is useful, then it can be defended independently of its descriptive nature. Take the idea of pan-Africanism. Provided that the idea is stripped of the falsehood of race, African scholars can adopt pan-Africanism as a useful idea urging for African solidarity.

Is utility enough to ensure the adherence of people to a belief? By deriving African identity from fixed racial and cultural components, the negritude movement avoids this kind of interrogation by involving the powerful impact of blood ties. Seeing that identities have the stubborn need to trace their roots to objective determinations, Appiah's pragmatic arguments are unlikely to dismiss the need for objective references: the usefulness of ideas may give people more reason to believe in those ideas, but it does not make them believe in the first place. Moreover, for the idea to be really useful, a galvanizing impact, mostly through the embellishment of the past, must stem from the belief. The invention of a dynamic identity is hardly possible if the representation does not convey the sense of being heir to a great and unique history. In short, the pragmatic criterion to which Appiah appeals calls for a mythical representation.

Even if pluralism concedes the need for a galvanizing vision, it is definitely ill-equipped to supply the vision, as dispersion and disunity seem to be the main message of pluralistic philosophy. Consider what becomes of pan-Africanism in the hands of pluralism. In place of the racialized unity, Appiah advocates a solidarity flowing from the sharing of the same continent and the consequences of colonialism and racism. The galvanizing idea of blood fraternity by which alone useful reasons for unity turn into a compelling force is thus neutralized, not to mention the difficulty that a merely useful African nationalism will have in subduing ethnic identities.

In the eyes of pluralism, all identities being inventions, ethnic personality is as valid as any other identity and the advocates of African unity would be well advised not to make the continental identity conditional on its dissolution. The fear that the new pluralist trend advocates "cultural Balkanization . . . breaking up the movement of the wholeness of the Black consciousness, which was precisely what founded this literature, which made it coherent and effective," is therefore quite justified.[27] Given the urge for a strong solidarity and an affirmative personality, the extent to which the promotion of multiple, divisive, and eclectic identities is liable to help Africa come out of its dependent status is open to question.

Whereas modernity promotes the building of a trans-ethnic community through the erosion of ethnic and traditional references, African pluralism upholds the dispersion of cultures and peoples. Worse yet, while the notion of history suggests the fulfillment of a destiny through a dialectical process involving rise and fall, pluralism subscribes to a movement largely determined by circumstances to the detriment of a goal-oriented process. As a critic writes:

> Hence where modernity promoted a proud confidence that human beings could at last take history into their own hands, shaping it in line with various aims or visions, postmodernism speaks of the "end of history," questioning all such large hopes, preferring to live without big goals, content with utility, communicability and an immediacy where there is not real past or future.[28]

To imagine how such down-to-earth thinking can become empowering is difficult. Utopian views being discarded as falsehood, the thinking takes away all passion from Africa.

Mudimbe has tried to overcome these deficiencies of pluralism, while remaining faithful to pluralist inspiration. This fidelity explains why he maintains the possibility of capturing, beyond the Western deformations, the authentic African past. As we saw, the notion of African difference is for him unquestionable, as the difference corresponds to given and distinct natural features and cultural characteristics. The possibility of rectifying the distortions of Western scholarship and recapturing the African difference cannot be excluded, provided African characteristics and beliefs are replaced in their original contexts following a radical deconstruction of the Western paradigm. If the work of deconstruction is properly done, "to reinvest worked objects with their own past from the context of their own society is, indeed, to revive the historical activity and the reactiveness of a culture with its motions and exemplary beauty."[29] Another anthropology that tries to capture the African originality instead of opposing the African to the Western is thus the task ahead.

4. Myth-Making and Construction

Notwithstanding the severe shortcomings of pluralism, one positive outcome is definitely the idea of identities as creations. The error of Hountondji is to believe that ethnophilosophers are really trying to revive the past. Had he suspected that the reference to the past is a way of creating a new identity that stands in the way of colonial categorization, he would have been better disposed to understand the reference as a legitimate act of differentiation.

The error of ethnophilosophers is to succumb to the objectivist illusion. Instead of seeing their discourse as a creative and free work, they assume that their view of the past is really reproducing Africa as it used to be. This descriptive concern has two major negative consequences. It brings ethnophilosophers round to the idea that their account must agree with anthropological findings, even though these findings are hardly flattering. Most of all, the objectivist claim introduces a state of complete separation between modern ideas and the African identity. The representation of the fusion of tradition and modernity being blocked by the restorationist intent, the mental movement fails to be creative by rewriting the past under the supervision of modern ideas.

Contrast the restorationist purpose with the inventiveness revealed by deconstruction theory. The term "invention" allows a greater freedom of maneuver than the revival of the past. Far from excluding the modern phase, it encourages the construction of identity in such a way that favorable and useful aspects of the past interact with modern elements. Construction is by definition strategist: it is out to create an assertive and competitive difference. The point is not to deny ethnophilosophy; instead, "going beyond the descriptive project of ethnophilosophy is the real challenge of philosophers engaged with the problems of contemporary Africa."[30]

The fact that the past is no more gives Africans a free hand to interpret the events of history in a way fitting their interests and ambition. Nothing is more wrong than the statement contending that the past cannot be altered, given that the past exists only through an act of remembrance that is bound to be interpretative. Furthermore, the continuity between generations that the historical interpretation establishes is anything but empirically verifiable. This impossibility of authentication explains why the interpretation of the past is not overconcerned with accuracy: the temporal link inherent in the scheme of continuity can neither be validated nor dismissed in the name of factual criteria.

The incompetence to refute does not warrant credibility. As we noted, postmodernism and the idea of invention are both wanting in persuasion and hence in empowerment. The creative act induces an element of arbitrariness and relativity that undermines conviction. Something more lifting and encompassing than the purposeful design of construction is needed, something that looks like a myth. Put otherwise, between realism and falsehood, there is place for a *sui generis* state of mind whose function is to provide an empowering reading of reality. The error of Appiah and Mudimbe is to have missed the peculiarity of this state of mind, which is reducible neither to knowledge nor to pure imagination. Henri Bergson defines it as "the myth-making function" the particularity of which is precisely to produce ideas that "counterfeit reality as actually perceived, to the point of making us act accordingly."[31]

Whereas other creations of imagination simply tell stories that transcend or run away from reality, the practical concern of the mythical type upholds actual actions through lifting representations. The function of the mythical is thus to empower human actions, not to provide an escape from reality by imagining an ideal world. Unlike products of pure imagination, the sense of reality is here crucial, though not in the empirical meaning of the expression.

The recognition of the autonomy of the myth-making function alone overcomes the conflict between subjectivism and objectivism. In the last chapter, we saw how Mudimbe, after exposing the relativism of science, faced the impossibility of discriminating between facts and representations. The

Bergsonian distinction shows that the problem originates from the inability to understand that a representation can be enticing while being beyond truth and error, to speak as Friedrich Nietzsche. In such a case, the representation owes its value to its empowering impact, not to its descriptive input.

This kind of mental production, which is therefore properly called mythical, requires the recognition of the separate status of the myth-making function, since neither the descriptive value nor the imaginary flight of the representation provokes the belief. The belief is about reality although in an uplifting sense rather than in the sense of independent existence or fancied representation. The obvious conclusion is: the failure to see the autonomy of the myth-function explains the main shortcoming of Appiah's theory of construction, namely, the great difficulty of arousing a galvanizing belief in the context of relativism. Willy-nilly, the myth-making function must step in for such a belief to occur when everything else bathes in the indifference of contingency and comparability.

The other merit of Bergson's theory is to avoid rejecting the descriptive dimension of science without denying the more pronounced ideological contents of social sciences. Provided a vigorous effort is made, the supervenient character of the mythical moment authorizes the distinction between facts and constructs. The dissociation amounts to discriminating between facts and their interpretation within a syncretic representation. The choice between construction and objectivity is not the only option: the separation of the given thing from its embellishing vestment is possible. Nor is the objection according to which the given presupposes construction admissible: without a bite into reality, however tiny it may be, no construct can be put into effect. The detection of facticity, of being given is precisely what triggers the interpretative work.

Construction is nothing if it does not yield the power of the myth. More exactly, the whole issue is to show how and when constructs assume a mythical ascendancy. Jahn expresses eloquently the condition of mythical thinking when he says:

> legend is not one of the forms, but rather the only form in which we can imaginatively consider and relive history. All history is saga and myth, as such the product of the state of our intellectual powers at a particular time: of our capacity for comprehension, the vigor of our imagination, our feeling for reality.[32]

Even though the representation is not factual, you believe in a myth because the myth paints the objective world in a way that echoes your actual subjective need. A characteristic example is religious belief, which colors the indifference of things with intentions designed to boost the confidence of human beings as well as their ability to influence them. Jahn's statement relates myth with reality less as vaporization of the factual than as actualization of a subjectivity geared toward the comprehension, imagination, or feeling of reality.

The statement seems to say that you reach the level of mythical thinking when reality is depicted in subjective terms, when the object is so interpreted as to coincide with the practical needs of the subject. One thing is excluded, though: the coincidence is not due to the objective reflection of the existing condition. The grasp of the situation cannot be described outside the vision so much so that the description itself appears as a reading authorized by the myth.

This approval recalls a notion that the first chapter has discussed, to wit, the Marxist conception of ideology as a production of falsehood for the purpose of practice. Marx characterizes religious, philosophical, political, and juridical ideas as "phantoms formed in the human brain," as opposed to the concreteness and objectivity of the material conditions of life.[33] Specifying further the distinct character of ideological thought, he adds that the phantoms, the ideological echoes are "sublimates of their [human beings] material life-process, which is empirically verifiable and bound to material premises."[34] This suggests that ideology gives a manipulated and idealized picture of the life process. Because the idealization remains unconscious, Friedrich Engels defines it as a mental process involving what he calls "a false consciousness."[35] The expression intimates that consciousness is not here merely mistaken about the real: the conscious state hides the falsehood from itself so successfully that it remains internally convinced of the veracity of its beliefs.

The trouble is that this denunciation of self-deception little harmonizes with other Marxist statements. When Marx tells us, "the dispute over the reality or non-reality of thinking which is isolated from practice is a purely *scholastic* question," he suggests that the value of an idea depends not so much on its likeness to reality as on its pragmatic outcome.[36] The real thinking being the one which empowers human action, to imagine such a promotion through thinking merely reproducing the given is hardly possible. The thinking must rise above the factual so as to have a perspective on things and a position of interpretation.

If so, the function of thinking is not to copy reality; it is to interpret reality in terms of our action. When Marx speaks of "phantoms in the brain," he is deserting the pragmatic stand for an objectivist or empirical concern. Whereas the pragmatic criterion only values the quantity and quality of action that the idea promises, the denunciation of false consciousness adds a superfluous objectivist criterion. Marx's usage of two incompatible criteria explains his inconsistency, defining thinking now pragmatically, now realistically. The concept of false consciousness is a direct product of the inconsistency, since the notion rejects a mental representation on objectivist grounds, without consideration for the action that is thereby promoted. What if said illusion is how reality is turned into a project of the subject?

At this stage, the Kantian distinction between the empirical and the a priori crops up as a possible way out. When Immanuel Kant writes that "reason has insight only into that which it produces after a plan of its own" and that knowledge is "constraining nature to give answer to questions of reason's own determining," he definitely indicates that the task of reason is to shape the world into a project of the subject.[37] According to Kant, this is done through the given being subsumed by pre-existing mental categories.

Doubtless, what Kant calls reason is quite remote from a mythical function if only because the atemporal nature of the categories of rational thinking contrasts with the idea of historical unfolding. The contrast is so true that for him the shaping of the empirical is essentially grounded on the apriority of the rational. All the same, the transcendental character of reason and its ability to shape the given denote the interpretation of reality in terms of the subject. Thus, space is not an empirical reality: it exists as "the formal character of the subject, in virtue of which, in being affected by objects, it obtains immediate representation, that is, intuition of them."[38] Space is thus something related to reality without itself being real. Its function is to give a mental form to reality, an assignment akin to myth-making. The Kantian approach justifies that we speak of representations pertaining to reality without these representations being themselves empirical.

Just as the Kantian space orders representations, the function of the myth is to organize events into a story. The myth goes from the present into the past so as to convert the present into a moment, a realization of the past, which then ceases to be merely anterior. In thus pouring events and happenings into a pre-established direction, the myth defies the determining impact of external events by depicting life as an unfolding process. The direction exists not because events are indeed occurring according to a pre-established plan, but because the myth so orders them by connecting the past with the present. Since the movement into the past is how the successive occurrence of events is molded into a story, the myth bears witness to the constitution of a historical subject. By generating a rolling process, the recollection movement promises the coincidence between the point of departure and the point of arrival. The movement becomes a self-realization, a transformation of the potential into actual, instead of being the product of external forces.

The capacity to tell a story determines the degree to which a nation controls its destiny. This is not simply a metaphoric way of stating things; the statement should be understood in a literal sense in that the story that a nation tells is how this nation projects its possible action, how it subsumes the objectivity of things and events under its will. What is crucial here is the principle of utility that the myth incarnates. As a story with a beginning and an end, the myth orders events and happenings according to a goal-oriented perspective. When events give the impression of being scattered and dis-joined, they denote a corresponding withdrawal of the control of these events. This withdrawal authorizes the conclusion that the loss of mythical represen-tation differentiates developed from underdeveloped nations. While the latter cannot tell a story because the obstacles against which their existence constantly bumps permeate their discourse with dots, the developed nations see their being as continuity, that is, as a swelling reality in which each moment actualizes a becoming.

No better way exists to connect the present with the past—which is no more—than the idea of a task which is being handed down from generation to generation. In effect, besides instituting a continuity between disparate events by identifying a permanent subject—without which history is merely the product of accidents and arbitrary encounters—the myth assigns a task whose result is the further specification of the subject. The myth invests the feeling of moving along a continuum with the idea of accomplishment. Accordingly, direction in history is best implemented through the idea of a calling: the mission that passes from generation to generation shapes the occurrence of events into an entelechy.

The reinterpretation of the past in light of present ambitions, which is, I repeat, a process characteristic of myth-making, explains the empowerment. The myth is empowering because it crystalizes ambition into destiny, aspira-tion into mission. The idea of passing a torch is how the ups and downs of life are assessed in terms of fidelity to or betrayal of an assigned mission. So construed, life rises beyond descriptive accounts, and any noted dissimilarity between the task and the actual behavior is naturally interpreted in terms of renunciation of mission. However, just as failure results from the surrender of the entrusted mission, neither is rise from decline excluded as a result of a change characteristically construed as a renaissance. Altering the usual meaning of change as a process of going out of oneself, the movement of rebirth portrays change as expiation, a return to the original inspiration. The idealized past, which can even go so far as to imagine a golden age, serves as a source dictating the obligation to be up to its standards. The mythical resto-ration of the past thus crowns change with the sense of duty, inviting an ethical understanding of modernization and change.

The more the past is described in glorious terms, the greater is the pres-sure on the present. Inasmuch as the representation exhorts people to inherit a great history, the glorified continuity plants the need for achievement in the culture itself. This is how July interprets the purpose of African restoration-ists: such scholars, he writes, "were concerned with reviving the past of their people precisely in order to build permanently into the popular mentality a sense of pride in age-old accomplishment as the basis for a new African nationalism."[39] The interpretation means that the power of history springs from the "ideology of heritage," which inculcates people with the need to be up to an established standard.[40] History is thus a process of duplication: the past that people imagine and to which they become heir is their self taking the form of commandment. Just as in our individual life we distinguish between body and soul, so too in our cultural life we establish a similar type of duplication through historicization.

The split between the present and the past inaugurates a process of self-creation such that the past is the self but which has grown into a guardian angel of the present. Change is then an endeavor of the subject to be up to expectations by working on itself. Traditionalism often wrongly opposes the past to the new when in reality the movement into the past is how the new is turned into a moment of an imagined and unfolding saga.

Where a saga is unfolding, situations of decline and loss of freedom are inevitable. In such cases, the return to the source counters the decline through a renewal of the original commitment. The temporal link that the return establishes between the past and the present posits the future as the time of redemption. This future ceases to be the unknown and becomes that which allows a given country the chance to revive its lost splendor. As a quest for restoration, change and progress come under a retrospective movement, for, as pointed out by an author, "there is no response to weakness and destruction save that of revivalism: the retrieval and restoration of the original qualities that made for strength and historical relevance."[41] While all superficial understanding opposes the new to the old and conceives of progress as going out of the past, as self-negation, the return to the past urges for fidelity. In thus framing change in terms of authenticity in lieu of self-denial, the return asserts that "the past is the accomplished future and the future is the past reasserted."[42]

5. African Attempts at Myth-Making

Some African scholars detect the empowering function of the myth. For instance, from the need to identify "a founding myth as the basis of our action and collective existence in modern times," Irele deduces "the continuing relevance of concepts such as Negritude and African personality."[43] He specifically defines the function of the myth as follows:

> It is thus not a matter of casting romantic glances back at the past which can no longer be fully operative for us, nor of a narcissistic enfoldment in the self, but rather of an openness to the future—of its implications for ourselves and for the rest of the world. It is a question of our regaining the historical initiative of which we were deprived as a people, and with it an originality of thought and action, with a meaning for ourselves in the first place and ultimately for the world with which we are today ineluctably involved in a common adventure.[44]

In reference to the same issue of resurrecting the past so as to reconnect with freedom and create a new future, Mudimbe quotes the remarkable terms by which Zoungrana Cardinal Paul, Archbishop, articulates the function of heritage:

> Beyond refusing all external domination, our wish is to link up in depth with the African cultural heritage, which for too long has been misunderstood and refused. Far from being a superficial or folkloric effort to revive some traditions or ancestral practices, it is a question of constructing a new African society whose identity is not conferred from outside.[45]

These are various ways of saying that Africans need myths to deploy the future, to regain the historical initiative. Since the future cannot be African if it is not expressed in African terms, the best way for doing so is to establish continuity with the African legacy through a movement into the past. As this reconstructed continuity cannot but present the colonial episode as an interruption, the reconstruction amends the broken heritage, and so dismisses the impression of being toyed by the Western engine. The return to the past is a return to initiative: the return decolonizes the mind as much as it steers the mind toward its own goal. According to Tsenay Serequeberhan, "documenting the traditional philosophies and worldviews of African peoples is fruitful only when undertaken within the context of and out of an engagement with the concrete and actual problems facing the peoples of Africa."[46] The whole question is to know whether this attempt to make the past usable for liberation and development can be anything other than myth-making. Being already dead, only in the form of a myth can the past incarnate whatever influence it is supposed to have on the present.

Though by no means a proponent of ethnophilosophy, the African author who resolutely engages in this line of thinking is undoubtedly Cheikh Anta Diop. His attempt to draw black peoples into the glory of ancient Egypt through the thesis of black Egypt associates the restoration of African history with the renaissance and modernization of Africa. For him, the renaissance is conditional on the restoration of the past, which restoration provides the most radical refutation of the colonial discourse. The battle for the past is highly important for Africans because the perception of the past conditions present capacity and ambition. This battle is how African scholars "restore the historical consciousness of the African peoples and reconquer a Promethean consciousness."[47] Africans must inherit a history of independence, initiative, and achievement for them to feel the obligation to restore that tradition. Since the purpose of the colonial discourse is to paint Africa as an "insolvent debtor," nothing could be more damaging than Africans acquiescing to the discourse by viewing themselves as merely borrowers.[48]

To invert this trend of thinking, Diop undertakes nothing less than the mutation of the insolvent debtor into an original and generous donor: hence the idea of the African origin of civilization. Given the admitted pioneering role of ancient Egypt, the thesis of black Egypt is thus liable to operate a salutary inversion by showing that "Europe and Asia were but junior variations on the original African theme in philosophy and science."[49] We catch the movement into the past in the actual work of myth-making. The point is to understand that little is gained even if ancient Egyptians were demonstrably black, for their connection and relevance to contemporary Africans would still remain as tenuous as if they were nonblack. The prevailing controversy over the racial origin of ancient Egyptians is enough for Diop to undertake an interpretative work that establishes continuity with ancient Egypt by racializing blackness, by suggesting that all black peoples partake in an unchanging black essence, regardless of time and place.

To define this black essence, Diop goes back into the past and stops at a time when a people geographically situated in Africa played a pioneering role. Sure enough, Africa could be defined by non-technicalness as well if the journey into the past ended in mediaeval or modern time, as for instance Senghor did. Diop prefers to pursue the journey into the past until he connects Africans with an event that crowns them as the creator of technical civilization. Thanks to this connection, he is also able to interpret African history in terms of rise and fall, its major implication being that the present destitution of Africa is only a transient decline. The fact of becoming conscious of the glorious legacy is enough to revive the African will to renaissance. No doubt, then, we are dealing with a myth: the movement into the past so reconstructs history that the future becomes the accomplishment of an entrusted mission. The insertion of a story changes the adverse objective world into a possible action of the African subject.

Another notable attempt at myth-making is the idea of African socialism. The idea depicts the future as an accomplishment of the African essence, as a return to the authentic past. Marx had suggested that the goal of class struggle is the realization of communism, which he understood as the retrieval of primitive communal society on the basis of modernized material production, that is, on the basis of a society that has overcome scarcity. This idea that the future accomplishes a given potentiality nicely fitted the assumptions of ethnophilosophers: African "primitiveness" and communalism appeared as the cultural premises of the future socialist society. To become socialist, the West had to put on many African values; especially, the West had to give up its individualistic and competitive spirit in favor of solidarity and equality.

This socialist requirement changes the direction of the civilizing mission: as the future of the world, socialism means that, not European capitalism, but African civilization is heading for the conquest the world. Since the movement of history pursues African traditional values, African socialism is also how Africans recover the initiative and accomplish themselves. The myth of African socialism thus transforms a whole people destined to acculturation and assimilation into a rising demiurge. The mythical work is all embodied in the movement into the past, which assimilates modern aspects of socialism into the African traditional traits. On the strength of this assimilation, J. K. Nyerere can write: "we [Africans] must, as I have said, regain our former attitude of mind—our traditional African socialism—and apply it to the new societies we are building today."[50]

What can we conclude from these examples of mythical thinking? Essentially that ethnophilosophy and professional philosophy are complementary in the very sense that rationality always teams up with myth. What is wrong with professional philosophers is their reductionist reasoning: they consider myth as an outdated state of mind, thereby missing the extent to which mythical thinking is coextensive with rationality. They fail to understand that rationality itself is elusive without a mythical background. Above all, their excessive and one-sided rationalism undermines the mythical power so that the peoples of Africa, thus divested of the power to believe, are unable to rise above challenges.

As to those who plead for the critical synthesis of tradition and modernity, they must admit that their critical stand presupposes the constructedness of identities. Such is the case of Kwasi Wiredu and all those who make the preservation of traditional features conditional on their prior critical assessment. Provided the criticism of Western concepts precedes the criticism of African traditions, all these theories are heading for the invention of Africa.

To the extent that postmodernism downplays rationality through relativization, besides emphasizing the constructedness of identities, it overcomes many of the weaknesses of professional philosophers. Unfortunately, postmodernism has no means to prevail over the skeptical drawbacks of its theoretical premises. In particular, the postmodernist thinker proposes invention, creation, without being able to have faith in its empowering impact. Because relativism cannot really arouse beliefs, it cannot lift up human ambitions and actions. Herein lies the strength of ethnophilosophy: apart from relativizing the West, it revalorizes feelings and beliefs, thereby stimulating the myth-making function.

The weakness of ethnophilosophy is to give in to the objectivist illusion to the point of missing the inventive nature of its original project. The project discovers the myth, yet does not know how to yoke it to reason because of the essentialist syndrome. It speaks of synthesis, which requires the giving up of the essentialist stand in favor of a creative approach. The return to the past is not an unearthing of the past; it is how the myth changes into reason, into an unfolding and conquering process, that is, into a forward movement.

When we ask the negritude thinkers to drop their descriptive intent in favor of a creative approach, we obtain the following result: Africans were non-technical by choice, for the sake of realizing a different mode of life. This corrected reading of negritude ascribes the African difference to choice rather than to racial provisions. The appeal to human freedom asks Africans to accept the past so interpreted because it results from freedom instead of backwardness. No sooner is the difference accepted as choice than the acceptance bounces into an appealing future: as Africans have opted for a specific life in the past, so too can they opt today for a new life, in particular for forceful technicalness. Nothing prevents them from doing so: as creators of their essence, the initiation of a new life, a new history depends on them. We see to what extent racialization was uncalled for: the endorsement of non-technicalness ceases to be demeaning and debilitating when non-technicalness is the product of choice instead of being the prescription of racial endowments.

The freedom of choice and its corollary, the inventiveness of identity, do provide the royal road to both the recovery of African dignity and its renaissance. Choice accords the idea of difference with the human essence by conceiving of Africans as creators of themselves through the choice of their own values. So contrived, the African difference does not go against any fact. The facts remain what they are; only their interpretation changes, which interpretation is nothing but how Africans assume their self, that is, appropriate their past and project their future. Only this freely assumed and constructed difference can neutralize the disparaging Western discourse. In other words, the same facts (African technological backwardness) are so constructed as to defend and stimulate Africans instead of depreciating them. We thus obtain an act of invention or sublimation that changes alleged defects into assets, into noble and higher causes.

To demarginalize Africa, the deconstruction of the idea of Africa is indeed crucial, provided it serves the purpose of inventing a new one, this time the inventors being Africans themselves. In so being, deconstruction avoids Diop's approach, which is another form of Westernization, as Africa is asked to compete with the West for the same values. Such an approach is negative for the main reason that it fails to be an invention giving the advantage to Africa. In becoming inventive, the method of deconstruction also turns away from Diop's racialization of Africans.

Specifically, the method pinpoints that Diop himself bumped into the construction of identity when he assigned the technological backwardness of Africa to a different choice of civilization. Although the negritude philosophers expressed the need to create a new emotion about Africa, yet they too failed to remove the distorting framework of racialist philosophy. Had Senghor emancipated himself from racialist categorization, he would have truly realized the transition that he promises when, after conceding, "Negritude is a myth," he adds that it is "a true myth."[51] Negritude would have become a true myth if it had succeeding in empowering Africans. It would have empowered Africans if it had appealed to their freedom rather than their racial characteristics.

To sum up, this long discussion on the constructedness of identities achieves one basic result, namely, the need to liberate the African power to believe. Whether we appeal to utility, as Appiah recommends, or relativize the West in the manner of Mudimbe, both ways presuppose the liberation of credulity, of myth-making. To imagine oneself according to the criterion of usefulness, the deconstruction of Western normativeness is a necessary prerequisite. To the extent that the deconstruction, the relativization of the West amounts to snatching the African subjectivity from objectification, the whole issue brings us back to the Kantian problematic of limiting knowledge to make room for belief. The emancipation of credulity follows from the perception of the transcendence of the African subject, which then springs from the limitation, relativization of Western *episteme*.

What has paralyzed Africans is their attempt to fit into the framework of a definition of the human essence that expressly bans as irrational all that shields them against the type of objectification framing them for the anthropological discourse. The perception of the framework as nothing more than domestication reconnects with freedom whose first act is to liberate the power to believe, since human beings are free only to the extent that the manner they define themselves coincides with how they imagine, embellish themselves. The Marxist depiction of the operation of false consciousness matters little, as the soaring above determinations will always remain the distinctive mark of human transcendence.

Seven

COLONIZATION WITHOUT COLONIZERS: THE PHENOMENON OF AFRICAN ELITISM

The crucial importance of the debate over the past finds another confirmation in the elucidation of a characteristic African phenomenon, to wit, the elitist attitude. For many scholars, colonialism and neocolonial policies remain the root causes of numerous African impediments, ranging from the persistence of poverty to the ravages of ethnic conflicts. Other scholars prefer to ascribe these impediments essentially to the persistence of traditional views and methods and to the lack of reforms radical enough to uphold a sustained process of modernization. The African philosophical debate suggests the overcoming of this either/or dispute by identifying the culprit as the rise of African elitism. This elitist phenomenon originates from the conjunction of externally and internally induced hindrances. I try to demonstrate the pertinence of my approach by showing how the major problems and impediments of African societies originate from a sociocultural condition that fosters elitism.

1. From Colonialism to Elitism

The determination of elitism as a characteristic effect of colonial rule is not hard to establish. Surprisingly, Placide Tempels is the first scholar to draw attention to the detriments of the phenomenon of elitism in Africa. In chapter two, we saw how, in addition to refuting the colonial allegation of irrational and immature peoples by arguing that Africans have their own philosophy, Tempels reflected on the evil consequences of denying philosophy to indigenous peoples. The trend of considering the African cultural legacy as a collection of irrational and absurd beliefs turns the clearing of the African mind of these beliefs into a prerequisite for the inculcation of Western ideas. Instead of dialogue and exchange of ideas, acculturation takes the direction of uprooting natives on the ground that they would become fit for Westernization only through the removal of their cultural legacy. Tempels consistently blames this colonial method for causing irreparable damages, especially for accelerating dehumanization and loss of centeredness among the Bantu. He writes:

> In condemning the whole gamut of their supposed "childish and savage customs" by the judgment "this is stupid and bad," we [missionaries]

have taken our share of the responsibility for having killed "the man" in the Bantu.[1]

A characteristic result of this inhuman method is the genesis of the *évolués*—a French term to characterize those natives who supposedly evolve into civilized Africans as a result of colonial education. Tempels has no kind words to describe the *évolués*. Besides blaming uprootedness for their degeneration, he speaks of these educated Africans as "empty and unsatisfied souls—would be Europeans—and as such, negations of civilized beings," as "moral and intellectual tramps, capable only, despite themselves, of being elements of strife."[2] All these severe flaws point the finger at colonial methods: molded to despise their legacy, these uprooted natives have so internalized the colonial attitude that they end up by nurturing a contempt for their own peoples similar to that of the colonizer.

To confirm that colonial education produces people with a colonizing turn of mind, Tempels stresses that the *évolués* "have no longer any respect for their old institutions, or for the usages and customs which, nevertheless, by their profound significance, form the basis of the practical application in Bantu life of natural law."[3] Since their primary function is to serve as a local instrument of colonial rule, their teaching, training, and mode of life dispose them to construe the dislike of their legacy as civilized behavior.

Partly reproducing the colonial greed and partly expressing their irreparable loss of commitment, these imitators of colonizers are obsessed with money: "money is their one and only ideal, their end and the supreme ultimate norm regulating their actions," writes Tempels.[4] When on top of being cut off from their society and pristine beliefs they feel in their bones the inhumanity of their colonial masters, what else could grow on them but the love of money? This obsession with money is how they display the cynicism that invades them when, for all the loss of commitment to their tradition they have gone through, the colonial society still rejects them. For these fresh converts, the duplicity of the colonizer, at first a source of dismay, easily turns into a general disbelief that unleashes the spur of greed. These would-be Europeans internalize all the vices of colonizer without assimilating any of the positive aspects of modernity.

Tempels fully understands the awkward position of the *évolués*: mesmerized by the power of the colonizer, yet repulsed by the racist ideology of colonialism. He defines them as "profoundly distrustful or embittered" by the obvious lack of "recognition of and respect for their full value as men by the Whites."[5] Because their hopes have been raised only to be dashed without mercy, humiliation is for these people a source of constant torment. So mortifying is their humiliation that they seek appeasement even in manifestations of eccentricity and megalomania. As a result, the need to impress the colonizer at all costs grows into an itch. Such conducts show that the opposition of the *évolués* to colonial rule hides deeper emotional disorders of the kind pushing them toward negative and destructive behaviors.

The error has been to take at face value the rebellious stand of the *évolués*. Even if their role has been decisive in the struggle for independence, one thing is to rise against an alien rule, quite another to develop an independent turn of mind and policy. To overlook this distinction is to miss the extent to which the perpetuation of the colonial rule under the guise of independence remains the appalling reality of Africa.

African elitism is born of the entitlement to an uncontested leadership inferred from the privilege of being exposed to modern education. The inference singles out the *évolués* as heirs to the civilizing mission, as though Westernization passes on to local elites the right to rule, that is, to continue the unfinished business of colonialism. To rule is still a civilizing mission with this difference that natives rescued from primitiveness assume the leadership. The entitlement to rule maintains the belief that Africans are really primitive, and so calls for methods of government similar to the colonial rule. Native rulers starting to think and acting like former colonizers make up the substance of African elitism. Basil Davidson describes well the process of its institution:

> The regimes installed at independence became rapidly subject to upsets and uproars. Striving to contain these, the multi-party parliamentary systems gave way increasingly, whether in theory or practice, to one-party system. Most of these one-party systems at this stage, perhaps all of them, decayed into no-party systems as their ruling elements became fully bureaucratized. Politics came to an end; mere administration took its place, reproducing colonial autocracy as the new "beneficiaries" took the place of the old governors.[6]

Colonialism remains the major source of hindrance not so much by its plunders and destructions—which though not negligible were nevertheless reparable—as by its ideological legacy. The colossal human wreckage caused by the internalization of the colonial discourse and so aptly personified by the *évolués* is how Africa was handed over to psychopathic personalities.

The main thinker of the school of professional philosophers, Paulin Hountondji, takes issue with Tempels over his critique of the *évolués*. Hountondji writes:

> In order to understand the meaning and real significance of this [Tempels's] critique, it is necessary to know that the rebellions and popular uprisings originated in this class of people, that the "agitators" of the rebellion, those who today we could call the African political leaders, came from the heart of this class.[7]

Besides confirming that the people that Tempels diagnosed as *évolués* form the main political and ruling force of present-day African societies, Hountondji reinstates his position linking the debate over the existence of African philosophy with the issue of power and the means of achieving modernization. Ethnophilosophy is charged with backing the views of the traditionalist or conservative, not to say reactionary, sector of African societies, while the rebuttal of ethnophilosophy is credited with modern and revolutionary options. What Hountondji and the proponents of the professional school particularly resent about Tempels and the school he inspired is, as we pointed out earlier, the promotion of the conservative policy of traditional elites through the attribution of a philosophical dimension to the traditional thinking. In the words of Hountondji:

> ethnophilosophy remains a fundamentally conservative discourse. By naming "philosophy" the ensemble of dominating collective representations . . . these representations are given a metaphysical consecration, turning a fact into a law and from then prohibiting all criticism.[8]

This aversion to traditionality exactly reproduces the colonial attitude toward the African legacy. Colonization and the advocates of Westernization all agree to characterize the African heritage as the main obstacle to development and modernization. The acquiescence of Africans to this colonial description of African tradition is what nurtures the elitist mentality by reviving the *évolué* sleeping in every "educated" African. The consent causes a characteristic blur assimilating the use of colonial conceptions and methods to an enlightened and positive approach. As a result of this mix-up,

> the indigenous societies of Africa will be not so much transformed as replaced by modern, secular societies; and the key agents of this process will be indigenous elites, including business elites or capitalists, conceive of as bearers of the necessary universal values of global modernity.[9]

As substitutes for colonizers and in default of being able to whiten themselves, the *évolués* resolve on a condescending and paternalistic attitude, which though different from racism, is nevertheless an entitlement to privilege and uncontested leadership. The great similarity existing between the colonial discourse on Africa and the analysis of professional philosophers of African legacy confirms the extent to which the discourse of the latter is in league with the view of colonizers. Because politics thus shifts to domestication, elitism is unthinkable without the assignment to modernize, which is then understood in terms of snatching the ignorant masses from traditionality. The conflict between tradition and modernity is, we know, the main *leitmotiv* of modernization theories, be they liberal, socialist, or Marxist. Entirely based on the colonial paradigm of civilizing mission, these theories assert that, in light of the larger society being immobilized by centuries of apathy, fatalism, and barbarism, salvation must come from outside, from the enlightened few.

One African scholar who has closely studied the phenomenon of elitism and its negative effects is V. Y. Mudimbe. To characterize the two African philosophers who have most vigorously criticized ethnophilosophy and defended the Western definition of philosophy, to wit, Hountondji and Marcien Towa, Mudimbe alludes to "elitism and Western dependency."[10] Both pander to the smearing of African past and legacy in the name of universalism, thereby giving support to the indoctrination of Africans by the Western idea of "man." The proven method of the indoctrination is the opposition between tradition and modernity whose consequence is to rule out the presentation of modernity as an extension, a continuation of tradition. Pushed to the other side of modernity, tradition appears as the major obstacle that must be liquidated for evolution to kick off.

To evince the irreconcilable opposition between tradition and modernity, the science of anthropology substantiates through extensive documentations and varied analyses that the disparity between European modernity and African traditions rises to the level of radical antagonism, the very one opposing the rational to the irrational, the civilized to the primitive, the good to the bad, and the dynamic to the static. The disparity could not but implant a desire for a conversion to Western views and methods deep down into the African soul. Make no mistake: this conversion has nothing to do with becoming modern; instead, the conversion is how Africans are conditioned to play a subordinate role in the colonial order. The absorption of the anthropological discourse produces the *évolué* as the one who, having a foot in both the modern and traditional worlds, best promotes the hierarchical order of colonialism by serving as a reliable liaison between colonized and colonizers.

Mudimbe gives a striking illustration of the mentality of the *évolué* in the person of Samuel Ajayi Crowther, a former slave and native of Yorubaland in Nigeria. Educated first in Sierra Leone and then in England, Crowther became in 1864 "the first Anglican bishop of 'the territories of Western Equatorial Africa beyond the Queen's Dominions.'"[11] In one of his missions in Niger, he is reported to have asked "whether the inhabitants of Gomkoi were Pagans or Mohammedans," if "the males wore some sort of cloth around their loins," even if "they were cannibals."[12] He had so internalized the Western narrative about Africa that he became unable to dissociate the images of "paganism, nakedness, and cannibalism" from the representation of his own race.[13] Instead of being the learning of modern methods and concepts, acculturation is thus essentially how natives learn to adhere to their allotted inferior rank and marginality through the depreciation of themselves and their legacy.

According to Mudimbe, the deconstruction of Western discourse is the only appropriate weapon against this induced self-debasement. Nothing genuinely African and good can be realized without the radical extirpation of the internalized colonial discourse. So long as the colonial idea of Africa survives—and the idea survives, nay, prospers through the Western education of young Africans—the conception of a truly African project of modernization is impossible, still less the design of policies and methods to turn modernization into reality. Mental decolonization is the key to Africa's numerous impediments and continuous marginality. This need to go from conversion to deconversion turns philosophical deconstruction into a *sine qua non* of African renaissance.

The deconstruction of Western paradigm must imply the rejection of the antinomy between modernity and tradition. Since colonial reading deforms the African past, no reason exists to endorse the opposition between tradition and modernity. Herein lies the main mistake of the school of professional philosophers. Their critique of the anthropological discourse and the denunciation of ethnophilosophy as an endorsement of that discourse give them the illusion of being revolutionary and committed to the emancipation of Africa. Little do they realize that their defense of the Western idea of philosophy and the subsequent denial of such philosophy to Africans reinstate the pretensions of Eurocentrism to be a model. They contest the anthropological discourse because anthropology deprives Africans of what the West values most, to wit, rationality. Yet their denial of African philosophy ends up by confirming the colonial allegation. Is not this reversal an endorsement of the colonial discourse, a resolute slide into the acceptance of inferiority and marginality?

Most interesting in this regard is Niamkey Koffi's position. He provides a tight and impressive criticism of Towa's and Houtondji's denial of African philosophy, but even more so he denounces elitism by unraveling its ascriptive claim to power. According to him, the rejection of African philosophy is not an innocent mistake, a mere oversight; the rejection is an ideology of power legitimation and conquest. It is how philosophy is mystified for the purpose of discrediting traditional thoughts as popular worldviews, as collective and uncritical beliefs. For the school of professional philosophers, to mistake philosophy for a vision of the world is to give the "concept a particularly vulgar meaning."[14]

So reversing the charge of consecration of the traditional thought made against ethnophilosophy, Koffi replies to Hountondji: your denial of African philosophy endorses Western hegemony, and you endorse Western hegemony because it advances your position as member of the intelligentsia. By vouching for the opposition between tradition and modernity, you play the game of the West and promote assimilation. By opting for a discontinuous process of modernization, you invest the Western educated elite with the exclusive right to rule.

The opposition between philosophy and traditional visions of the world is how philosophy denounces false knowledge. In thus stigmatizing tradition as false knowledge, the defense of the Western definition of philosophy imposes a complete silence on the vision of the world, on the thoughts of African peoples. To say that a vision of the world is not philosophy is to take position against said vision; it is to demean the vision so as to justify its suppression. The distinction between vision of the world and philosophy

> at once hides and reveals a secret struggle for power, a battle for domination of Science against pseudo-Science, a battle of philosophy against the vision of the world. This struggle is in the last instance the expression of the will of the carriers of knowledge to overthrow the carriers of alleged false knowledge so as to appropriate their authority.[15]

Instead of organizing the opposition of the dominated, the Western definition of philosophy that Towa and Hountondji defend consecrates the victory of the West through the devaluation of their legacy. In defying this devaluation, ethnophilosophy exhibits the commendable goal of not only affirming the existence of African philosophy, but also of demonstrating the specificity of this philosophy *vis-à-vis* the West.

The ultimate intention of the valorization of modernity, philosophy, and science is, Koffi insists, to initiate a struggle for power by taking all legitimacy away from tradition. For Towa and Hountondji, ethnophilosophy is a false philosophy, a non-philosophy, not a different philosophy. In so thinking, they fail to see the relationship between their philosophical productions and "their class position of elitist intellectuals" refusing the title of philosophy to thoughts originating from their people.[16] For one thing, they miss the occasion to criticize the West by showing that the myth of philosophy, born in Greece and developing logically through the history of the West, is nothing but a construct elaborated in favor of the hegemonic West for apologetic purpose. For another, the rejection of past beliefs and institutions without a concrete and unbiased assessment of their nature and the option for discontinuist ideologies feed on the "intellectualist snobbery" of the elitist position.[17]

Some such position is not in line with the real interest of Africa and its search for freedom, since it intimates that Africans can profitably use the Western type of philosophy. How could it be so when, as a property of the West, Western philosophy is specifically designed to promote the hegemony of the West? Whenever Africans use such kind of philosophy, they do not liberate but submit Africa to the capitalist order. The riddle is solved, however, if we read into the support for the colonial description a justification for the political ambition of the African intelligentsia. The support is how African intellectuals present themselves, in the words of Davidson:

as those who were to be the instruments of applying the European model to Africa, and therefore as the saviours of the continent. Being sure of the values of their Western education, they were convinced of their superiority over their vast majority: who but they, after all, possessed the keys to the powerhouse of knowledge whence European technology and conquest had flowed?[18]

The savors of Africa turned out to be its plunderers and a complete disillusionment took hold of Africans. Economic crises, perpetual political instability, and social tensions, together with rampant corruption and nepotism, became the defining features of Africa. If anything, the depravity and predatory nature of the postcolonial elite testify to the complete loss of its sense of accountability to society. One explanation is uprootedness: because uprootedness dilutes respect and commitment, it takes away the sense of obligation to the people from the political elite. When perceived as essentially inadequate, society is likened to a raw material that must be fashioned at will, it inspires no obligation to its demiurges. As a result of ceasing to belong to the native society on account of its Western education, the intelligentsia panders to patronization whose conspicuous result is the collapse of all ethical relationship with the social community.

To summarize, the elitist attitude echoes the colonial mentality means that the moral bankruptcy of the educated elite is a direct consequence of the endorsement of the idea of primitive Africa. The act by which Africans welcome Western education is the act by which they acquiesce to the colonial discourse on Africa: the one is inseparable from the other. As a result, educated Africans are unable to adopt a moral standard: the contempt—mostly unconscious—that they feel for Africanness totally deprives them of ethical relationships with themselves and their original society. Disdain and non-accountability appear to them as the only way by which they demonstrate their complete emancipation from their legacy. Imperative, therefore, is the recognition as a major explanation of African numerous impediments the fact that modern African states have simply replaced the colonial states. Because "Africans replaced the Europeans officials right to the top of the bureaucracy" without the prior dismantling of the colonial state and methods, especially without a far-reaching decolonization of the educated and political elites, small wonder the same structure and turn of mind usher in similar results.[19]

2. The Elitist Drift of Ethnophilosophy

So far we have shown how the internalization of colonial discourse produces elitism. But what about ethnophilosophy, which argues against the colonial discourse by defending the idea of African philosophy? The rehabilitation of African traditions suggests an orientation that should ward off elitism: instead of imposing the imitation of an external model, the thinking should be committed to building modernity on African realities and centrality.

Most ethnophilosophers, such as, Léopold Sédar Senghor, Kwame Nkrumah, and Julius Nyerere, refer the future of Africa to the idea of African socialism. The reference implies the inadequacy of the Western model; it also pledges to rehabilitate "the traditional social order and to seek salvation in the pristine values of our [African] ancestors."[20] Since the Western model is inadequate, Africans must return to their source. This return is all the more necessary as the search for authenticity provides a solution to African failure. The delay of modernization suggests that the path to socialist development alone is suitable for African personality. Above all, the revival of tradition and the reconnection of Africans with the idea of a free precolonial Africa are perceived as the best way to decolonize the African mind. Decolonization is impossible so long as Africans do not rediscover and reconcile themselves with the idea of a free Africa.

Granted these positive inspirations, the truth remains that ethnophilosophy did not escape the ascendancy of the colonial discourse. Deeply upset by the denial of philosophy, ethnophilosophers began a frenzied search of philosophy no matter where, in African languages, myths, and proverbs. Given the Western hegemony, the attempt to refute by all means the colonial denial of philosophy amounts to a plea for recognition addressed to the colonial master. The refutation simply demands that the master recognizes philosophy in the African thinking even if the thinking is not genuinely philosophical. What is the purpose of this plea? The following observations of F. Eboussi-Boulaga explain:

> In the dominated society of Africa, philosophy also belongs to those types of knowledge that have no other contents than to bring nearer to the master, to make the liberated worthy to succeed the master, to confer legitimacy on him. Philosophy is an attribute of power. Well, the West holds (and distributes) power.[21]

The linkage of ethnophilosophy with power, more exactly with the justification of power evinces its purpose. To be recognized by the West as having a philosophy is to be worthy of power. The recognition is how the emancipated ruling elite becomes entitled to rule, to replace the colonizer. Ethnophilosophy tries to obtain the mandate to rule for the African elite from the West perceived as source of power. Notwithstanding its confrontational language, ethnophilosophy has never been against Western hegemony; it was seeking its blessing instead.

Even if the accusation of collusion with Western hegemony made against ethnophilosophy is evidently excessive, ethnophilosophers' attempts to decolonize the African mind are not crowned with success. One explanation for the failure of the ethnophilosophical discourse is that it revels in a rosy description of the African past under the pretext of decolonization and rehabilitation. Ethnophilosophy speaks of a return to the source without making sure that the unearthing of the past does not hamper the number one priority of Africa: modernization. In advocating a return to an unrecreated past, ethnophilosophy itself turns into an elitist position. Succumbing to the objectivist illusion, ethnophilosophy endorses the colonial idea of African otherness and attempts to define Africans in terms counter to Westerners.

Implicit in the defense of a collective philosophy is the stigmatization of individualism, diversity of views, and dissent as un-African. What else is this stigmatization promoting but a resurgence of the traditional notion of chief? The so-called positive traits of Africans tend to describe a society entirely cut out for the uncontested authority of the chief. The fact that the new chief is armed with an ideology (socialism) according to which society is fashioned only reinforces the elitist inspiration of ethnophilosophy. That many African political leaders were also theoreticians of ethnophilosophy is not sheer coincidence. The sincere intent of valorizing African values should not lead us astray: since what ethnophilosophers valorize is the Western view of Africa, they are unable to rise above the assumptions of colonial policy, and so call for the same policy of authoritarian imposition. Moreover, their equal expertise in the knowledge of traditional and Western philosophies allegedly gives them the unique ability to modernize African societies through a synthetic approach. As expedient leaders, power accrues to them as an exclusive entitlement.

Recall Hountondji's insight linking the ethnophilosophical discourse with power. Delving into the reason why African scholars insist on calling traditional thoughts philosophy, Hountondji detects a valorizing intent, an apology. In view of the meaning of vulgarity and un-sophistication attached to the popular or the traditional, the attribute of philosophy surely imparts majesty and prestige. The hidden purpose of calling African philosophy what is after all a mere collection of uncritical and collective beliefs is the valorization of unanimity and its interpretation as a genuine African trait. As Hountondji states, "the belief in unanimism . . . is the real cornerstone of ethnophilosophy," since the sole purpose of naming popular beliefs philosophy is to hail the unanimity that they advocate.[22] As an outcome of philosophy, the unanimity of beliefs rises to the level of a norm.

Let us retrace how Hountondji proceeds to expose ethnophilosophy as an ideology of unanimism and conservatism. He begins by showing that the notion of collective philosophy is a lure; in reality, individual philosophies are paraded as collective philosophies. Once the camouflage is taken off, the profoundly totalitarian and conservative purpose of ethnophilosophy appears clearly. Since the appeal to an implicit and collective worldview contains the imperative of unanimity, the apology of ethnophilosophy turns into a ruling stating that in African societies "there can never be individual beliefs or philosophies but only collective systems of belief."[23] The idea of collective philosophy is then how an individual thinking invokes the authority of tradition, of that which is authentically African and permanent, to impose itself.

Thanks to the "myth of unanimity," the individual view soars high above any critical examination and demands the mere capitulation of dissident positions in the name of authentic Africanness.[24] This apology of unanimism is a justification for dictatorial regimes and undemocratic methods of ruling. The ideology of the one-party system, the rejection of individualism as un-African, the praise of the collective, the ostracization of dissident views, all work toward the goal of consecrating absolute power as an African virtue.

Unanimity presupposes the debilitating notion of race. Inherited from colonialism, the notion is responsible for illusory conceptions of unity that lose sight of African social, tribal, and cultural diversity. From the alleged racial unity the belief that all Africans think alike is easily deduced. In the name of this racial unanimity, African despots have stifled differences and initiatives: all that was dynamic, plural, and democratic was stigmatized as un-African. Again take the idea of African socialism. The idea rests on strong racial presuppositions of the kind decreeing that Africans are socialist by nature. Communalism, in the strong sense of implicating the absence of acquisitiveness and individualism, is therefore their inborn characteristics.

Consequently, class differentiations and conflicts should be considered as alien and detrimental. Thus, rejecting the Marxist interpretation of class struggle, Nyerere speaks of African socialism as being "opposed to doctrinaire socialism which seeks to build its happy society on a philosophy of inevitable conflict between man and man."[25] According to him, the revival of the former, precolonial attitude of mind is enough to dissolve all the acquired capitalist attitudes whose exclusive birthplace is the West.

The discovery of this ideal and normative Africa confers on Western educated Africans a messianic role, a historic mission that quickly degenerates into elitism. Already many African leaders had opted for socialism because of the prestige socialist ideology had in Europe, especially among intellectuals. The prospect of obtaining the support of the now defunct socialist camp was another consideration. Yet no reason was as appealing as the elitist image of rescuer: dragged from their natural inclination and confounded by an alien situation, Africans needed nothing more than a political tutelage that would put them back into their natural socialist milieu.

The spectacle of Nkrumah, for instance, forcefully implementing African socialism on a people that he otherwise termed socialist by tradition gives a good evidence of elitism. His elitist slip clearly transpires when he makes the success of the anticolonial struggle dependent on the intervention of those who control knowledge. He writes: "this triumph must be accompanied by knowledge," which means: "it must be socialist in form and content and be embraced by a mass party."[26] The imperative of a mass party guided by the enlightened few is how power and knowledge fall into the same hands, and government, thus armed with an ideology, changes into tutorship.

The other muddled goal that the racialization of Africans has inspired is the idea of pan-Africanism. I am not denying the great merit of African continental unity. The common history of slavery and colonialism and the added syndromes of prolonged marginality give Africans enough reason to make common cause. Moreover, the idea of continental unity works against dispersion: unity being force, Africans have a better chance of combating marginality and poverty if they unite. The argument according to which the political unity of the African continent will favor peace by solving the problems of divided tribes and arbitrary borders is also worth considering.

All these attributes of unity, however positive, do not change the fact that pan-Africanism remains an endorsement of the colonial discourse. More than the common experience of domination, the idea of Africans belonging to the same race, sharing common physical and cultural traits, cements the ideology of pan-Africanism. To show that pan-Africanism echoes the colonial racialization of African, Frantz Fanon reminds: "for the colonist, the Negro was neither an Angolan nor a Nigerian, he simply spoke of "the Negro."[27] Nothing evinces better the internalization of the colonial discourse than this propensity of African educated circles to echo racist philosophies.

Fanon reveals the principle at work when he notes: "the efforts of the native to rehabilitate himself and to escape from the claws of colonialism are logically inscribed from the same point of view as that of colonialism."[28] Thus, to the continental and racial characterization and defamation of the colonizer corresponds the racial response and rehabilitation of the ethnophilosophers. Nowhere do these thinkers say: racialization being where the distortion and insult originate the African response would be well advised to challenge the idea of race. Repulsed by the idea of national cultures and states and in perfect accord with racism, Africans too speak of African culture only and place the future of Africans in the hands of the Negro continent and the Negro state. Is there a better illustration of the failure of decolonization than this propensity to echo racist characterizations of Africa?

Not only does pan-Africanism welcome the racialization of Africans, but it also puts a severe strain on existing African states by contesting their legitimacy. Emphasizing the particularity of African nationalism, Nyerere writes: "the African national State is an instrument for the unification of Africa, and not for dividing Africa, that African nationalism is meaningless, is dangerous, is anachronistic if it is not at the same time pan-Africanism."[29] Already stigmatized as artificial entities imposed by external colonial forces, the existing African states lose the little legitimacy they had against the racial state of pan-Africanism Yet the reason why Africans would obtain better results in a larger unit than in smaller ones is not clear. Without mentioning the huge problems of organization, communication, and harmonization of a vast continent, we can say that a larger unit is not better equipped to resolve what is essentially a problem of democracy and economic efficiency.

The likelihood is that unity on the scale of the continent will only multiply and amplify the same problems to the point of making them insolvable. Rightly Fanon warns: "this historical obligation in which the men of African culture finds themselves to racialize their claims and to speak more of an African culture than of a national culture will tend to lead them up a blind alley."[30] Compared to the wisdom of creating organizations that initiate and support cooperation in all fields between African states so as to make them interdependent, the racialization of the pan-African state only succeeds in undermining the existing African states. The progressive, step-by-step integration of African states will have the incomparable merit of positing unity as a choice, a construction rather than a derivative of racial identity.

At this juncture, a characteristic default of elitism transpires: the preference of utopia to practically achievable goals. By making their claims racial, ethnophilosophers miss the African states as political realities. When existing states are overtaken by the concern for Africanness in general, which is abstract and devoid of political reality, the movement of African renaissance is doomed to remain a wishful thinking, an unattainable ideal. In thus being cut off from the concrete life of people and actual political realities, talk about African renaissance verges on mere utopia. Since the rehabilitated culture comes against liberation by standing in the way of positive change, Fanon rejects the return to the source of negritude as a misguided attempt of a colonized elite to reconnect with the masses.

The corrosion of African states by the elitist discourse of pan-Africanism easily shifts to the no less elitist discourse of ethnicity. This is to say that pan-Africanism as much as ethnic separatism flows from ethnophilosophy. What connects the two ideologies is clear enough: the way pan-Africanism removes legitimacy from existing African states is also how it encourages the rise of ethnic politics. In addition to race leading directly to ethnicity, the promotion of ethnicity joins the main stream of African elitism. First, the passive, unimagined return to the past rediscovers and revalues ethnic membership. Second, the tendency to base union and solidarity on relatedness, derived from the pan-Africanist moment, easily yields to ethnic calling because both thinks that blood, kinship favors a better, more solidaristic social life and organization.

Fanon gives a good illustration of the logical connection between race and ethnicity. Elaborating on his warning that the mere replacement of colonial rulers by African ruling classes will only indulge in a dependent policy reproducing the syndromes of colonial governments, he notes: "we observe a falling back toward old tribal attitudes, and, furious and sick at heart, we perceive that race feeling in its most exacerbated form is triumphing."[31]

Fanon analyzes the rise of ethnicity as a bourgeois inspired ideology. Inherited from colonial mentality, ethnic ideology is nothing more than an exasperated racism. It is a cheap racism, racism in the African style. Ethnicity is definitely an expression of colonized mentality in that it classifies, separates, excludes peoples on the basis of natural characteristics. In the words of Fanon, it is "a racism of defense, based on fear. Essentially it is no different from vulgar tribalism."[32] Most importantly, ethnicity is the weapon of the dependent bourgeoisie: unable to accomplish its national historic mission, the African elite finds no other means to hold on to power than through the politics of division and exclusion, which exclusion, in turn, activates the ethnicity of the excluded. Recourse to ethnicity only confirms the lack of strength of the national bourgeoisie: the amputation of its role as a result of dependency compels the African bourgeoisie to rule through disunity and exclusion in line with the colonial principle of divide and rule. To show that the dependent African elite exactly reproduces the principle of colonial rule, Fanon reminds us how "by its very structure, colonialism is separatist and regionalist. Colonialism does not simply state the existence of tribes; it also reinforces it and separates them."[33]

The elitist content of ethnicity becomes particularly glaring when we pay attention to the manner ethnic ideology justifies power. Scholars have been struck by the modernist language of ethnicity: ethnic claims speaks in terms of justice, democracy, and self-determination, and educated groups are the most ardent supporters and leaders of ethnic movements. Because of this modern content, many scholars rightly warn against any identification of ethnicity with tribalism. Yet behind the modern and democratic language, there looms an ascriptive entitlement to power. As one scholar notes, "the rigidity of ascriptive characteristics that define ethnicity compared to the fluidity of alternative bases of identity (especially class) accounts for the comparative advantage of ethnicity in sustaining group solidarity."[34]

In going back to the past, elites discover a new form of entitlement: the ascriptive right of kinship. According to this right, the representatives of ethnic groups exercise power as a matter of natural rights, of belonging to the same natural group. They are the natural representatives of the group; their entitlement is in the blood, in the ethnic belonging. No other people have the right to represent them: others are precisely outsiders. Nor is there a more compelling principle of unity than natural solidarity; this type of unity transcends even classes and common economic interests. Class mobilization maintains the entrenched disadvantages by subordinating particular interests to common interests when what excluded groups need is the defense of their particularity. Because the alleged common interests usually favor the dominant ethnic group, minority groups prefer ethnic mobilization to class unity.

Ethnicity is where the ideology of unanimity achieves a perfect expression. The ethnic group is obviously the embodiment of unanimism: in addition to having common characteristics and history, members of an ethnic group are supposed to think alike and to have a common interest beyond class and status divisions. Most of all, ethnic solidarity is presented as a normative behavior with the assumption that kinspersons are the best possible representatives of the ethnic group. No better way exists to deliver a whole people in the hands of elitism than to brandish the possibility of a breakaway ethnic state or a state functioning on the basis of ethnic solidarity.

The logic that pushes Nkrumah to argue in favor of the one-party system because such a system "is better able to express and satisfy the common aspirations of a nation as whole, than a multiple-party parliamentary system" works beautifully well for ethnicist politicians whose basic credo is the origination of common aspirations from ethnic membership.[35] Ethnic solidarity replaces class solidarity, the dividing line being between the ethnically related and the alien. Additionally, the notion of diversity is believed to be detrimental to the struggle. The same enthronement of the enlightened few, who alone illuminate the road to freedom, follows as a matter of course. The ideology of the return to the source gives them a messianic stature, turn them into deliverers from ethnic oppression. Once ethnic solidarity becomes the principal rule, it stifles all dissident views by authorizing the characterization of all internal opposition as a betrayal of common interests. The ruling exactly institutes unanimity around the leadership canonized as the sole interpreter of the interests of the ethnic group.

This analysis of ethnicity must not be interpreted as a condemnation of ethnic politics in Africa. The fact that an excluded group organizes itself and fights the exclusion cannot be rejected without going against democratization. The inclusion of pluralism strongly favors the development of modern values by stimulating openness and competition. What is adverse, however, is the tendency of ethnic politics to harbor a separatist spirit by identifying the nation with the ethnic group. The use of ethnicity to break up the state confuses what is essentially a problem of democratization with the emergence of a new ethnic state whose democratization is yet to come. Having ethnically related people control the state does not eliminate issues pertaining to democratization and modernization. On the contrary, the ideology of relatedness can even get tougher to democratize inasmuch as it is little prone to the impersonalization of the state.

The question is to know to what extent the defense of the ascriptive rights of ethnicity is compatible with the principle of modernity, given that modernity decrees the dependence of the status and place of individuals on their achievement. Unless the entitlement promoted by ethnicity is reconciled with the principle of merit and achievement, the style of household politics will prevail to the detriment of public accountability and democratic rules.

3. Power as Tutorship

We have enough elements to define better the phenomenon of elitism. Take the case of Fanon. We saw how pertinent his critiques of the racialization of Africans are, and yet he personifies elitism to the highest degree. D. A. Masolo correctly writes:

> Fanon considered elitism to have a key role in the revolutionary process. The intellectual and political elites must exist and unite to give leadership to the masses. For him, as much as the masses need to be led into political activism as an uncompromising revolutionary force, they also need to be educated about the proper political and cultural awareness.[36]

What produces elitism is precisely this normative union of knowledge with power, this assumption that those who get involved in intellectual work should also rule. Behind this entitlement to rule, we find the ethos of the *évolués* who, having internalized the Western discourse, take on the task of rescuing their society from barbarism and ignorance. Because of the perception of modernization as a passage from savagery to civilization, knowledge or enlightenment entitles the Westernized African to power.

This entitlement completely redefines the role of the state. According to the influential liberal theory, modern states implicate a contract of citizens among themselves and with the government as a result of which the latter becomes accountable to the people. Classical Marxist theory insists that the contract does not involve the working people, given that governments protect the interests of ruling classes. The attribution of a modernizing role to the state adds a civilizing mission to the normal administrative and political functions of the state. Following the colonial paradigm, from representative of social forces the state thus grows into a tutor. And who can direct this state if not those natives who have access to Western knowledge? Since civilization must come from outside, power must become tutorship. This equation produces elitism in all its various forms.

The ancient precursor of this association of power with knowledge is none other than Plato. In the *Republic,* Plato uses the term guardians to define the intellectuals who assume the political task of reforming and guiding the society. They are those who, having contemplated the world of ideas, return to the visible world with the firm intention of modeling it in the image of the eternal truth. The specific normative terms by which Plato confirms the salvationist role of intellectuals and reserves the right to rule only to those who know are as follows:

> The society we have described can never grow into a reality or see the light of the day, and there will be no end to the troubles of states, or

indeed . . . of humanity, till philosophers become kings in this world, or till those we now call kings and rulers really and truly become philosophers, and political power and philosophy thus come into the same hands.[37]

Let no one object by saying that the specific reference to philosophers underlines the imperative of moral standard so that Plato has in mind a new type of political leadership quite distinct from ordinary politics. In the modern versions of political leadership too, the requirement to combine political power with knowledge advocates high moral integrity and commitment to the people. As stated by Daniel Chirot, what is common to modern tyrannies is "an absolute sense of moral superiority based on an ideology, or a religion that claims to explain everything perfectly."[38]

Such is particularly the case of Leninist ideology, and significantly so, since nowhere does elitism reach a more influential form than in the Soviet system. In his book, *What Is To Be Done*, V. I. Lenin develops the principle that intellectuals, going beyond their normal role as bureaucrats, technicians, researchers, educators, and critics, should also become political leaders. His argument that power and knowledge must come into the same hands is all based on his assumption that, left to itself, the working class would only develop a trade-union consciousness. Lenin writes:

We said that *there could not yet* be Social-Democratic consciousness among the workers. This consciousness could only be brought to them from without. The history of all countries shows that the working class, exclusively by its own effort, is able to develop only trade union consciousness. . . . The theory of socialism, however, grew out of the philosophic, historical and economic theories that were elaborated by the educated representatives of the propertied classes, the intellectuals. . . . Similarly, in Russia, the theoretical doctrine of Social-Democracy arose quite independently of the spontaneous growth of the labour movement; it arose as a natural and inevitable outcome of the development of ideas among the revolutionary socialist intelligentsia.[39]

Other Marxist intellectuals, such as, Antonio Gramsci, Mao Tse-tung, and Fanon, add their voices to turn the conjunction of power and knowledge into a credo of revolutionary movements in the third world. The Leninist principle is little in agreement with the original ideas of Karl Marx, who did not think that intellectuals should have a special role, still less a dominating role, in the transition to socialism. Marx assumed that socialism being what the working class creates as the struggle of workers unfolds, there was no need for external organizers or leaders. The subject, the maker of the process remained the working class, and this standing of the class excluded the idea that socialism could be a process imposed from outside.

Many African thinkers and African leftist movements in the 1960s and 70s fully adopted the Leninist principle. All agreed that unless the struggle of the people is organized and radicalized by committed intellectuals, it will have no positive outcome, especially it will not steer toward socialism. Thus, after contesting the capacity of the peasantry, urban petit bourgeois social formations, and workers to wage a revolutionary struggle, Amilcar Cabral emphasized "the need for a revolutionary (as opposed to simply nationalist) vanguard party led by a politically conscious elite."[40] In a chapter of his book, *Revolution in Guinea*, characteristically titled "The Weapon of Theory," Cabral goes so far as to define the unique historical role of such an elite by its propensity to "committing suicide as a class in order to be reborn as revolutionary workers, completely identified with the deepest aspirations of the people to which they belong."[41] This myth of an elite entirely committed to the cause of the people—a myth echoing the Platonic ideal of the philosopher-king—would not have been possible without the belief ascribing its transfiguration to the possession of a revolutionary theory.

The flourishing of the Leninist principle, first in backward Russia and then in third world countries, reveals the social condition that fosters elitism. The condition is a perceived social impasse conferring on an enlightened group the right to seize power in the name of a class or a large section of the people conceived unfit to conquer political hegemony. The group claims to have the mandate for tutorship until the people become mature enough to assume the task of self-government. To have an idea of the shift of the role of intellectuals in third world countries, recall the position of European intellectuals fighting the feudal order. When one reads the political writings of Jean-Jacques Rousseau, François-Marie Arouet de Voltaire, and John Locke, other than the purpose of enlightenment and the suggestion of an alternative social organization and evolution, no goal to seize power in the name of a class or a people suffuses their works. On the contrary, they think that the new emerging bourgeois class, once properly enlightened and armed with alternative views, is perfectly liable to establish a new and progressive social order.

Different is the theory that produces the phenomenon of Leninism or elitism: the theory stipulates that underdeveloped societies are so disrupted that they are devoid of progressist social forces. Being in a deadlock, such societies call for outsiders, saviors (intellectuals, military officers) from outside traditional as well as modernized sectors of production. For these outsiders to appear as saviors, to acquire the entitlement to rule, a theory of history is needed from which they draw the calling, the mission. The purpose of the theory is to establish and explain the deadlock.

Once more Lenin gives a perfect example of such a theory. In defining imperialism as the stage of "parasitism and decay of capitalism," his theory announces the exhaustion of bourgeois forces and revolution.[42] The hegemony of this parasitic capitalism on peripheral societies prevents the rise of regenerative social forces, thereby investing intellectuals with the historic mission of guiding the liberation movements. This historic role legitimizes elitism as the self-appointed delegate of the people. The clear impact of imperialism being the paralysis of the inner process of evolution while generating a small yet active enlightened sector, this social impasse passes on the role usually ascribed to classes to the enlightened few.

Whereas the liberal view of modernization assigns the leading role to the bourgeois class, the socialist version thus favored an intellectualized elite. Entirely based on the colonial paradigm of civilizing mission, the socialist option asserts that, on account of the larger society being immobilized by centuries of ignorance and fatalism, salvation must come from the enlightened few. In thus hailing the revolutionary role of organized intellectuals, Marxist theoreticians do no more than advocate a revamped version of the colonial rule. What prevents these scholars from seeing the colonial inspiration of their theory is the illusion of possessing the science of social evolution. In their eyes, the application of a science, however disruptive and remodeling it may be, is absolutely distinct from the demeaning and exploitative changes introduced by colonial rule. African intellectuals are here victims of the false promise according to which "it is possible to formulate perfect social and economic models, and that society can be 'engineered.'"[43]

This analysis equally applies to the other elitist drift incarnated by ethnophilosophers and promoters of ethnicity. The socialist option of ethnophilosophy requires the enthronement of an educated elite, since the communalist goal excludes the leadership of a particular class. Whereas class leadership structures society on the basis of economic interests and goals and promotes contractual relationships among people, elitism proposes a programmed and politicized course of action whose main outcome is to take initiative and freedom away from social life. Little wonder the same communalism easily shifts to ethnicity perceived as the embodiment of group solidarity. That is why among the promoters of ethnicity many were at one point Marxist so that ethnicity is for them a substitute for the now outmoded theory of class struggle. Most of all, the organization and mobilization of people around ethnic issues is a political option that justifies elite ascendancy. Just as in the case of class interest, the belief is that, left to themselves, the masses are unable to fight consistently for their ethnic identity and interests.

The political leadership of intellectuals is necessary to turn the ethnic group into a self-sufficient, free, and self-governing movement. Only when intellectuals assume the leadership can the group change from mere entity into subject. The secessionist alternative is only an exasperated form of the resolution of local elites to claim the exclusive right to represent a group of people. We find the same Leninist idea that positive developments cannot emerge from the people themselves unless those who are conscious and organized exercise the necessary tutelage to bring the ethnic group round to the idea of its distinct identity and interests.

In all the considered cases, whatever the chosen path, a decisive role is accorded to intellectuals because they appear necessary to impose developments whose origination from within social life is ruled out. In line with the colonial reasoning, progress must come from outside and must be imposed on the people. The difference between the colonial paradigm and the elitist model boils down to the burden of "the white man" becoming the burden of the native intellectuals, of the *évolués*.

Essential is the grasp that the social condition of the intellectual feeds on elitism. African intellectuals cannot reflect one moment on themselves and the backwardness of their society without thinking that they incarnate freedom and emancipation while all the rest is in darkness. They invariably think of themselves as liberators, and so develops what we can call the demiurge complex. Everything conspires to nurture this belief, for it is inscribed in their modern education. Being Western educated is how they see themselves in a sea of ignorance and barbarism. They cannot give credence to their modern education without secretly acquiescing to the image of primitive Africa.

This tacit consent explains the vulnerability of Africa to leaders that quickly change into monsters. Among the explanations of the propensity of African societies to fall under the rule of ruthless and buffoon tyrants, particularly exemplified by Idi Amin of Uganda and Jean Bedel Bokassa of the Central African Republic, only those which take resentment against colonial masters as a major cause of erratic behaviors escape the usual racist stereotypes of African savagery. These studies suggest that these infamous tyrants had in common the hatred of African intellectuals as a result of their poor education, but were at one point used by colonial powers and then ignored in favor of more educated Africans.[44] Thus Bokassa, who fought loyally for France in Indochina, was a highly decorated officer in the French army. Idi Amin was also a loyal professional soldier with a long and distinguished career in the British colonial army, which used him to crush the Mau Mau rebellion in Kenya.

The truth about these two tyrants is then that they had prostrated themselves before their colonial masters whom they faithfully served. On account of their servility and intellectual mediocrity, former colonial powers helped them seize power when events required the intervention of loyal natives. Both their lack of intellectual aura—a necessary attribute to win the legitimacy of power in Africa—and their deep resentment against their former masters drove them to the dangerous path of trying to impress at all costs their compatriots as well as former colonizers. Bokassa's Napoleonic farce was clearly designed to strike the imagination of the French and of his French-educated compatriots.

Likewise, Amin's expropriation of Indians, anti-Western rhetoric, and wrongheaded economic measures together with his alliance with anti-Western Arab leaders were meant to anger the West and rally Ugandans behind him. At first an attempt to impress and gain legitimacy, their extravagance and megalomania soon changed into brutality as their unrealistic and inconsistent policy pushed more people into opposition. These extreme cases clearly grow from a sociocultural situation in which the failure to have the intellectual legitimacy to rule—a requirement entirely derived from the colonial discourse—can look for compensation even in insane policies and behaviors.

I am not suggesting that all African leaders belong to the species of the two mentioned tyrants. Nonetheless, the intellectualization of power is fraught with many dangers, and the inability to devise a correct and self-empowering course of action is the most common peril. African leaders may not be aware of their inheritance of the colonial discourse; they can even have the impression of systematically combating colonialism. Yet a glance at their practices reveals the unconscious belief that makes them fall back on the colonial view. Such recurring and detrimental practices as the liquidation of democracy and the institution dictatorial powers point to the propensity of African leaders to assume a civilizing role. Their conversion to modern views has been basically a conversion to the colonial view of Africa: the perceived need for tutors bears witness to this internalization of the colonial contempt.

No other explanation to the recurring penchant of Africa for dictatorial regimes comes to mind than the megalomania of the *évolué* using all means to pull the people into civilization. Such leaders cannot rely on the consent of the governed; they know what is best for them. This political suckling has an economic version: nationalization, centralization, and household management style are all ways and means of taking initiative away from the society in favor of the enlightened leadership. Complete centralization and paternalism are believed necessary to extirpate traditionality and implement the most basic elements of modernization. Once a situation of massive ignorance and apathy is posited, the undivided, forceful, and providential leadership of the enlightened few appears as the only remedy.

This paternalistic model is doomed to failure for the simple reason that paternalism cannot internalize the colonial contempt and yet give birth to a positive outcome. The truth is that the model leans toward negative policies because both its inspiration and methods come up against constructive courses. In this system where the governed are assimilated to tutees, failure and disaster are part and parcel of the governing task. Whereas a sane policy would require nothing less than the rejection of the colonial discourse, elitism must engage, under pain of losing justification, in destructive policies. The distorted relationship of elitism with the people stands in the way of devising sound policies. The manner ethnic conflicts, the mismanagement of the economy, and the spread of bribe and corruption plagues African social life is how elitism recreates its legitimacy.

To conclude, the internalization of the colonial discourse, be it in the ethnophilosophical form of racialization or in the evolutionist sense of professional philosophers, provokes thoughts and practices that are detrimental for the simple reason that the internalization repeats negative notions of Africans. Just as professional philosophers tend to assign modernization to the tutorship of the few, so too are ethnophilosophers reproducing the same syndrome of elitism through the endorsement of collectivism. All these views stand in the way of democracy and a creative path to modernization with an active participation of the people. The reconnection with the past, as envisaged by ethnophilosophers, should be preserved on condition that the objectivist illusion is abandoned in favor of free creation. Only some such approach can avoid the trap of the colonial discourse, while providing Africans with an empowering idea through the revelation of their freedom. The next chapter shows how this creative approach conceptualizes the issue of ethnicity and ethnic conflicts in Africa.

Eight

ETHNICITY AND STATE FORMATION: THE MYSTICAL ROOT OF NATIONHOOD

The issue of ethnicity is at the forefront of the preoccupation of many social scientists. The numerous conflicts in Africa, allegedly unleashed by ethnic claims, explain the growing need to understand the origin and nature of ethnicity in the hope of finding a solution to Africa's lack of stability. This practical concern also extends to philosophical preoccupations: besides its social and political impact on African societies, ethnicity raises deep philosophical queries of the kind having a direct bearing on the classical problems of philosophy. The aim of this chapter is to show how some of these problems relate to the important questions of the foundation of the state and the constructedness of identities.

For a growing number of scholars, the phenomenon of ethnicity discloses a movement of protest against the notion of the nation-state, such as the notion has developed through the history of most Western countries. Some go so far as to suggest that the rise of ethnicity testifies to African otherness, thereby urging African societies to find a new form of association in which purposeful organizational arrangements would institutionalize ethnic pluralism. The proposal toys with the idea that the nation-state may be unfit for African societies. Whether this proposal is characterized as postmodernist or as a variation on the same theme of the nation-state, African ethnic problems, together with the diversity inspired by gender issues, have the conspicuous impact of staining the universality of philosophical concepts with the spatters of diversity. Far from being symptoms of backwardness, these problems point to the need of organizing pluralism into a new form of association. Let us first review the standing of ethnicity in the African philosophical debate.

1. Ethnicity and the African Philosophical Debate

Unlike social scientists, African philosophers have not been so eager to deal with the phenomenon of ethnicity. The prevailing tendency understands ethnicity either as a characteristic display of the conflict between tradition and modernity or as little more than a supervenient expression of localism against an overwhelming background of racial oneness. While the notion of race has inspired diverse and worthy philosophical investigations, in particular by Afro-American philosophers in their attempt to understand the foundations of racism, the special type of exclusion inherent in ethnic alignments has solicited far less philosophical attention. True, ethnicity does not cross the threshold of the belief in racial superiority. It prefers to settle for closed groups in the name of cultural integrity or as a reaction against social inequality, without indulging in racial grading. Still, it involves exclusion of such nature as to question the assumed racial fraternity of Africans.

That the explanation for the persistent postponement of the ethnic issue is the racialization of Africans is not hard to establish. Even though the impact of ethnicity forces its way in the debate about the existence of African philosophy by the coinage of the term "ethnophilosophy" or "folk philosophy," the prevailing view continues to think that racial unity overrides ethnic disparities. Surprising as it may sound, ethnophilosophers failed for some time to deduce the substantiality of the tribe or ethnic group from the idea of collective philosophy. In order to counter the colonial denial of the existence of an African philosophy, their arguments took the direction of legitimizing the claim of a collective philosophy that transcends ethnic differentiation. Moreover, the determination to uphold the racial communality of Africans led them to stress the common values and conceptions of Africans.

As we saw in the previous chapters, such notions as vital force, mysticism, and communalism have become binding characters over and above ethnic identities. A radical expression of this oneness is negritude with its "abstract and absolute conception of a black essence related to a certain spirit immanent in African culture, with the suggestion of a constancy of such an essence impervious to the historical process."[1] This idea of a unified African culture is designed to dismiss the image of division and fragmentation suggested by ethnic ascendancy.

The opponents of ethnophilosophy have less reason than ethnophilosophers for taking ethnicity seriously. Their commitment to the Western inspired view of philosophy only deprives ethnic groups of philosophical significance by affixing on the commitment to ethnic identity the type of prescientific and uncritical form of thinking characteristic of traditional societies. Above all, we saw how in the eyes of Paulin Hountondji the attribution of a philosophical status to traditional thinking amounts to its consecration. The cause of modernization requires a resolute crusade against the unanimist trend of the ethnic group.

To cut the ground from the feet of all revivalist tendency, the crusade must begin by showing that no philosophical ethos of any kind animated the traditional thinking of Africa, with greater reason the ethnic group. The strategy of this African anti-revivalist school is obviously to undermine ethnic references through the discredit of the form of thought closely associated with them. The demonstration that "traditional cultural values cannot be accommodated by the ethos of the modern scientific culture and so cannot be reconciled with it" depicts ethnic loyalties as a thing of the past, as a form of resistance to modernity and the rise of the nation-state.[2]

The combined pressure of postmodernist ideas and the serial failures of postindependent African states persuade African philosophical consciousness into addressing the issue of African ethnic diversity. Such thinkers as V. Y. Mudimbe and Kwame Anthony Appiah quickly point out the contradictions of ethnophilosophy as well as of its opponents. The apology of race, they argue, is an internalization of the Western construction of Africa. The conceptualization of African philosophy as the thinking of the black race fighting for the recognition and rehabilitation of its otherness is bound to gloss over ethnic groups. Yet, the notion of collective philosophy is defensible only through the reality of the ethnic group whose linguistic unity allows its members to "share concepts, and thus those a priori beliefs whose possession is constitutive of a grasp of concepts."[3]

As to the opponents of ethnophilosophy, because their fascination with universalism prevents them from measuring the full impact of Eurocentrism hiding behind universalist notions, both Hountondji and Marcien Towa walk away from pluralism, and so deny themselves the opportunity of reflecting on "the surprising persistence of these 'premodern' affiliations."[4] Instead of being content with a critique of ethnophilosophy that is impregnated with elitism and its dependent thinking, some such reflection urges opponents of ethnophilosophy to denounce the alleged normativeness of Western experience. The denunciation, in turn, exhorts them to come up with a better understanding of the resistance of traditional identities.

Once ethnic groups are established as African realities, we can confidently say that all political theory that fails to integrate the groups as an inevitable element of African political life is on a straying course. The straying includes those theories that have nothing better to say than to characterize ethnicity as a residue of past history. A serious reflection on ethnicity in Africa must reach the conviction that no political modernization is adapted to African realities if it does not incorporate ethnic groups as the cornerstone of nation-building. In the words of Francis Mading Deng:

> Africa has cornered itself into rejecting *ethnicity* as an *organizing concept* in the process of nation-building. The challenge then is whether it is possible to reverse the mindset so that ethnic groups, which are African realities, can be seen as resources or building blocks that can provide a sound foundation for sustainable political and socioeconomic development from within.[5]

The ethnic issue gives momentum to the charge that much of African predicament is caused by the imposition of the Western model and the subsequent alienation and satellization of African societies. African events increasingly exposing the plight of the nation-state in its dealings with ethnic identities give evidence of the drawback of the model. While the pan-Africanist and universalist trends of African philosophy continue to detect a stalled unity in these events, the postmodernist tendency of African philosophy, in conjunction with the concrete orientation of social sciences, sees more the rise of pluralism than a delayed unity. According to Crawford Young, the rise of cultural pluralism means:

> the world enters a period of exceptional fluidity—of the sort which historically has usually come about through the dislocation of a major war. Nation and state, as we have known them, are interrogated by history and alternative visions of the future. In this process, the politics of cultural pluralism will influence the outcomes in many important ways.[6]

The breakup of the state in the former Soviet Union and many socialist countries, the threat of secession in such countries as Canada and Belgium, and the growing disaffection with assimilationist policy in various parts of the world are salient manifestations of a universal drift into pluralism. This trend is most potent on the African continent which mixes the end result of the breakup of the state (Ethiopia and Somalia), with past or ongoing armed struggles for the control of the state (Nigeria, Sierra Leone, Liberia, Burundi, Sudan, Congo, Rwanda, and Ivory Coast), sporadic clashes (Kenya and Namibia), and latent or apparent tensions as in Cameroon, Uganda, and Central African Republic. The resulting hindrance to the development of Africa adds a major implication to the multiplication of ethnic conflicts: every time that the effort to implement the nation-state only succeeds in reinvigorating ethnic identities, the equation of modernization with Westernization comes into question.

What most scholars find puzzling is the salience of ethnic references in the middle of the process of modernization. Theories of modernization, be they liberal or Marxist, on the strength of the universal model of modernity extracted from the experience of Western countries, had predicted the dissolution of local attachments in favor of the nation-state. The resilience of ethnicity in Africa casts doubt on the universality of the proposed model as well as on the pertinence of the paradigm of modernity. If facts indicate that "ethnic competition is a consequence of modernization," or better, "the pursuit of politics in the modern era," then the reluctance of African societies to follow the model of the nation-state questions the assumption making the dissolution of localism into a condition of modernity.[7] Speaking of the Western model, Bruce J. Berman writes:

> Development theory has thus treated Western experience as "history," making it difficult to see it as a particular historical conjuncture, one of several potential trajectories of human development. The unilinear evo-

lutionary assumptions contained in these theories have universalized Western experience and abstracted it into structural models.[8]

Herein lies a major philosophical problem. Each time theorists characterize the model of development as unilinear and Eurocentric, they also disclose the reason for its failure. Because the model is an external imposition, it commits two mistakes: it is alien to the concerned peoples and, most of all, it scorns their freedom and subjectivity.

Theories of development have the strange habit of suspending human subjectivity, though they rely on subjectivity to unfold their schemes. The idea of a model implies that peoples having different values, historical experience, and environment should conform to a pattern extracted from a particular set of historical experience, cultural premises, and environment. The model is judged workable through the assumption that values and cultural characteristics can be altered according to the requirements of the external model. In particular, the introduction of institutional, technological, and economic devices is believed to trigger a process of social change that brings indigenous idiosyncrasies into line with the stipulations of the model. This forceful process, otherwise known as Westernization, assumes that "economic and technological innovations . . . are the most powerful levers that change traditional society."[9] Once the Western model is unleashed, it is bound to have a total effect, including the melting of traditional identities in accordance with the idea of the nation-state.

This approach, which Alfred Schutz says, "intentionally eliminates the actor in the social world with all his subjective points of view," lands Africa more in the impediments of underdevelopment than in the stimulating course of development.[10] Its implication is the growing appeal of scholars to read into African underdevelopment not so much a failure as a protest against the denial of the African self. However clumsy and self-damaging the protest may be, it bears witness to a subjectivity refusing to play in a game whose end result is its own demise. Understood as a "fearful resistance to development projects conceived in the West," underdevelopment may very well be "the last impulse of self-preservation" hiding behind passivity and retreatism.[11] Chief in this challenge is the furious attempt of ethnicity to shake off the imposition of the nation-state through the revival of past identities.

The intensity of ethnic conflicts in Africa could not but bring along major repercussions on the manner scholars theorize about modernization. One such effect is the growing appeal, in line with the ethnophilosophical approach, to explain the failure of the Western model in Africa by the divergence of Africa's cultural premises from those of the West. This notion of African difference induced thinkers and political leaders to look for a form of modernization more adapted to African personality. Recall how the need to avoid the imposition of an alien model so as to allow the full expression of

African personality led to the project of African socialism, the assumption being that socialism is best suited to the communal traditions of Africa. The failure of African socialism should not obscure the actual philosophical significance of the project, that is, the defense of human pluralism, whether pluralism is due to race or cultural orientation.

In their attempt to understand the genesis of Western modernity, many Western scholars underline the particularity of the cultural premises and value-orientation of Western societies, thereby suggesting that the nation-state is itself a product of the application of Western rationalism. The Senghorian distinction between Western rationality and African emotion thus finds a renewed application in the resilience of African ethnic identities. The determination to homogenize identities by the dissolution of local attachments is certainly in keeping with the universalist claim and abstractionist method of Western rationalism. Explicit in the stress on the resilience of ethnic identities is the idea that the Western type of national consciousness is inseparable from the cultural premises and the particular historical context that have shaped Western experience.

Once scholars admit the dependence of the Western trend on historical contingencies, the crucial question becomes that of knowing whether the model can be transposed to other cultural personalities and historical trends, especially whether it can work "without a firm anchorage in the Judeo-Christian religious heritage."[12] Neither the noticeable lack of strong individualist commitments in Africa, nor the fact that "few African peoples had ascetic traditions" augurs the rapid ascendancy of national cultures over localisms.[13] In short, the Western model fails in Africa because it does not encounter the necessary cultural environment. The issue is less African backwardness failing to measure up to Western superior achievements than dissimilarity in terms of values and goals preventing the merger of alien trends. Properly diagnosed, the rise of ethnicity in Africa is African integrity grappling with the model of the nation-state imposed by the West.

2. Primordialism and the Naturalness of Ethnicity

However dominant the reductionist trend may have been in Western scholarship, the existence of a counter school committed to defending ethnic particularism as a universal standard must not be overlooked. Known as primordialism, this school begins by likening the resurgence of ethnic alignments to the resistance of natural or primordial feelings. It grounds ethnic ties in deep biological and affective prods, similar to those involving kin. To quote a prominent exponent of primordialism, Pierre L. van den Berghe, "ethnicity . . . is extended kinship."[14] The involvement of relatedness entails that ethnic ties are "more basic and 'primordial' than social groups organized on the basis of class."[15] Seeing that besides resisting the tide of change and the melting-pot ideology, ethnicity causes violent conflicts, so powerful a motivation, primordialism argues, must involve deeper drives of the kind emanating from biological and psychological bias.

This bias constitutes groups, since mutual exclusion is how groups come into being. Turning its back on those theories deriving ethnic loyalty from a stand against social discrimination, primordialism thus gives primacy to the "affective dimension of the problem."[16] Far from proposing methods of managing ethnic conflicts, the theory simply takes note of existing differences and advises the breakup of African states, in agreement with the principle of self-determination, whenever differences aspire to separate existence.

According to primordialism, the ethnic phenomenon is not exclusively African: all modern societies, with their large class divisions based on impersonal economic criteria and integrated into the no less impersonal order of the nation-state, are artificial. African societies are better equipped to resist de-ethnicization because of the recentness of their modernist venture. Even Western countries are never guaranteed against the resurgence of ethnicity: the slightest national ordeal is enough to rekindle old identities, as witnessed by the recent redrawings of borders in Eastern Europe. Though predictions that "ethnic sentiments would become increasingly vestigial, and that 'modernity' would engulf petty particularisms" were current, in reality "few, if any, of these expectations came to pass."[17]

A host of philosophical assumptions underlies the primordialist position. Let us limit ourselves to the assumptions pertaining to the relationship between nature and culture and the historicity of human beings. In the eyes of primordialism, only small and homogeneous societies are natural for human beings. Such societies are based on primary sentiments of attraction and repulsion, making human gatherings into meaningful ensembles. Human beings perform better when their groupings accord with natural inclinations. Large and heterogeneous societies are cumbersome and ill-sorted gatherings little fit for lasting achievements, as evinced by the repeated collapses of empires. The higher the homogeneity of the social tissue, the nearer the social order is to the form of organization wished by nature, and the better is its performance. As Richard Rosecrance states, "dynamic qualities inhere in small cohesive nations, countries which are not so multifarious internally that they cannot reach agreement on social and international missions."[18] Witness the superior performance of Japan and of East Asian countries—Taiwan, Hong Kong, South Korea, and Singapore—whose characteristic is to associate smallness with cohesiveness.

An important lesson follows from the virtue of cohesiveness: African countries must come round to the idea that their failure to catch up with development and modernity is due to their internal ethnic heterogeneity. Lacking in solidarity and unity of purpose, their inability to cope with modernity is little surprising. The political borders, artificial and imposed by colonialism, as

Africans themselves admit, call for a serious revision in accordance with natural affinities if Africa is to be put on the right track. So long as African countries remain in their present borders, all their efforts will be consumed by internal disputes and incompatibilities instead of being used to further progress.

Given this harmful outcome, ethnicization turns into a condition of Africa's entry into the path of successful modernization. It is so because ethnicization has a vital human message: of all human motivations, nothing is more powerful than sentiments. The primordialist position thus encounters the protracted philosophical debate about the ascendancy of feelings or reason in human motivations. Its attempt to account for the resurgence of ethnicity in the modern world concurs with the position of David Hume according to which "since reason alone can never produce any action, or give rise to voli-tion . . . the same faculty is as incapable of preventing volition, or of disputing the preference with any passion or emotion."[19] The survival of ethnic identi-ties is thus another challenge to the primacy of reason: the rationality of the larger ensemble of the nation is powerless against the lure of natural affinity.

3. Instrumentalism and the Constructedness of Ethnic Identities

To the opponents of primordialism, characteristically referred to as instrumen-talists, social inequalities instead of primary feelings explain the persistence of ethnic alignments, there being no doubt that enduring social discrimina-tions encourage "the continued salience of racial and ethnic criteria."[20] Struc-tured social inequalities so operate that excluding groups use selected charac-teristics (physical, linguistic, or religious) to define and justify their hegemony, while excluded groups extol their differences to establish solidarity among themselves and contest the hegemony. Biological, cultural, and psychological traits provide the circumstance, not the substance of ethnic coalitions. At any rate, they can explain neither the revival nor the persistence of ethnicity. As an outcome of fractured social relations, ethnicity is thus accountable in rational terms.

Two important implications issue from this rationalization. (1) Ethnicity has its roots in social inequalities; as such, it is an expression of group inter-ests competing for an increased share of scarce resources. To quote Young, ethnic groups are "calculating, self-interested collective actors, maximizing material values through the vehicle of communal identity."[21] The implication of interests in ethnicity ascertains the ascendancy of rational considerations over affective attachments. The school of constructivism further disentangles ethnicity from primordial sentiments by identifying ethnic groups with what Benedict Anderson called "imagined communities."[22] The emphasis is then less on the congenital character than on the manufactured nature of ethnic identity, making it into "an innovative act of creative imagination."[23]

This difference of approach between instrumentalism and constructivism does not affect their agreement on the strategic content of ethnic identity; for both of them ethnicity is accessible to rational analysis inasmuch as it is a strategic assertion. (2) The rational content of ethnic identity allows a rational treatment of ethnic conflicts. Instead of sanctioning the breakup of existing states, instrumentalism proposes the management of ethnic conflicts. According to Harvey Glickman, instrumentalism argues:

> ethnic conflict is not incompatible with institutions of democratic government if it finds expression as a group interest among other interests, and if the means of expression provide openings for rewards and not merely sure defeats.[24]

The error is to try to ignore, worse eliminate ethnicity through the use of force or the imposition of the one-party system. This way of dealing with ethnicity actually betrays a primordialist conception, since the approach assumes that ethnicity is not disposed to negotiate. Yet conceive of ethnicity as a product of social inequalities whereby groups of people, turned into competitive actors, aim at maximizing their interests through ethnic mobilization, and the inherent possibility of a negotiated settlement stands out clearly. In this regard, the frequency of ethnic mobilizations in some areas need not lead us astray: depressed and underdeveloped economies, instrumentalism clarifies, are most likely to inspire ethnic mobilizations if only because the scarcity of resources tends to invite larger forms of exclusion. In conditions of scarcity, ruling elites are inclined to use the centralized power of the state to fashion a social system all geared toward the reward of supporters and the repression of competitors.

The strategic content does not make ethnicity any less stringent. For instrumentalism, any attempt to downplay demands will only harden the secessionist option. The best method to deal with ethnicity is to design a political and social system liable to satisfy its deep aspirations. Since ethnic references represent group interests in competition, greater democratization, rising to the level of power sharing, should organize these interests into a form of peaceful competition. In other words, "moving away from a unitary government offers the potential opportunity to channel ethnic conflict into peaceful competition by dividing power at the top and by distributing it between center and region."[25] Whether the solution contemplates federalism, regionalism, rotation of power, or any other form of power devolution, the thinking grounds the political system on a coalition of ethnic parties such that real power goes to ethnic instances at all levels.

This solution differs from known forms of power devolution, as nothing less than a federation of ethnic states is proposed in lieu of the usual separation of powers within the unity of the nation-state. In the obscure, if not contradictory, words of Glickman, the solution is a "federalism that maintains a stake on a strong central government, so that regionally strong ethnic parties can find coalition partners at the level of central government."[26]

In upholding the rational content of ethnicity against the view of primordialism, instrumentalism promotes the idea of peaceful solution to ethnic conflict. Provided the appropriate rational method is used, partition, instrumentalism says, is not the inevitable outcome of ethnicity. This idea of management of ethnic strife leans on the assumption that human beings tend to settle their disputes peacefully as soon as their interests are made convergent. The harmonization of interests can require new forms of association; the point is to be innovative to the end. The institutionalization of ethnicity promotes greater democratization whose outcome can only be the accelerated modernization of African societies.

Facts do not seem to corroborate the benefits that instrumentalism expects from the institutionalization of ethnicity. Recent history shows how the issue of democratization in some former socialist countries led to secessions, either peacefully or by means of violent conflicts. In this regard, the breakup of the former Soviet Union suggests an invaluable lesson. Just as is the case of the United States, the Soviet Union had adopted a federal system. The great difference between the two countries, however, was that, unlike the American system, which is a federation of states, the Soviet system was a federation of ethnic groups. While the American democratic and liberal federalism spatially fragments ethnic political expressions, the Soviet system implied what one scholar called a "centralized ethnofederalism" as a counterpart to the regional concentration of ethnic political expressions.[27] What largely explains the breakup of the Soviet Union is the regional identification of ethnic political expressions resulting from the institutionalization of ethnicity. The usual objection imputes the collapse of Soviet federalism to the absence of democracy rather than to the institutionalization of ethnicity.

The objection overlooks that even in democratic countries such as Canada and Belgium, the management of ethnicity has not overcome the specter of partition. What is more, the absence of democracy does not directly correlate with the demise of a political union, given that grievances against a social system normally incline people to rebel and reform the system, not to break away from the system. Instead of facilitating the integration of groups, the institutionalization of ethnicity really drifts them apart. The provision of a territorial basis is a sure way of changing ethnicity into ethnonationalism.

As concerns Africa, the guess is that the institutionalization of ethnicity will entail a redrawing of political borders in line with ethnic definitions. May it be, then, that primordialism is not totally wrong after all? All the more so as larger communities offering more economic opportunities than smaller ones, this preference for partition of ethnic groups suggests, if not an irrational behavior, at least an attitude not fully congruent with rational calculation.

What if, as primordialism maintains, something irreducible exists in ethnicity, something that activates feelings and biological prods?

Compelled by facts, instrumentalism ends by earmarking partition for a possible solution to ethnic conflicts. "At the same time," Glickman concedes, "we must also be prepared to recognize the state-breaking threat of ethno-nationalism."[28] When the stage of ethnonationalism is reached, peaceful partition becomes the only rational solution. This happens, Glickman assures us, whenever circumstances politicize ethnicity, without however telling us whether his idea to provide ethnicity with institutional expressions is not a sure way of politicizing it. Be that as it may, the main idea of primordialism is surreptitiously accepted. In order to control ethnicity, a new state, called multiethnic state, based on the coalition of ethnic parties and rejecting the principle of majority rule, must be erected. The shortcoming of majority rule is that, in separating winners from losers, it empowers the former in a situation of extreme polarization. Majority rule changes defeat into a consecration of exclusion. Such is the case every time ethnic minorities confront majority groups in electoral contests.

One question comes to mind: Is this project of a democratic system going beyond majority rule realistic? The truth is that even developed countries cannot afford so radical a democratic change. The proposal amounts to turning partition into the inevitable lot of all those societies suffering from scarcity. Is there anything in the whole proposal to which primordialism would not subscribe? Ethnic issues are so primordial that they dominate the whole life of the state, which state is nothing more than a hostage of ethnic parties.

4. Ethnicity and the Legitimacy of the State

The regression of instrumentalism to primordialist beliefs is fraught with philosophical questions. In particular, the regression enables us to pose in an interesting way a question with which philosophy has wrestled since its inception, to wit, the question of the legitimacy of state power. The relevance of ethnicity to the issue of state legitimacy is not hard to establish. Clearly, people would not desire the breakup of the state, were they not doubting its legitimacy. Another state, a state yet to be born, appears to them more legitimate than the existing one.

Let there be no misunderstanding: the question of legitimacy does not arise because of the projection of an ideal state. Were people simply dissatisfied with the existing state, they would want to change the system, not exchange the state for another unreal state. We must distinguish between an uprising due to discontent and a secessionist drive. For the latter, only the imagined state appears legitimate, while the existing state is declared illegal, even regardless of performance. In light of the momentum of ethnic strife in

Africa, let us see whether the most representative schools of political philosophy can bring clarity into this transfer of legitimacy.

The set of theories deriving the state from the need of one dominating group to hold in check other groups have little to say regarding our question. Be they as crude as the approach of Thrasymachus in Plato's *Republic,* or as refined and elaborate as the Marxist conception of the state, such positions hardly deal with the issue of legitimacy. For Marxism, the fact that the state represents the most advanced class is in a sense a source of legitimacy, so long as the class remains progressist. However, no state is legitimate, all states resting in the final analysis on violence and the imposition of a particular class interest on the general interest. That is why, pushing the idea of the state being "merely the organized power of one class for oppressing another" to its logical conclusion, Marxism defines communism, the final stage of the history of class struggle, by the withering away of the state.[29] The day the state uses no violence and imposes no particular class interest is the day of its demise. Even the state of the workers, characteristically called the dictatorship of the proletariat, must assume dictatorial powers to defend the interests of the working class.

Regardless of the issue of legitimacy, Marxism is well equipped to explain the rise of ethnicity as a form of protest. We can even say that the instrumentalist approach to ethnicity owes its theoretical orientation to the Marxist elucidation of the forms of social protest. First, the strong economic content of ethnicity on account of which instrumentalism upholds both the rational character and the manageability of ethnic conflicts is indebted to the Marxist theory of social struggles. Second, the construction of identity around shared attributes, such as, language and religion, reproduces the Marxist notion of ideology. Just as Marxism insisted on "the *derivation* of political, juridical, and other ideological notions, and of actions arising through the medium of these notions, from basic economic facts," so too instrumentalism reads into ethnic identities a form of protest due to social exclusion.[30] The Marxist influence is greater in the approach of constructivism, since the act of creative imagination which manufactures identities tallies with the Marxist characterization of ideological ideas as "reflexes and echoes" of the life process, as "phantoms formed in the human brain," as "sublimates" of the material life process.[31]

Despite its strong influence, Marxism departs from these schools in sharp terms. Because it advocates the ascendancy of class distinctions over idyllic relations, Marxism relegates ethnicity to a secondary level of struggle. It argues that ethnicity is a provisional form of protest, soon to be superseded by the real conflict, the very one dividing and opposing people along economic lines over and above cultural or racial commonness. Whenever ethnic alignments persist in keeping the lead to the point of obstructing the mobilization of people along economic lines, Marxism denounces them as reactionary attitudes that block the process of class struggle. Thus, when a scholar, speaking of ethnic divisions in Africa, recommends, "the best antidote to tribalism is the politics of class," the Marxist confidence in the primacy of economic interests over cultural idiosyncrasies is taken for granted.[32]

Notwithstanding the Marxist primacy of class conflicts, movements claiming obedience to Marxism have nevertheless waged struggles against national oppression. They fought for self-determination, even against regimes claiming to be socialist, arguing that the issue of the nation is not reducible to class solidarity. The point is that Marxist theory has never been consistent with the issue of ethnicity. Instead, an opportunist attitude was adopted, now justifying secession, now condemning it in the name of class solidarity. The cause of self-determination was considered revolutionary when it antagonized a bourgeois or a feudal regime, but reactionary if the regime in place happened to be socialist. In both cases, ethnicity was subordinated to the cause of international communism instead of being considered for its own sake.

This opportunism is scarcely surprising: Karl Marx did not approach the issue of ethnicity directly, confident as he was that the spread of the bourgeois revolution in the world will sweep away all localisms in favor of the nation-state. His followers had to deal with situations in which capitalism simply merged with traditional societies, and so failed to erase traditional identities. In addition to the difficulty of thinking ethnicity as a modern phenomenon, this unusual combination imparted to their thinking its own indecisiveness.

The Marxist theory of the state was coined to counter all those theories tending to place the state above classes and particular interests. Unlike Marxism, these theories are well placed to discuss the issue of the legitimacy of state power. The alleged transcendence of the state over particularism provides the main criterion for establishing the legitimacy of the state. Legitimacy accrues to the state when it incarnates the universal, when through laws and their enforcement the general interest prevails over particular interests. The more the state is transcendent, the higher is its legitimacy.

According to G. W. F. Hegel, the state is the incarnation, better the objective realization of reason; it is reason in power, legislating and ordering the life of individuals, making their life conformable to the universal by bringing actions and motives under the rule of laws. To quote Hegel, "the state is absolutely rational inasmuch as it is the actuality of the substantial will which it possesses in the particular self-consciousness once that consciousness has been raised to consciousness of its universality."[33] While the presence of the divine will was formerly the guarantee of the transcendence of the state, for Hegel, the theological conception is a mere moment in the realization of the inner transcendence of the state.

Otherwise known as impersonalization, this notion of transcendence brings out the rational principle of the nation-state, namely, the principle of one uniform and consistent law. Marx gives us a good idea of the notion when he writes:

> The bourgeoisie, wherever it has got the upper hand, has put an end to all feudal, patriarchal, idyllic relations. It has pitilessly torn asunder the motley feudal ties that bound man to this "natural superiors," and has left remaining no other bond between man and man than naked self-interest, than callous "cash payment."[34]

The intentionally disparaging language put aside, what Marx calls here "self-interest," "cash payment" has been theorized by other scholars as the replacement of privileges and ascriptive rights by the order of competition and achievement. Privileges of nobility or protections of kinship relations through such practices as favoritism and nepotism no longer decide the place and status of individuals; disparities due to particularisms and local customs are not tolerated either. Inasmuch as exclusions due to birth, kinship relations, and customs are countered, the establishment of non-mercantile bonds institutes the impersonal order of the free market, which, in turn, determines the place of individuals.

My purpose agrees with Claude E. Welch's view: "the acceptance of the state as the impersonal and ultimate arbiter of human affair" points to what is really at stake every time instrumentalism calls for the management of ethnicity.[35] Pushed by the state-breaking impulse of ethnicity, instrumentalism proposes to found the state on a coalition of ethnic groups, conceived of as an advanced form of democratization and power sharing. The whole question is to know whether in such a coalition the sum will be greater than the parts, whether the state will have an authority transcending the parties. So pronounced is the exclusiveness of each ethnic group that the merger of parties is unlikely to constitute a whole. Instead of an association resembling the state, the ethnic parties seem to form at best a partnership with multiple centers of decision. What is most missing in this partnership is the idea of sovereignty, that is, of "a single authority both for making laws and with force to sustain them within a sharply defined and consolidated territory."[36]

This idea of sovereignty is particular to Western history. It coincides with the rise of the nation-state in the very act of dissolving the entrenched local powers of the nobility and clergy. Given that the background of European feudalism accounts for the rise of the nation-state, where no similar social evolution occurred, the model of the nation-state should be left aside in favor of new forms of association. The suggestion forgets that the whole issue is whether the modern state can function without the idea of sovereignty. Though particularism is rightly stressed, it must never be allowed to dismiss the regularities inherent in the modern state. In the suggested coalition, each party has its particular interests in mind to the point of making its participation in the life of the central state dependent on the promotion of those interests.

Where are the common goals and the transcending authority? Where is the impersonal order of competition as a result of which people, stripped of natural ties and protective bonds, appears as individuals in the market? And if each ethnic party has the power to hold the coalition to ransom through the threat of secession unless its exclusive demands are met, the coalition is scarcely tantamount to the idea of state. In lieu of being the sovereign, the state is the hostage of ethnic parties, which then represent sovereign entities.

Relevant though transcendentalism is to understand the requirement under which an association becomes the state, it does not tell us how to achieve the transcendence of the state. Take the theory of convention, be that of Jean-Jacques Rousseau or Thomas Hobbes. The sovereign is constituted by the surrender of natural rights in exchange for peace and civil liberties. According to Rousseau, the foundation of civil society is that *"each of us places his person and all his power in common under the supreme direction of the general will; and as one we receive each member as an indivisible part of the whole."*[37] For Hobbes, too, the contractual surrender of natural rights is how individuals generate the state in exchange for peace and security. "The only way to erect such a common power," writes Hobbes, is when people "confer all their power and strength upon one man, or one assembly of men."[38] The surrender begets the rights of the state, but also its duties to protect the civil rights of individuals under pain of invalidating the contract. Individuals obey because through the submission of their freedom they have created a transcendent body, which body, in turn, is obliged to protect them because they have become its members.

Contrast this principle of the prior surrender of natural rights with the coalition of ethnic parties as conceptualized by instrumentalism. Neither the notion of coalition nor the commitment to particularism brings us anywhere near to the surrender of rights. Ethnic specificity is not handed over; it is brandished at the state as an inalienable right. Though belonging to the collective domain, the specificity is not a civil right that the state defends according to laws. It is an affiliation that escapes the authority of the state. The state cannot have jurisdiction over a right that is not put into its care in the first place. Everything appears as though sovereign states were entering into a coalition instead of one single state coming into being. In a coalition of nations no one state loses its sovereignty; in the coalition of ethnic parties too unity is revocable if one of the partners decides to pull out. The paradox is that the emanation of the state from ethnic parties confers on them the right of sovereignty. In thus supporting ethnonationalism in its very womb, the state is simply preparing its demise.

The state can legislate for the rights placed in its hands only in the form of individual rights. Take the case of religious pluralism. The separation of church and state, characteristically designed to cope with religious conflicts, meant not so much the acceptance of factionalism as the entrustment of the right to believe to the state. According to this arrangement, the state warrants freedom of belief as an individual right. It does so by the entrustment barring the state from serving any particular belief. Individuals are free to worship any belief and to organize for that purpose. The state cannot grant a freedom of this nature without transcending particular beliefs, and so without being committed to secularism. It springs to mind that the foundation of this beyondness of the state is none other than the prior surrender of exclusiveness: the state can soar above particularity because it is made into the guardian of all particular beliefs without embracing any of them. In this secularized state, no religion can be imposed and individuals cannot be discriminated because of their belief.

A crucial question follows: if religious conflicts required the secularization of the state, how comes it that in the case of ethnic conflict scholars are proposing the ethnicization of the state? Let there be no talk of religious beliefs being private while ethnicity would settle for nothing less than power sharing. The purpose of religious conflicts in Europe and elsewhere, be it recalled, was also the control of state power. Groups cannot share power with the sovereign without the latter ceasing to be sovereign. Instead, groups have rights conferred by the sovereign on its members, the essential foundation of the operation being the membership itself. While the state thus accords individual rights to its members, the condition for nonmembers to be so treated is still the surrender of their rights, not the claim to inalienability or to share power. Since the relinquishment makes up the membership, the dissolution of exclusive entities into universal individual rights is the manner the authority of the state is shaped and individual rights warranted. In other words, pluralism, whether it is religious or ethnic, can only be enjoyed as a universal entitlement, an individual right. Pluralism cannot be made into an inalienable and exclusive right without undermining the authority of the state.

Besides transcendence and social contract, the government of the best has been one influential way of founding the legitimacy of the state. Plato has discussed the main ingredients of the theory in the *Republic*. The state, Plato says, has its origin in the necessity of the division of labor. This necessity wants that important functions, especially governance and material production, devolve upon different people. Human beings can hardly contest the necessity of dividing labor, though they can and must make the most of it by wishing that governance be entrusted to the best of them. While for Aristotle, the best regime is "a form of aristocracy," provided that the governing body is "dedicated to the pursuit of virtue," Plato goes further with his idea of "the philosopher-king."[39] According to him, only when human society is governed by people who have the passion of philosophy can it hope to reach the best government, for only then can the rule of the good become the justification of the state. When political power and philosophy come into the same hands, the state achieves its best form.[40]

The relevance of this theory to the issue raised by ethnicity becomes evident when we see that both instrumentalism and constructivism have their point of departure in the idea of bad government. More specifically, they attribute the rise of ethnicity in Africa to post-independence disillusionment, right after the short-lived euphoria of national integration. Whereas in other countries bad government has favored the rise of internal revolutionary or reformist forces calling for greater integration, in Africa defective regimes led to ethnic alignments, that is, to social constructs establishing common interests and solidarity along ethnic lines. The idea of the government of the best, necessary to justify the authority of the state, shifted from the existing state to sub-states whose characteristic is to equate the best with the ethnically related.

Ethnonationalism emerges from this switch of loyalty and ideality to a secessionist state on the ground that relatedness warrants commitment to the common good. Peter F. Sugar suggests that the term "natioethnicism" is preferable to "ethnonationalism," since as a breakaway nationalism, ethnicity "retains the nation—Swiss, British, etc.—but transfers primary loyalty and concomitant political power to its constituent smaller units—cantons or lands like Scotland, Wales, England."[41]

Many theoreticians ascribe the ethnicization of social conflicts in Africa to the immaturity of its modernization, notably to the fact that "the loyalty of most rural and many urban people is still to tribe rather than nation."[42] Various aspects of the past are still present in Africa, but this cannot explain why ethnic consciousness is most vivid among the educated and modernized elite. The easy capitulation of African educated elite to ethnic sirens is the main reason why theoreticians conceptualized ethnicity as a modern phenomenon. From this conceptualization has risen the instrumentalist idea that the best approach is to diagnose ethnicity more as a social protest and construct than as a mere persistence of tradition. This social construct is intelligible only if the background of disillusionment of postcolonial regimes is maintained. Ethnonationalism is then the search for an ideal state whose characteristic is to break away from a conglomeration imposed by ill-disposed colonial rulers. Ethnic nationalism wants to substitute ensembles based on natural affinity and concern for the ill-sorted colonial collections.

Ethnonationalism turns ethnicity and ethnicization into a condition of good government. Just as for Plato the qualities of the philosopher guarantee the best regime, so too do ethnic homogeneity and rule for ethnonationalism: in providing concern and solidarity, they bring about the best government. Multiethnic states are ill-assorted gatherings, more inclined to exhaust their energy in inter-ethnic conflicts than to pursue the common good. By contrast, ethnonationalism maintains, ethnic homogeneity activates natural solidarity and, through the enhancement of unity, the concern for the best regime.

The persistence of bad government in Africa is largely due to the discordant amalgamation of different peoples at the expense of natural affinity. The solution is the ethnicization of African states by which alone they can hope to become viable, and hence legitimate. The rise of ethnicity in Africa thus aims at putting an end to the plight of "heterogeneous peoples living within the artificial boundaries imposed by the European master."[43] Ethnic politics is simply the continuation and the conclusion of the decolonization of Africa. Its main purpose is to create modern and viable nations in place of the self-destroying amalgams.

5. From Ethnicity to Nation-State: The Mystical Moment

Despite different approaches, the theories about the legitimacy of the state that we have so far discussed have, with the exception of Marxism, one thing in common: transcendence is the condition of the legitimacy of the state, the foundation of its authority. Whether scholars believe that the state represents the general soaring above the particular, or is the trustee of the rights of individuals, or embodies the rule of the best, the idea is that it fulfills a superior function that neither individuals in isolation nor their mere sum can achieve. Attachment to the state is loyalty to a set of values crucial to human realization. Disloyalty begins when people doubt the capability of the state to promote these values. The doubt progressively leads to the ideal of a breakaway state.

If the movement is toward nationalism and back again to ethnicity, the following assumption becomes legitimate. Theories propose different approaches because they confuse two different realities: the primary social organization as such and the process of its further enlargement. The revival of ethnicity appears as a retreat, as a process of falling back on the natural after the attempt to open up proved deceiving. This suggests the need to posit two societies: the natural, inscribed in the very nature of individuals, and the historically acquired, which depends on non-biological thrusts. This acceptance of a natural society corroborates an aspect of primordialism: in being natural, society does involve primary feelings. Most philosophical theories originate human society from the need of cooperation, from the manifest lack of self-sufficiency on the part of individuals. Based on the necessity of cooperation Aristotle, for instance, concludes: "the state is a creation of nature, and ... man is by nature a political animal."[44]

This naturalness, rightly deduced from the necessity of material cooperation, does not paradoxically extend to the cultural components. Abandoning the natural explanation, many philosophers assume that the idea of convention better explains the nature of social consciousness. Yet a group would fail to exist as a unit if cultural factors (religion, language, and social customs) do not endow the group with a specific personality. The content of the personality may be due to convention, not the structure of the personality whose function is to establish the cohesion of the group through the exclusion of other groups. In defending the existence of primary feelings, primordialism states the need to posit the structure, that is, exclusion as a constitutive act of the group. Even if ethnicity does not coincide with the primary social organization, the ethnic group undoubtedly revives and mobilizes the spirit of primary formations.

Henri Bergson's notion of "closed society" provides a philosophical endorsement of primordialism. Arguing that nature ordains human society, Bergson holds that the structure of the closed society is how the ordinance comes into effect.[45] The essential function of the structure is to constitute groups by means of mutual exclusion. This biologically conditioned society rests on the tribal mentality, which uses the pressure of characteristic beliefs and sentiments to obtain the insertion of individuals into distinct groups. The war-spirit, disposition to hierarchical organization, xenophobia, and all the ingredients of tribal religion are the most salient methods of the closed society. They all work toward strengthening internal cohesion through the rejection of other groups.

According to Bergson, this closed mentality shows that "man was designed for very small societies," but also that "the original state of mind survives," regardless of the enlargement it has undergone.[46] A pertinent example of this survival is the rise of the feudal system in Europe. It ensued from "the suppression of the force which was preventing the breaking-up of society," that is, from the decomposition of the Roman Empire whose extended duration was due, in the first place, to the combination of force with a semblance of independence granted to the conquered populations.[47]

The suggestion that "there is a natural human society, vaguely prefigured in us," goes against all those theories deriving society from convention in the manner of Rousseau or Hobbes.[48] The proposal also maintains that theories defending the origination of society from the need of material cooperation do not go far enough. The cooperation presupposes the tribal mentality, "the general plan of which fitted the pattern of our species as the ant-heap fits the ant."[49] The error of instrumentalism and, with greater reason, of constructivism, is to overlook the natural existence of a tribal mentality. In equating social identities with mere constructs, both theories forfeit the paradigm of natural society, alone able to account for the resiliency and powerful appeal of a breakaway state.

Does this mean that primordialism is right all the way? No, because "nature, which ordained small societies, left them an opening for expansion," so that on the edge of the closed society, there exists the pressure of the "open society."[50] Human history is a constant effort to open up the tribal society. In various parts of the world, a *modus vivendi* was reached, resulting in the appearance of modern nation-states, in default of embracing all humanity.

What makes the unclosing difficult is the impossibility of passing from the tribal society to the open society by a mere process of expansion and addition, as verified by the fragility of empires. According to Bergson, only the force of mysticism can overpower the resistance of the tribal mentality, the very one that patriotism incarnates:

> If great nations have been able to build themselves up firmly in modern times, this is because constraint, a cohesive force working from without and from above on the complex whole, has little by little given way to a principle of unity arising from the very heart of each of the elementary societies grouped together, that is to say, from the very seat of the disruptive forces to which an uninterrupted resistance has to be opposed. This principle, the only one that can possibly neutralize the tendency to disruption, is patriotism.[51]

Larger communities, often resulting from expansion and conquest, survived because they were supported by a mystic drive. Without the rise and cultivation of a sentiment strong enough to overcome the narrow-mindedness of the tribal mentality, none of these nations would have endured. "Imitating the mystic state" and merging memories and hopes with poetry and love, a "noble . . . sentiment" as patriotism lured the primary loyalty into upholding larger communities.[52]

This appeal to mysticism to explain a political reality may generate a reaction of surprise. The idea of the nation-state seems to refer to rational considerations implicating contract, utility, or a higher stage of human evolution. In any case, so secular a notion resents being referred to a sentiment exclusively concerned with religious aspirations. Some such objection overlooks one key element of the problem, to wit, the need to involve the power of sentiment wherever rational deliberations confront the resistance of natural tendencies. *Mysticism stands for human invention* such as it is bound to step in each time natural tendencies stand in the way of progress.

According to Bergson, the foundation of larger communities is mysticism, there being no doubt that the natural only yields to the mystic. Insofar as human society is natural, all theoretical attempts to show how human beings moved from the natural state to social life raise a false problem. Just as is the case of natural sentiments, primary organizations do not need any justification other than the impact of nature. Radically different is the issue of the enlargement of primary organizations: in default of natural supports, we must appeal to human made or invented devises. To speak in a fashionable way, larger communities come under human construction.

The question is to know why the construction should involve mysticism instead of secular sentiments. For instance, Kwame Gyekye believes that the best remedy for ethnonationalism is to show that ethnicity is a fiction, an invention. "The perception of 'ethnicity' as invented," he writes, "should favor the pursuit of nationhood in the multinational (multicultural) state in the contemporary world."[53] The dismissal of the idea of a common ancestry is liable to mitigate the powerful sentiment of relatedness so that "people will feel bound to one another more by social and professional interests than by ethnic considerations."[54] Yet the demonstration that ethnicity is an invention does not make the multinational state any more attractive: if the fact of being invented reduces the commitment to ethnicity, then how much more so it may be for the multinational state whose constructiveness is far more conspicuous.

When the construction is of such nature as to implicate the love of and commitment to a higher body, as patriotism does, a greater reason exists for saying that purely secular motivations are hardly sufficient. You cannot turn a contractual or mercantile reality into an object of devotion without radically altering its nature. The devotion must draw its breath from a state of mind similar to the one that fused the natural gods of mythology into one unique and transcendent God. This parallel with mythological thinking is all the more pertinent since tribal societies were also religious communities worshiping different and often hostile gods.

The only way to shun a mystical explanation is to appeal to evolutionary arguments of the type suggesting that a transition to a higher stage of development dissipates the primary organization. Bergson rejects the evolutionary explanation by underling that nothing is more questionable than "the admittance that habits of mind acquired by individuals in the course of centuries can have become hereditary, modifying nature and giving a new mentality to the species."[55] The idea of different human races rests on the improbable transformation of acquired characteristics into hereditary traits. The same doubtful evolutionary assumption sustains Lucien Lévy-Bruhl's notion of primitive mentality, given that the notion implies that the thinking of the civilized European has long ago escaped from the drawbacks of the primitive mentality.

While human efforts can expand the natural, the fact remains that the natural cannot be neutralized, still less permanently removed: the primitive mentality, understood as the basic structure of human social organization and conceptions of things, is as present in "the white man" of the twentieth century as it is in the peoples defined as backward human beings. What human inventiveness can do is to work on the natural so as to channel it into new directions. It can invent neither new feelings nor new motivations. Patriotism is one such product of human creativity expanding the limits imposed by the natural. In making patriotism into a mystical drive, Bergson only emphasizes the manner human creativity gets around natural feelings by enticing them into different goals rather than attempting to uproot them. That is why societies keep up the new fervor by constantly mobilizing the whole process of social acculturation, which they nourish with poetry, legends, and futuristic embellishments.

The point is to understand that the goal of keeping together basic and self-sufficient elements cannot be thoroughly explained by rational considerations. Not that rational considerations are absent or entirely powerless, but because they become arguments in favor of unity only once the egoism of primary organizations has been somewhat tempered. Take the case of the contract theory. Behind the thinking rationalizing the state as an emanation of contractual relationships, we find the forceful assertion of the value of freedom and equality. If we push our investigation further, freedom and equality will appear as a crystallization of a mystic inspiration, the very one propagated by Christianity. Bergson writes: "democracy is evangelical in essence and . . . its motive power is love."[56]

One approximate way of translating this mystical inspiration into a political reality may be the idea of contract. The proposal making the consent of the governed into the real source of authority does raise subjects to the level of legislators, and hence restores the dignity of human beings. If we ask Rousseau, for instance, what is the justification for restoring such dignity, his answer is that human beings "are born free and equal."[57] This assumption of Rousseau does not seek factual supports; it draws its validity from a vision propagated by the evangelic inspiration. Without the background of the mystic requirement of love, the emergence of modern nation-states with their consensus on democratic values would have appeared as an eccentric outcome. More generally, every time that the Judeo-Christian roots of Western civilization are emphasized, the understanding is that, as a characteristic expression, the nation-state also feeds on the same legacy.

Nothing could be further from the thinking of primordialism and instrumentalism than this suggestion that the foundation of modern nation-states is a mystic sentiment. Primordialism sticks to the primary loyalty and considers any enlargement as artificial. It overlooks how successfully this loyalty can be overcome by a sentiment that, artificial though it may be, can possess the power unleashed by human creativity. By contrast, instrumentalism and constructivism insist on the manufactured nature of social identities. The identities are enlarged or narrowed according as integration proves gratifying or not. While the notion of construction rightly applies to the larger community, which is thus truly an imagined community, or to use Bergson's more felicitous expression, a mystic community, it is not so with the tribal mentality. Ethnicity is, therefore, easily characterized as retreatism—occasioned by deception—to a safer, more reliable community whose configuration is borrowed from the tribal mentality. In the face of ordeal, the communal or natural does appear safer than all human constructs.

In view of deception encouraging retreatism, the approach translating ethnicity into a modern idea is certainly valid. It means that ethnicity is a product of disillusionment after the euphoria of independence, if we take the case of African countries. Since the larger community did not deliver its promises, people tend to fall back on the smaller organization whose natural-ness seems so appropriate to harbor a no less natural search for a meaningful community. This is another way of saying that mysticism is at the root of modern nations. Disillusionment signifies the decline of the mystic power: modern African societies do not arouse any emotion, still less are they cred-ited with stimulating ideals. They are accepted for want of other alternatives, or they are viewed as jungles in which people strive to survive. The poetry is gone, and cynicism is the general attitude. Little wonder people imagine new communities to appease their urge for solidarity and social ideals. When they do so, they simply revive, in form if not in content, the dormant tribal mentality.

This revival discloses the connection between African elitism and ethnicity. The previous chapter approached ethnicity as an expression of elitism, and so intimated its constructedness. The involvement of Westernized elites with modern ideas of democracy, justice, and self-determination and the use of group identity for political mobilization targeting the conquest of power establish beyond doubt the constructedness of ethnicity. Still, human construction does not work *ex nihilo*; it presupposes materials handed down by nature. Elitism in the precise sense of modern ideas tapping the natural tribal mentality makes up, therefore, the substance of ethnicity. Ethnic ideology is a return to the past but in such a way that the legacy is entirely shaped and reinvented by modern projects. The mobilization of natural sentiments explains the resilience of ethnicity while the modern language and vestment of ethnicity display the impact of politically ambitious elites.

The understanding is that both ethnicity and nationhood are constructs. Nonetheless, one essential difference emerges: while nationhood is mystic in the very sense of enlarging, going beyond natural limitations, ethnicity falls back on the natural solidarity. When nationhood tries to lift an obstacle, ethnicity leans on the same obstacle to counter the lifting movement. The one is an opening, a calling, the other a retreat, a backing out. That is why nation-hood is harder to achieve than ethnic commitment: it is an ascending, expanding movement when ethnicity is merely a retraction. The nation has the advantage of responding to the sense of greatness, of concurring with the human aspiration to transcend the limits of nature.

Gyekye's argument that the best antidote to ethnicity is the exposure of its artificiality would acquire strength if it were placed in the context of two constructs competing for human allegiance. While ethnicity appeals to the sense of natural protection, nationhood offers the much more exacting and no doubt more thrilling task of building a home of one's choice. Only as an issue involving human choice can ethnicity lose its grip on the mind of people. Some such disenchantment, in turn, clears the way for a humanly acceptable resolution of ethnic conflicts. Africans have the choice between recreating themselves through the generation of larger associations or limiting the horizon of their life by confining themselves to inherited characteristics.

If the rise of ethnicity in Africa is due to the decline of the mystic inspiration of African states, the creation of ethnic coalitions, as instrumentalism suggests, cannot resuscitate the attachment to larger communities. The cold calculation of interests and the sharing of power hardly favor the rise of the missing emotion. The coalition is likely to intensify the sense of heterogeneity, thus adding fuel to a tendency already too inclined toward nepotism, ascription, and cynicism. In proposing a coalition of interests, scholars only succeed in divesting the larger society of the sense of community to the delight of ethnic identification. The concept of power sharing is not enough to manage ethnic conflicts either. Sharing power can even escalate the idea of competition when what is needed is the invigoration of the sense of oneness.

The power of emotion is the only antidote to the selfishness of each ethnic group. To lean toward the idea of merger and unity, Africa needs poetry, not cold calculation of interests; it needs communion, not the institutionalized competition of exclusive ethnic groups. The role of mysticism is to endow the larger group with the sense of community, without which no nation can appear.

What is said here is not new. The expression "the founding fathers of nations" singles out the contribution of some individuals as being of such nature as to bestow a mystic flavor on ensembles often emerging from violent conquests or mercantile interests. When America is defined as the land of opportunities, what else is portrayed but the appeal of a generous idea? In Africa too, some leaders felt the need to cement the unity of the new states with galvanizing ideas. Such was, for instance, the aim of African socialism. Not only did these leaders feel that the best way to bring together tribal identities was through the appeal of a generous idea, but they also understood that the solidarity inherent in tribal ideology was best captured if the new larger community was committed to its extension.

The mystic of socialism failed, partly because of wrong policies and betrayals, partly because of structural inadequacies. Yet the failure of socialism did not incite African leaders and theoreticians to look for a substitute, except perhaps through the gruesome proposal of the free market economy, which does no more than annul any communal entitlement to the larger community. While competition between individuals remains the proven method to achieve economic growth, the idea of organizing ethnic groups into competing partners drops the substance for the shadow. The ethnic competition will develop along the line of disparate and exclusive identities, less so in the direction of national integration. To be sure, African leaders and scholars also speak of democracy, though they never explain why the larger community is better suited than the smaller one to achieve the ideal of democracy.

The African poet, thinker, and statesman, who verges on the Bergsonian view is Léopold Sédar Senghor with his idea of the modern nation as a humanization of the tribe. This appeal to Senghor may appear surprising in light of his eminent role in the promotion of the idea of immutable and uniform black essence of negritude philosophy. Not so if we maintain that he was bound to feel the pressure of African tribal differentiation sooner or later. Senghor begins by asserting: "all frontiers are artificial, even in Europe. They have been drawn by history."[58] This artificiality argues against primordialism: modern nations are not founded on ethnic purity; they are all a mixture of ethnic groups realized by conquest and assimilation. By contrast, the tribe, called by Senghor the homeland, has a natural basis. The tribal group is "the heritage handed down to us by our forefathers; land, blood, a language, or at least a dialect, manners and customs, a folklore and an art, a culture, in fact, rooted in one particular area and given expression by one race."[59] These references to localism and exclusiveness recall the Bergsonian description of the closed society.

In addition to assigning a natural basis, Senghor conceives of the nation as the act of transcending nature, of pushing back its boundary. As such, the nation involves human inventiveness and freedom. Using words reminiscent of Bergsonian analyses, Senghor writes:

> the nation is superior to the Homeland. It is a quintessence of the values of the Homeland, a sublimation of them formed by transcending them, and thus a *humanization*. For it belongs to man to heave himself up from the earth, to lift himself up from his roots, in order to unfold in the sun, to escape by a free act of *freedom* from the determinism of nature.[60]

Humanization stands for invention of the kind capable of bending the determinism of nature; it corresponds to the role that Bergson assigns to mysticism. The definition of the nation as the sublimation of the homeland also rediscovers the historicity of the process, the progressive extension of the tribal loyalty to a transcending appeal. The sublimation of tribal identities— what Bergson calls patriotism—is then a mystic act in the precise sense of opening up the constraint of nature and transferring the attendant feelings to a transcendent, imagined community. Without the transference of the natural sentiment, the larger community, however rational or useful its justification may be, remains a cold reality unable to attract the devotion of its members. This lack of attraction easily changes into repulsion whenever the conviction is reached that the larger community is an inherently deficient gathering.

The instrumentalist proposal ignores this obligation to transfer allegiance from the tribe to the nation. The institutionalization of ethnicity has the conspicuous implication of shutting up what needs to be unlocked. Let no one be misled by thinking that the utility of the arrangement will end up providing the missing devotion. While human beings can perfectly, let us say it once more, expand, transfer, and embellish natural feelings, whether they can create new feelings, still less counter natural feelings without first luring them away from their natural purposes, is more than doubtful. Appiah faces and then evades this problem when he admits that the constructedness of identities falls short of tallying with the seriousness of those who believe in them. For him, the intervention of the myth-making function is not necessary inasmuch as the power of conviction and commitment can be unleashed by utilitarian or pragmatic considerations. If the invented identity empowers us and works for us, then the new identity is enough to generate the attending commitment and belief.

Had this line of thinking been true, the evolution of ideas and feelings would have been so multifarious and disparate as to exclude any permanence and stability. The truth is that human creativity must be understood not so much as an invention *ex nihilo* as an embroidery on the canvas supplied by nature. Poetry, legends, and mythologies are all directed toward the purpose of inciting the natural to overstep its boundaries, there being no doubt that nature can be lured, not dismissed altogether. The secret of sublimation, or to speak like Bergson, of mysticism lies in this art of seducing natural fervor into an accomplice of supra-natural goals. The great merit of Bergson's approach is thus to combine instrumentalism and primordialism. While the positing of the primary organization satisfies the requirement of primordialism, the mystic factor provides the inspiration for enlargement, and so endorses the role that instrumentalism attributes to human inventiveness.

To summarize, the rise of ethnicity in Africa originates from the decline of galvanizing ideas, that is, from the inability to convince peoples that they will be better off in larger communities than in smaller ones. The proposal to harness the state to a coalition of ethnic parties working in the framework of a decentralized system of power is not a solution so long as the question of why ethnic groups should share power when they can have their state has no answer. African nations are dying because their mystic source has dried up, mostly by the accumulation of failures. Unless the multiethnic union achieves a higher ideal as opposed to the ethnic one, the unification never solidifies for want of meaning and function, all the more so as the success of East Asian nations seems to say that smallness and ethnic homogeneity condition achievement. Nor can some such galvanizing ideal emerge without people beginning to look beyond their interests and ethnic horizon, without their insularity opening up to a higher appeal.

Such an appeal is likely to come if the African mind is decolonized to the point of rekindling the mystical impulse suppressed by the fascination for Western rationality, which in any case remains elusive without some idealism. Hence the importance of ethnophilosophy inasmuch as the ethnophilosophical discourse invites Africans to pick up the mystical fervor as a way of countering the ascendancy of the West. There remains the integration of professional philosophy: the integration occurs when the mystic of the Negro settles down to the task of finding secular expressions, a characteristic example of which is nation-building.

This chapter shows that the challenge of ethnicity indicates the extent to which the African power to believe is undermined. The best way to recover the power is to become aware of the involvement of choice in what passes for natural conditionings. The awareness of freedom revives availability, and so prepares for the inspiration. To rise from ethnicity to nationhood is to give birth to a conquering mysticism, a mysticism that develops into reason as a result of craving for worldly validation.

Nine

HARNESSING MYTH TO RATIONALITY

The purpose of this last chapter is to suggest a solution to what appears as an African dilemma. From the attempt to rehabilitate Africans various philosophical schools arise whose paradox is that they endorse some of the implications of the colonial discourse even as they try to refute it. Before attempting to develop a solution, let us spell out the terms of the dilemma by a rapid review of the basic arguments of each school.

1. The African Dilemma

We are familiar with the charge that ethnophilosophy is an endorsement of the colonial discourse. The attempt to refute the characterization of Africans as prelogical by the assertion of difference only succeeds in ascribing a non-rational mode of thinking to the African self, the consequence of which is the perpetuation of marginality. Thus, Léopold Sedar Senghor's advocacy of emotion as an African specificity compromises the prospect of African modernization. Scientific and technological orientations are incompatible with a turn of mind dominated by emotional connection with the world.

Though the professional philosophers initiate the above criticism of ethnophilosophy, they do not escape the charge of endorsement of the colonial idea of Africa. Their commitment to the universality of the human mind cannot but establish a contrast between Africa and the achievements of the West such that the African difference appears as a lag, thereby resurrecting the evolutionary terms of backwardness and prelogicality. Though the conception promises that Africa will catch up with the West, the assent given to the idea of backwardness hampers the march toward progress.

The merit of the deconstructionist school is to have understood the extent to which the internalization of Western representations blocks the African initiative. Freedom can return to Africa only if Africans disengage from Western definitions. However, since the price for the disengagement is the acceptance of relativism, the freedom that the deconstructionist promises lacks the sense of its objectivity, and so is wanting in conviction and power. Without power, decolonization is not effective.

One appealing exit is to reject the path of difference by putting the blame for African retardation on the West. Cheikh Anta Diop follows this road when he ascribes the paternity of rationality to Africa via Egypt. The idea of the stolen legacy attributes the lag of Africa to a protracted war waged against the black race. Modern slavery and colonialism are only recent episodes in this long crusade to deprive the black race of its rightful place.

Everything appears as though the Marxist notion of class struggle could be extended to include the phase of racial confrontation resulting in the reduction of a creative race to servitude. In addition to being immersed in the controversial thesis of black Egypt, Diop's view sanctions the idea of human races with all the drawbacks that the notion entails.

Is there a way to maintain the West as a culprit while avoiding the racialization of the conflict between oppressors and oppressed? Such a thesis would emphasize that Africa and Europe were at a comparable traditional stage until the breakthrough of European modernity accelerated the gap. Europe used this advance caused by circumstances to block the progress of Africa by the hemorrhage of slavery and the imposition of colonial rule. Frantz Fanon's theory of a polarized and terminal conflict between "the wretched of the earth" and colonizers fully approves an approach blaming the West for Africa's underdevelopment. Similarly, Kwasi Wiredu's concept of comparable traditionality between the West and Africa can be interpreted as supporting the idea of Western culpability.

Maurice Delafosse remains the incontestable precursor of the view blaming Europe for Africa's social and technological retardation. To dispel the belief that the black race is intellectually inferior, Delafosse argues that a historical review of the African continent clearly shows that many African societies had attained a level of civilization comparable to the stage reached by European countries during the time of Charlemagne. The rise of West African empires, such as, the Ghanaian, the Songhoy, the Mandingo, and the Mossi empires, with their high degree of state organization and their centers of religious, philosophic, and scientific studies, the most famous being Timbuktu and Gao, gives evidence of the advances accomplished by the African medieval age. The question that comes to mind is why the advancement was not pursued.

Delafosse's answer considers two interrelated matters. (1) He asks us to appreciate that whatever Africans have accomplished, they have done so without outside help. While other peoples were able to advance thanks to contacts with and borrowings from other civilizations, Africans present the unique case of complete isolation imposed by the formidable barrier of the Sahara. To quote Delafosse:

> the Negroes of Africa, isolated from that Mediterranean lake which, during millenniums, has been the only vehicle of world civilization, were not able, in the absence of the emulation created by constant contacts with the outside world, to progress in a way that was possible, for example, in the case of the Gauls under the influence of Roman civilization.[1]

(2) He underlines the sad and unfortunate fact that, when technological progress finally overcame the natural obstacle and ended the African isolation, the purpose of the people who landed on the shores of Africa

> was first to tear away, anew, thousands of slaves, then, to inundate them with alcohol, and finally, without preparation, to thrust a civilization of the nineteenth century in the midst of other civilizations which had remained contemporaneous with Charlemagne.[2]

No lengthy demonstration is necessary to admit that the Western predilection for slaves and colonies turned out utterly degrading for Africans.

Those African scholars, Marxist or otherwise, who attribute African underdevelopment to Western domination and exploitation support the thesis of the culpability of the West. Their approach agrees with the analyses of the neo-Marxist school known as the dependency school. For André Gunter Frank, the main thinker of the dependency school, traditionality or backwardness simply means "nondevelopment," whereas underdevelopment is the product of the satellization of third world countries.[3] As a mechanism of surplus appropriation, satellization ensures the enrichment of centers at the expense of peripheries. Implicit in this analysis is the abstention of the dependency school from sanctioning the idea of difference. Nor does it put the blame for African retardation on the African past. This exculpation of the past avoids the endorsement of the prelogicality of precolonial Africa.

Notwithstanding the promise of positive gains, the rejection of African difference passes over the distinction between tradition and modernity. Worse, the approach supports the Hegelian notion of unilinear history. It simply substitutes the idea of peoples reduced to underdevelopment for the notion of retarded peoples. Some such substitution does not challenge the Hegelian scheme: underdevelopment is a confiscated, suppressed modernity, not a state of affairs prompted more by cultural divergences than by impediments or primitiveness. Not only does this conception of underdevelopment completely underrate the crucial role of change in the generation of modernity, but also endorses the universality of modernist ventures.

The same oversight weighs down Delafosse's approach. The thesis concedes that Africans were on the same track as the West until isolation prevented them from performing as well as Westerners. Compelled to invent everything by themselves, they have lost much time, and so lag behind. The understanding of the African situation in terms of lag definitely intimates that Africans would have reached a level of development similar to the West were they not hampered by environmental obstacles and, most of all, by European conquest and colonization. Delafosse sees Western civilization, not as a product of specific choices emanating from a no less specific historical orientation, but as a natural target of human beings wherever they are. So he speaks of lag instead of difference.

This universalist approach prevents the perception of the real meaning of modernity. It does not allow the radical understanding of the Western venture, the singularity of its inspiration, and the formidable challenge that the venture poses to non-Western cultures. The comprehension of Western scientific and technological ventures as natural products of growth that other cultures would produce were they not dominated glosses over the painful choices and sacrifices implied in change as well as over the original disparity of cultural orientations.

To become aware of the need to change is to reconnect with one's specificity so as to map out a new direction in which a recovered centrality inspires borrowings from and dealings with the West. The power to change too is dependent on the reconnection with specificity, since historicity—without which no sense of mission arises—feeds on continuity. This backward journey into the past is how the new and the past fuse into a new synthesis. But then, the best way to get out of the African dilemma is neither to assert nor deny the African difference; it is not to look for an uncontaminated vision of the past essence either. The recognition of the concomitance of myth and rationality, of traditionality and modernity, is the appropriate way to diffuse the African dilemma. No better refutation of the colonial discourse is to be found than in the exposure of complementarity in the alleged contrast between myth and reason.

The position that myth and rationality are concomitant makes room for African difference without succumbing to otherness. It posits an original orientation by which a culture makes sense of life and assigns a specific task to rationality. The assignment suggests that the way rationality is used can vary from one culture to another. In this regard, Placide Tempels's approach is exemplary: he argues that the way the mind of the Bantu functions is different because rationality is harnessed to a different purpose, not because it lacks rationality. To redirect rationality toward science and technology, the correct path is less to initiate discontinuity through the relegation of the past to prelogicality than to reformulate the inspiring myths of the culture in accordance with present needs. The reformulation is the recovery of historicity, which transcends the conflict between otherness and sameness by the very act of making tradition pregnant with modernity.

Let us insist on the ability of historicity to succeed where universalist and relativist definitions of Africa fail. The universalist option necessarily brings back evolutionary concepts; the strategy of otherness takes rationality away from Africa, while the relativization of commitment dilutes the particularism of deconstruction. The different approach of historicity starts by stating that what is wrong with negritude is not so much the claim to difference as the ascription of the difference to racial attributes. If instead of drawing the difference from racial, natural characteristics, negritude had attributed it to an act of choice, it would have moved in the direction of historicity. The intervention of choice invalidates the debate over the racial reality or non-reality of the black essence. What is accomplished as a result of choice refers to freedom, and so excludes objective determinations. The accomplishment, however specific, does not bar other human potentials; it simply springs from different utilizations of universal human aptitudes as a result of divergent historical choices.

If depending on the initial value orientation or choice of a given culture, rationality can assume different forms, the opposition that negritude reads between the African and the European approaches to nature loses its demeaning connotation. Choice avoids excluding the rationality of Africans. By removing the racial barrier, it also warrants the possibility of changing lanes, of passing from one conception to another through an act of choice. Most importantly, choice moves away from the evolutionary approach: if differences are accountable to choice rather than to backwardness or natural characteristics, the relativity of civilizations becomes unavoidable. Choice is always relative in that the selection of some goals entails the suppression or the giving up of other equally valid goals. The Western option "to become master and possessor of nature" is paid by the loss of other ways of relating with nature. This drawback revalues the African legacy by construing non-technicalness as a pursuit of a different purpose with its positive and negative sides.

This rehabilitating reading confirms that the way out of the African dilemma is the divergent conception of evolution. Contrary to the universalist and stage-producing-stage conception of evolution, divergence implicates splits within the same unity such that the process, in the words of Henri Bergson, "splaying out like a sheaf, sunders, in proportion to their simultaneous growth, terms which at first completed each other so well that they coalesced."[4] This dissociation of the original unity achieves particular outcomes, which are complementary rather than hierarchical. The one outcome does not represent a higher stage, but a divergent course with positive and negative attributes. In light of the complementarity of the divergent courses, the human target should be less the frenzied pursuit of one direction—which is what Westernization is forcibly accomplishing—than the attempt to achieve a harmonious development of human potentials by integrating the positive characters of the divergent courses.

The relativization of the West, not its normativeness, opens the African path to modernity. When the West is presented as the norm, Africans are reduced to imitators, or to speak a more familiar language, to dependency. When the West turns relative through a divergent conception, it becomes an object of assessment, better still, of free choice. With the intervention of choice, the instruction to copy the West gives way to utilitarian questions: What can

Africans learn from the West? What must they reject? How can they integrate their borrowings into their continuity? The identification with a rehabilitated past provides the detachment that allows the deployment of such questions. Developing this type of pragmatic relation with the West means the prior decolonization of the African mind, which is neither more nor less than the recovery of freedom. The questions are the very ones that Africans would have raised were they not colonized.

The normativeness of the West has far-reaching detrimental implications. As imitators rather than creators, Africans become totally dependent, and lose their ability to think and act in a steadfast, systematic, and creative manner. A copy never reaches the perfection of the model, and the copyist has less passion and commitment to execute the project. Since imitators already accept their inferiority and do not strive to deliver their own making, they fall short of being passionate and resolute about their undertaking. What they do is always very second-rate; it may even be deliberately messed up out of the naughtiness that comes along when grownups and old cultures stoop to the status of children undergoing a process of domestication under Western tutorship.

No sooner do Africans decide to become imitators than they expose themselves to faulty executions of the model. Since imitation is an admission of inferiority, the act by which copyists revere the model is the very act by which they suppress their capacity, thereby putting themselves in the position of committing mistakes. No other way exists to acquire the requirements and the virtues of the model than to deviate by avoiding repetition. You equal the model when you become creative or original, and not when you imitate.

The "essence of progress," as defined correctly by Edward W. Blyden, is the attainment of *"difference."*[5] All that is not unique, original is deficient because it owes its existence to a reduced ability. When creativity takes the lead, the model loses its normative stand and becomes an inspiration. The great difference between inspiration and imitation is that imitation makes a person passive, subordinate; it is lowering and debilitating. Not so with inspiration, which is an appeal to rise to the same standard, if not to go higher. Inspiration is stimulating and emboldening while imitation inculcates self-lowering and dependency.

This analysis sheds some light on the mystery of Africa's apparent inability to go forward. Though African societies adopt Western institutions and values, none of these borrowings seem to function properly. One way of explaining this stagnation is to suggest that imitation commits Africans to failure. Externally, African societies appear to be doing all that is necessary to modernize, but they do it as learners, apprentices who commit mistakes. Unfortunately, these mistakes soon turn into internal blockages that stand in the way of advancement. Just as undigested meal hampers our body, so too the faulty imitation of the West leads to drawbacks that impede the progress of modernization. Take the case of the state. On the assumption that a strong and centralized state is necessary to implement modernization, the conditions of dictatorship are put in place, which conditions conflict with other admitted goals, such as democratization, and prove tougher to remove later.

When the path of dependency is discarded, the attainment of self-reliance emerges as the *sine qua non* of modernization. According to the basic belief of the modernization school, modernization occurs when traditional values, beliefs, and ways of doing things give way to innovative views and methods. In the words of Bert Hoselitz, "in order to have economic advancement, the practice of assigning economic role by ascription, or according to status, must be replaced by the standard of achievement."[6] The resurgence of innovative ability has its prime condition in the practice of self-reliance.

The definition of modernity by the liberation of innovative capacity has the interesting twist of putting the blame for Africa's failure to modernize less on the persistence of tradition than on the erection of Western experience as a normative model. Though Hoselitz underscores the role of innovation, he does not hesitate to ask "in what way the study of the social and economic history of the more advanced countries provides a series of hints for the construction of models."[7] Nothing is more contradictory than to emphasize the role of creativity and self-reliance in achieving modernity, and to expect the birth of these same qualities through the imposition of a model whose major defect is to bar self-reliance.

In light of these drawbacks of imitativeness, the central question becomes: what encourages self-reliance? To rely on oneself presupposes the attainment of self-respect and confidence in one's ability, which has to do with self-representation. Empowering self-representations bring in the role of ideology so that, as stated by Norman Long, "re-interpretations of ideology are essential prerequisites to creating a modern society and economy."[8] If modernity is equally tributary of rationality and ideological representations, we need to understand the condition under which rational thinking and ideological beliefs come to collaborate instead of impairing each other.

2. The Complementarity of Myth and Rationality

Where choice intervenes, invention is most active. So is myth-making as a characteristic instance of invention. One major result of the previous chapters is that the return to the past is not so much the reproduction of the past as a reconstruction, an imaginative movement into the past. Its purpose is the deployment of historicity: the involvement of a mission supposedly handed down from the past connects the past and the future in such a way that the bond unleashes the myth of an unfolding subject, which sustains the theoretical construct of all historical consciousness and development theories. The need for such a myth becomes all the more compelling when peoples come under the marginalizing effect of a prolonged domination. This explains the emergence of African ethnophilosophical discourses, which advocate a return to the source as a way of reviving the historicity of the African subject. {PRIVATE }

With the involvement of inventiveness, the African ethnophilosophical discourse ceases to present mythical thinking as antithetical to rationality; instead, it comes out in favor of their complementarity. Still less does the discourse racialize Africans, since the refusal to set myth against rationality explicitly invites Africans to assume their freedom. In claming what the West despises, Africans redefine themselves as negativity, as the antithetical subjectivity intent on recreating humanity by the insertion of values and beliefs extracted from the experience of marginality. Just as Christianity created a new sense of being human by valorizing the poor and the weak, so too the wretchedness of Africans is out to create a new sense of the human person.

That this creative power exists is easily established if we pay attention to the impossibility of reducing the mythical faculty to mere imagination. Closely following the arguments of Bergson, I endorse the autonomous existence of the myth-making function together with the empowering purpose of the function, the understanding being that excessive valorization of rationality results in the complete asphyxia of the power of the mind. The basic error is to define myth in terms of knowledge, be it as false knowledge or as construction. While ethnophilosophers change myth into a different type of knowledge, that is, into a discrete epistemological orientation, their opponents argue for the distinction between mythical thinking and rational knowledge, and advocate the eradication of the former. For V. Y. Mudimbe too, to the extent that myth is a construction of the world, mythical thinking fulfills the function of knowledge, even if he denies the objectivity of such knowledge.

Of all the theories exposing the involvement of ideological biases in an epistemological orientation claiming to be objective, Marxism provides clear-cut means to denounce the operations of false consciousness without thereby espousing relativism. Provided that certain principles, such as, materialism, scientific attitude, and class position, are put to use, Karl Marx believes in the possibility of discriminating between objective knowledge and partisan or biased approaches. These principles guarantee that

> we do not set out from what men say, imagine, conceive, nor from men as narrated, thought of, imagined, conceived, in order to arrive at men in the flesh. We set out from real, active men, and on the basis of their real life-process we demonstrate the development of the ideological reflexes and echoes of this life-process.[9]

Unlike Marx, Mudimbe has no provision for universalizing instances. By reducing indiscriminately everything to construction, he deprives himself of the opportunity of differentiating between ideology and objective conceptions. His emancipated view of Africa is thus condemned to be an invention confronting another invention. My argument does not criticize the idea of invention; it simply points out that relativism clashes with Mudimbe's search for authentic Africa.

As for Marx, his attempt to shun ideological thinking altogether betrays an objectivist commitment that treats mythical thinking as false knowledge. His approach is totally deaf to the suggestion that the involvement of invention does not necessarily entail the impossibility of objective knowledge. If the role of myth is less to deform or conceal reality than to provide galvanizing representations, the assumption that myth complements reason becomes a legitimate statement. Instead of usurping the role of reason, the function of mythical representations is to enclose knowledge in an uplifting vision. What blocks the perception of mythical thinking acting as a buttress rather than a rival to reason is the stubborn tendency to depict mythical thinking in terms of knowledge.

A little reflection suggests that myth is not knowledge. Wiredu gives a hint when he remarks that myth and science coexist, that even in the contemporary world, including among scientists, mythical representations resist the impact of rationality. Alluding to the stubborn resistance of religious beliefs, Bergson writes: "experience may indeed say 'that is false,' and reasoning 'that is absurd'. Humanity only clings all the more to that absurdity and that error."[10] Had mythical thinking been a form of knowledge, the progress of enlightenment should have entailed the dismissal of religious beliefs, especially among educated people. Seeing to what extent idealist thinking dominates Western philosophy and that those called great philosophers are overwhelmingly idealists, it springs to mind that the major object of philosophy is the defense of religious ideas. We saw that for Immanuel Kant the purpose of philosophy is to limit science to the phenomenal so that there is room for faith.

The materialist doctrine itself makes sense only as an antithesis, as an attempt to refute idealist positions. A case in point is the Marxist idea of defining philosophy by the conflict between idealism and materialism over the basic question of the primacy of spirit or matter. According to Friedrich Engels:

> those who asserted the primacy of spirit to nature and, therefore, in the last instance, assumed world creation in some form or other . . . comprised the camp of idealism. The others, who regarded nature as primary, belong to the various schools of materialism.[11]

The stubborn resistance of spiritualist beliefs raises the question of knowing whether mythical thinking does not have a proper function, more exactly, whether the function of the myth is not to counter the representations of reason every time these representations fail to support life. This explanation is the path that Bergson takes when he defines religion as a *"defensive reaction of nature against the dissolvent power of intelligence.*"[12] The definition certainly gives a new understanding of the connection between reason and myth. The dissolvent power of intelligence is most apparent in representations connected with the inevitability of death, the appearance of selfishness in a being designed for social life, and the uncertainty of projected actions in a mechanical, unfriendly world. Religious beliefs counter these depressing representations of intelligence through mythical beliefs that paint death as transition to another life, social rules as sacred obligations protected by gods, and mechanical determinism as animated by forces endowed with intentions.

Let me illustrate the role of mythical thinking through a direct confrontation with the Marxist notion of ideology. In *The German Ideology*, Marx uses the context of Germany's technological lag *vis-à-vis* British and French advances to uncover the mode of thinking characteristic of ideology. At a time when British and French philosophical views increasingly assumed earthly contents, those of Germany, Marx notes, remained bogged down in religious and idealist explanations. A good example is the way Georg Wilhelm. Friedrich Hegel and the Young Hegelians conceptualize historiography: "while the French and the English at least hold by the political illusion, which is moderately close to reality, the Germans move in the realm of the 'pure spirit,' and make religious illusion the driving force of history."[13] Marx has no doubt that the true explanation for this mythical infatuation lies in the "connection of German philosophy with German reality."[14] In particular, Germany's lag in terms of commerce and industry compels its intellectuals to focus on speculative achievements, and thus to revel in illusions, in events and accomplishments taking place in the realm of pure thought.

This German reaction appears totally inadequate to the requirements of the situation. When a resolute industrialization is the only appropriate response, strange is the German preference for spiritualistic escapades. The production of illusions totally ineffective in dealing with the situation is little intelligible, since the admitted impact of the illusions is to intensify the lag, even to the point of blocking its removal. Insofar as this negative role makes no sense, it requires an explanation that associates the production of beliefs and ideas with the need to respond to a challenging situation. Such an explanation defines mythical thinking less by the tendency to flee reality than by the vocation to support or enhance the resolution to cope with adversity. Instead of opposing mythical thinking to science and rationality, the explanation conceives of them as forming a team.

In light of the disadvantageous reality exposing the industrial lag of Germany, the recourse to mythical thinking to counter the challenging situation is indeed a better explanation than the assumption of a thinking determined to escape from reality, which assumption fails to account for the suitability of the response to the existing situation. The thesis of the complementarity of reason and myth reads into the religious interpretation of history the need to spiritualize economic pursuits for the purpose of both reinstating continuity with German cultural trend and infusing vigor and determination into the industrialization process. The great impact of Hegel's theory making "the History of the World" into the "process of development and the realization of Spirit . . . the justification of God in History" is the reconciliation of capitalism with religion.[15] No better way could be found to attune the German mind to capitalist methods and values than a conception of history greeting modernity with the blessings of religion.

Another influential endorsement of the need to harness knowledge to myth is found in Friedrich Nietzsche's normative characterization of such a bond as the pillar of all viable human civilization. All the more reason for the endorsement to be quite significant is that, dealing specifically with the meaning of the German romantic reaction to the Enlightenment, Nietzsche notes, "the cult of feeling was erected in place of the cult of reason."[16] This reference to the romantic cult of feeling irresistibly evokes Senghor's pronouncements. Nietzsche praises the romantic reaction as a positive phase, as the birth of an autonomous German mind escaping the ascendancy of British and French advances.

According to Nietzsche, the preservation of the sense of mystery and transcendence within the routine and techniques of everyday life is a general requisite for the sustenance of civilization, given that the freedom and audacity of the will depend on the maintenance of a line of communication with a fabulous world. What is at stake is the empowering impact of the myth, for as a "concentrated picture of the world . . . as abbreviature of phenomena," the myth "cannot dispense with wonder."[17] A necessary conclusion follows: since "without myth . . . every culture loses its healthy creative natural power," the protection of the mythical inspiration is the number one priority of any civilization.[18]

For Nietzsche, a pertinent case is again the orientation of German thinking: "Kant and Schopenhauer made it possible for the spirit of *German philosophy* . . . to destroy scientific Socratism's complacent delight in existence by establishing its boundaries," he says.[19] This necessity to earmark the sense of transcendence shows that the glory and rebirth of a civilization depend on the control of knowledge so that knowledge serves life instead of the opposite. Is not wisdom, the great pursuit of philosophy, the control of knowledge?

When Wiredu notes that Western thinking is not free of mysticism, he should have added that Western thought has produced mystics as has no other culture, as evinced by the sweeping mysticism of the Middle Ages. The great self-deception of ethnophilosophy is to reserve mysticism to Africa while perfectly knowing that Europe reached unsurpassed levels of mysticism, and this deliberate oversight obstructs the assessment of the role that mythical thinking played in the history of the West.

A pertinent example of this role is found in Max Weber's analysis of capitalism. On the strength of the Hegelian spiritualization of history, Weber, a most serious student of economic development, does not hesitate to ascribe the rise of capitalism to a mystical inspiration, to the need to appease the religious anxiety spread by Protestantism. His approach goes beyond reconciling religion with worldly pursuits; it attributes to the religious anxiety the release of such a systematic and insatiable pursuit of worldly success that human beings become "dominated by the making of money, by acquisition as the ultimate purpose of . . . life."[20] If Europe owes the power to colonize the world to a mystical inspiration, then Africans must understand that what colonizes them is less their deficiency in rationality than their repudiation of mythical callings for fear of ratifying the colonial discourse.

3. The Particularism of Freedom

The discovery that mythical thinking has a different function challenges Lucien Lévy-Bruhl's evolutionist reading, and establishes the complementarity of myth and reason and their equal coexistence in non-Western as well as Western peoples. Does this coexistence mean that no difference exists between Westerners and other peoples? Even though differences are apparent, they do not reside in the way the mind functions. We can say that the progress of science and technology reduces the need for mythical representations among Westerners; we can also add that mythical representations assume an exaggerated role among traditional peoples. Even so, the truth remains that if we take away all acquired habits, the same nature persists in Western and non-Western peoples.

The ethnophilosophical argument according to which the African mind functions differently from the Western mind is not receivable for the simple reason that mythical thinking is not a form of knowledge opposed or different from scientific knowledge. Paulin Hountondji's characterization of mythical thinking as a false, unscientific or prescientific knowledge is not receivable for the same reason. As to Mudimbe's position, the fact that the mythical and the scientific do not have the same target justifies their distinction: objective knowledge aims at the control of things, while mythical thinking focuses on beliefs that counter those representations of rationality that depress life. One important lesson follows, namely, the need to keep myth and rationality tied together. The neglect of reason discourages technicalness, and the rejection of mythical thinking kills confidence and belief, without which nothing great can be accomplished.

The colonial discourse is dangerous to Africa not so much by the depreciating intent of the discourse as by the misleading belief that the highest, the most advanced expression of life is rationality. In addition to hiding the mythical foundation of Western thinking, such a belief paints mythical thinking as an expression of backwardness. Acculturated Africans desire nothing less than the complete extirpation of mythical thinking. This one-sidedness, this growth of rationality unsupported by mythical inspiration takes the sense of wonder away from African thinking. The belief in the immortality of the soul is a good example of what is meant by wonder. To aspire to life beyond the bodily existence, the natural realism of the intellect must be overtaken by a great proclivity for awesome encounters. Without this bent for the extraordinary urging us to assume that life can be more than what it appears to be, life after death would have been unthinkable.

The tendency to censure ideology confirms that awesome inspiration increasingly withers away among Africans. Witness Alpha O. Konare, first elected President of Mali, recently writes: "Young people no longer believe in ideologies, but they do believe in the values of democracy, justice, work, solidarity."[21] The statement evades the question of knowing how the great values of democracy and justice can crop up in a mind confined to down-to-earth pursuits. The departure of the sense of wonder suppresses the very motivation to undertake great things, to become ambitious and surpass oneself. We see instances of this motivation in matters connected with nation-building and construction of identity. Only when reason is backed by those beliefs that stir up the emotional force of life does it become daring and ambitious. As Bergson states, emotion is:

> the source of the great creations of art, of science and of civilization in general. . . . Not only because emotion is a stimulus, because it incites the intelligence to undertake ventures and the will to preserve with them. We must go further. There are emotions which beget thought.[22]

Excess of intellectualism cripples intelligence, and this is exactly the impact of colonial discourse on Africa. The stigmatization of mythical thinking, that is, the association of myth with backwardness, talks the educated African into the exclusive valorization of rationality, which then becomes a tool divorced from belief, and so a source of dissolvent representations. Following different premises Ali Mazrui makes a similar diagnosis of African intellectual impotence when he writes: "the sense of awe towards the West becomes a foundation for subsequent intellectual dependency."[23]

Consider the relativist arguments of the deconstructionist school. The enthusiasm for relativist philosophical premises may well be an imprint of mental colonization, given that the relativization of the West as the sole avenue to shake off Eurocentrism leaves the bitter aftertaste of generalized incredulity, not to say cynicism. This outcome reiterates the imperative to accompany the attempt to refute the universalist claim of Eurocentrism by a corresponding effort to renew the power to believe. That the dethronement of the West is paid by the risk of being prone to skepticism and cynicism is a major African dilemma whose only antidote is the revival of myth-making consequent upon the disclosure of how closely the rational and the mythical work in tandem.

The revelation of complicity removes the discredit thrown on whatever is not rational. This idea of complicity achieves a higher result than the relativization of the West: it particularizes Eurocentrism without indulging in skepticism. While relativism excludes universalism, particularism grasps difference as a discrete arrangement of the universal. By inserting the universal into a context characterized by a selective and inventive receptivity, it grounds universality on a founding myth, and so particularizes it.

Particularism inaugurates historicity, that is, the creative unfolding of an initial choice, of an original arrangement. The unique and irreplaceable value of the particular lies in this creative originality, which likens identities to works of art. Hence the importance of continuity: it is loyalty to a choice that is unique and inaugural and thanks to which existence assumes a task, defines itself as a moment in the realization of a vision. Moreover, because the idea of collusion between the mythical and the rational underlines the intervention of choice, it encourages the revival of the power to believe. Nothing is more apt to unleash enthusiasm and instigate belief than the discovery of our freedom: the disclosure of our agency calls on our commitment and paints the world in rosy colors.

If as a result of acquiescing to the colonial discourse, Africa becomes totally overwhelmed by the analytic ascendancy of the West to the point of losing the power to believe, this asphyxia, otherwise known as mental colonization, calls for the revalorization of the power to believe. Mazrui appeals for "derationalization," which, he explains, "is, from a nationalist point of view, a call for a cultural revival."[24] The irreverent attitude to Western rationality of the negritude thinker appears as a necessary moment: to make up stories and believe in them, people must rise above the objectivist repute of scientific thinking. That is why empowering stories require the act of limiting knowledge, which is then an eminently philosophical task. By diluting all forms of one-sided rationalism and postmodernist skepticism, such a philosophical inquiry fosters a state of mental availability liable to reactivate the myth-making function. Properly understood, the ethnophilosophical project is in keeping with the Kantian purpose of limiting knowledge to make room for belief, provided that the objective is to emancipate the African power to believe from Western objectifications.

This goal of liberation encourages the understanding of the defense of otherness in terms of disengaging the African subject from Western *episteme*. Liberation targets the decolonization of the African mind, a prerequisite to the rekindling of the mythical impulse suppressed by the fascination for Western rationality whose paradox is that it is itself inaccessible without some idealism.

Deploring "the complete absence of idealism," Stanislav Andreski notes that "the higher ideals which have inspired those who made Western civilization what it is appear . . . devoid of any motivating force" to Africans.[25]

Though a necessary moment, the attempt of ethnophilosophy to contain the overwhelming ascendancy of the West through the assertion of African otherness is neither sufficient nor free of negative fallouts. There remains the next step, that is, the integration of the objection of professional philosophers. Hence the need for an African philosophy that continues and transcends ethnophilosophy by infusing the desire for rational expressions into the mythical fervor. The defense of particularism, defined as a unique blend of rationality and mysticism, is the best way to realize such a goal.

Of all the main aftermaths of the Western conquest of Africa, the imposition of the cult of rationality as a result of which Africans lost the power to believe seems to me the most pernicious. Recall that this cult is at the root of the endorsement of the unilinear theory of history by which Africans consent to their marginality. Unless the power to believe is liberated, I maintain that Africa cannot have the will to rise above its marginal existence. The attacks against ethnophilosophy express the end product of Westernization essentially manifested by the rise to leadership of Africans trained in rational thinking unattended by mythical inspiration. Insofar as the training puts the blame for African technological lag on the mythical past, it produces an analytic mind totally alien to the sense of wonder in addition to internalizing colonial stereotypes about Africa.

Though the deconstructionist school attempts to dethrone these stereotypes, the relativist premises of deconstruction theory prevent the recovery of the sense of wonder. To decenter the West so as to recenter Africa, much more than deconstruction is required. Likewise, all those theories advocating Afrocentrism call for something higher than the mere removal of oppression, as shown by the very inspiration of Diop, who changed Egyptian pyramids into Negro testimonies.

Negritude comes close to the sense of wonder, a characteristic example of which is found in Aimé Césaire's poetic theme of the return to the source. Relativizing the Western glorification of the conquest of nature, the inspiration invested Africa with the unique metaphysical vocation of playing with the world. Unfortunately, negritude thinkers drew back from integrating the rational moment, and so fell short of transforming their vision into reason, into a program of action. They spoke of synthesis with the West, thereby failing to foster a demiurgical orientation from the bosom of negritude itself. Such a synthesis was *per force* devoid of competitive spirit, being but an external linkage with the West. Unable to activate worldliness, the mythical inspiration dried up.

Negritude thinkers would have promoted worldliness, had they consented to lose their blackness so as to recover it in a developed form. In this way, the thinking would have grown into an odyssey, the return to the source being this time the imagined future. The adherence to a descriptive, racially determined notion of negritude, instead of the freely created one, prevented this course of thinking. In surrendering the right to a free definition of negritude, the thinking misses the opportunity of changing the past into a future. For the rewriting of the past in light of present ambitions is how an unfolding subject endowed with the sense of mission moves toward a concocted future.

NOTES

Chapter One

1. Lucien Lévy-Bruhl, *How Natives Think*, trans. Lilian A. Claire (Princeton, N.J.: Princeton University Press, 1985), p. 35.
2. *Ibid.*
3. *Ibid.*, p. 78.
4. *Ibid.*, p. 43.
5. *Ibid.*, p. 79.
6. *Ibid.*, p. 36.
7. *Ibid.*, p. 78.
8. *Ibid.*, pp. 129–130.
9. Paulin J. Hountondji, *African Philosophy: Myth and Reality* (Bloomington, Ind.: Indiana University Press, 1983), pp. 43, 45.
10. Placide Tempels, *Bantu Philosophy*, trans. A. Rubbens (Paris: Présence Africaine, 1969), p. 50.
11. Léopold S. Senghor, *Prose and Poetry*, trans. John Reed and Clive Wake (London: Heinemann, 1976), pp. 29–30.
12. Lévy-Bruhl, *How Natives Think*, p. 44.
13. *Ibid.*, p. 56.
14. Sigmund Freud, *The Freud Reader*, ed. Peter Gay (New York: W. W. Norton & Company, 1989), p. 143.
15. *Ibid.*, p. 165.
16. Blaise Pascal, *Pascal's Pensées*, trans. H. F. Stewart (New York: Pantheon Books, 1950), p. 91.
17. Heraclitus, *The Presocratic Philosophers*, ed. G. S. Kirk and J. E. Raven (Cambridge, England: Cambridge University Press, 1975), pp. 189–190.
18. Friedrich Engels, *Herr Eugen Dühring's Revolution in Science*, ed. C. P. Dutt (New York: International Publishers, 1966), pp. 28, 132.
19. Henri Bergson, *The Two Sources of Morality and Religion*, trans. R. Ashley Audra and Cloudesley Brereton (Notre Dame, Ind.: University of Notre Dame Press, 1986), p. 144.
20. *Ibid.*, p. 145.
21. *Ibid.*
22. *Ibid.*, p. 146.
23. *Ibid.*, p. 164.
24. Friedrich Nietzsche, *The Twilight of the Idols*, trans. Anthony M. Ludovici (New York: Russel & Russel, 1964), pp. 17–18.
25. Paulin Hountondji, *African Philosophy*, p. 61.
26. V. Y. Mudimbe, *The Invention of Africa* (Bloomington, Ind.: Indiana University Press, 1988), p. 20.
27. Jean-Paul Sartre, *Existentialism and Human Emotions*, trans. Hazel E. Barnes (New York: Philosophical Library, 1957), p. 15.
28. *Ibid.*, p. 41.

29. Friedrich Engels, "Letters on Historical Materialism," *Basic Writings on Politics and Philosophy*, ed. Lewis S. Feuer (Garden City, N.Y.: Anchor Books, 1959), p. 408.

30. W. E. B. Du Bois, "The Conservation of Races," *W. E. B. Du Bois: A Reader*, ed. David L. Lewis (New York: Henry Holt and Company, 1995), p. 25.

31. Hountondji, *African Philosophy*, p. 66.

32. Jean-Jacques Rousseau, *The First and Second Discourses and Essay on the Origin of Languages*, ed. and trans. Victor Gourevitch (New York: Harper & Row, Publishers, 1986), p.7.

33. *Ibid.*, p.9.

34. *Ibid.*

35. *Ibid.*, p. 237.

36. *Ibid.*, p.220.

37. Arthur Schopenhauer, *The World as Will and Representation,* trans. E. F. J. Payne (New York: Dover Publications, 1969), vol. 1, p. 109.

38. Henri Bergson, *Creative Evolution*, trans. Arthur Mitchell (New York: Random House, 1944), pp. 182, 194.

39. Søren Kierkegaard, *Kierkegaard's Concluding Unscientific Postscript*, trans. David S. Swenson (Princeton, N.J.: Princeton University Press, 1964), p. 171.

40. Stanley Diamond, *In Search of the Primitive* (New Brunswick, N.J.: Transaction Books, 1974), p. 120.

41. Samuel Oluoch Imbo, *An Introduction to African Philosophy* (New York: Rowman & Littlefield Publishers, 1998), p. 5.

42. Richard Rorty, "Philosophers, Novelists, and Intercultural Comparisons: Heidegger, Kundera, and Dickens," *Culture and Modernity*, ed. Eliot Deutsch (Honolulu: University of Hawaii Press, 1991), p. 4.

43. *Ibid.*

44. *Ibid.*

45. *Ibid.*, pp.5–6.

46. Martin Heidegger, *The Question Concerning Technology and Other Essays*, trans. William Lovitt (New York: Harper & Row, Publishers, 1977), pp. 129–130.

47. *Ibid.*, p. 22.

48. *Ibid.*, p. 27.

49. Martin Heidegger, "Letter on Humanism," *Basic Writings*, ed. David F. Krell (New York: Harper & Row, Publishers, 1977), p. 221.

50. Friedrich Nietzsche, *Beyond Good and Evil*, trans. Helen Zimmern, in *The Philosophy of Nietzsche* (New York: Random House, 1954), p. 382.

51. Nietzsche, *The Genealogy of Morals*, trans. Horace B. Samuel, in *The Philosophy of Nietzsche*, p. 792.

52. *Ibid.*, pp. 742–743.

53. Michael Paul Gallagher, *Clashing Symbols: An Introduction to Faith and Culture* (New York: Paulist Press, 1998), p. 88.

54. *Ibid.*, p. 89.

55. Clinton M. Jean, *Behind the Eurocentric Veils* (Amherst, Mass.: University of Massachusetts Press, 1991), p. 4.

56. D. A. Masolo, *African Philosophy in Search of Identity* (Bloomington, Ind.: Indiana University Press, 1994), p. 127.

57. *Ibid.*, p. 128.

58. Imbo, *An Introduction to African Philosophy*, p. 5.
59. Rorty, "Philosophers, Novelists, and Intercultural Comparisons: Heidegger, Kundera, and Dickens," p. 12.
60. Gallagher, *Clashing Symbols*, p. 90.
61. Ruth Benedict, *Patterns of Culture* (Boston: Houghton Mifflin Company, 1959), p. 223.

Chapter Two

1. D. A. Masolo, *African Philosophy in Search of Identity* (Bloomington, Ind.: Indiana University Press, 1994), p. 67.
2. Theophilus Okere, *African Philosophy* (Lanham, Md.: University Press of America, 1983), p. 47.
3. Masolo, *African Philosophy in Search of Identity*, p. 47.
4. Placide Tempels, *Bantu Philosophy*, trans. A. Rubbens (Paris: Présence Africaine, 1959), p. 109.
5. *Ibid.*, p. 119.
6. John S. Mbiti, *African Religions and Philosophy* (New York: Frederick A. Praeger, Publishers, 1986), p. 15.
7. *Ibid.*
8. Tempels, *Bantu Philosophy*, p.13.
9. *Ibid.*, p. 14.
10. *Ibid.*
11. *Ibid.*, p. 110.
12. *Ibid.*, p. 17.
13. Gordon Hedderly Smith, *The Missionary and Anthropology* (Chicago: Moody Press, 1945), p. 26.
14. *Ibid.*, p. 27.
15. Tempels, *Bantu Philosophy*, p. 17.
16. *Ibid.*
17. *Ibid.*, p. 16.
18. *Ibid.*, p. 19.
19. *Ibid.*, p. 113.
20. V. Y. Mudimbe, *The Invention of Africa* (Bloomington, Ind.: Indiana University Press, 1988), p.53.
21. Tempels, *Bantu Philosophy*, p. 20.
22. Lucien Lévy-Bruhl, *How Natives Think*, trans. Lilian A. Clare (Princeton, N.J.: Princeton University Press, 1985), p. 38.
23. *Ibid.*
24. Tempels, *Bantu Philosophy*, p. 51.
25. *Ibid.*, p. 52.
26. *Ibid.*, pp. 51–52.
27. *Ibid.*, p. 51.
28. *Ibid.*, p. 60.
29. *Ibid.*
30. Paulin J. Hountondji, *African Philosophy: Myth and Reality* (Bloomington, Ind.: Indiana University Press, 1983), p. 77.
31. Masolo, *African Philosophy in Search of Identity*, p. 57.

32. Mudimbe, *The Invention of Africa*, p. 151.
33. *Ibid.*, p. 141.
34. Aristotle, *Aristotle's Metaphysics*, trans. Hippocrates G. Apostle (Grinnell, Iowa: Peripatetic Press, 1979), p. 83.
35. Tempels, *Bantu Philosophy*, p. 35.
36. *Ibid.*, p. 43.
37. Masolo, *African Philosophy in Search of Identity*, p. 49.
38. Léopold Sédar Senghor, "On Negrohood: Psychology of the African Negro," *African Philosophy: Selected Readings*, ed. Albert Mosley (Englewood Cliffs, N.J.: Prentice-Hall, 1995), p. 127.
39. George Berkeley, *The Principles of Human Knowledge and Three Dialogues between Hylas and Philonous* (New York: Meridian Books, 1963), p. 66.
40. Tempels, *Bantu Philosophy*, p. 115.
41. See Abiola Irele, *The African Experience in Literature and Ideology* (London: Heinemann, 1981), p. 80.
42. Henri Bergson, *The Two Sources of Morality and Religion*, trans. R. Ashley Audra and Cloudesley Brereton (Notre Dame, Ind.: University of Notre Dame Press, 1986), p. 104.
43. *Ibid.*, p.151.
44. Gerald Broce, *History of Anthropology* (Minneapolis: Burgess Publishing Company, 1973), p. 13.
45. Tempels, *Bantu Philosophy*, p. 112.
46. *Ibid.*, p. 110.
47. *Ibid.*
48. *Ibid.*
49. *Ibid.*, p. 113.
50. *Ibid.*, p. 114.
51. *Ibid.*, p. 110.
52. *Ibid.*, p. 65.
53. *Ibid.*, p. 105.
54. Smith, *The Missionary and Anthropology*, p. 43.
55. Tempels, *Bantu Philosophy*, p. 110.
56. *Ibid.*, p. 116.
57. *Ibid.*
58. *Ibid.*
59. *Ibid.*, p. 120.
60. *Ibid.*, p. 121.
61. *Ibid.*, p. 120.
62. *Ibid.*
63. E. E. Evans-Pritchard, *Theories of Primitive Religion* (Oxford: Oxford University Press, 1966), p. 15.
64. Jean-Jacques Rousseau, *The Basic Political Writings*, trans. and ed. Donald A. Cress (Indianapolis: Hackett Publishing Company, 1987), p. 53.
65. Stanley Diamond, *In Search of the Primitive* (New Brunswick, N.J.: Transaction Books, 1974), p. 102.
66. Tempels, *Bantu Philosophy*, p. 77.
67. *Ibid.*, p. 112.
68. *Ibid.*

69. Clinton M. Jean, *Behind the Eurocentric Veils* (Amherst, Mass.: University of Massachusetts Press, 1991), p. 20.

70. See Ruth Benedict, *Patterns of Culture* (Boston: Houghton Mifflin Company, 1959), p. 223.

71. Dominique Zahan, *The Religion, Spirituality, and Thought of Traditional Africa* (Chicago: University of Chicago Press, 1979), p. 5.

72. *Ibid.*, p. 6.

73. Bergson, *The Two Sources of Morality and Religion*, p. 269.

74. *Ibid.*, p. 274.

75. Heinrich Fries, *Revelation* (New York: Herder and Herder, 1969), p. 26.

76. Aylward Shorter, *Revelation and Its Interpretation* (London: Geoffrey Chapman, 1983), p. 248.

77. Evans-Pritchard, *Theories of Primitive Religion*, p. 2.

78. James B. Wiggins, *In Praise of Religious Diversity* (New York: Routledge, 1996), p.15.

79. Tempels, *Bantu Philosophy*, p. 18.

Chapter Three

1. Kwame Anthony Appiah, *In My Father's House: Africa in the Philosophy of Culture* (New York: Oxford University Press, 1992), p. 176.

2. G. W. F. Hegel, *The Philosophy of History*, trans. J. Sibree (New York: Dover Publications, 1956), p. 99.

3. Cheikh Anta Diop, *The African Origin of Civilization: Myth or Reality?* (New York: Lawrence Hill & Company, 1974), p. 4.

4. John Reed and Clive Wake, "Introduction," Léopold Sédar Senghor, *Prose and Poetry*, trans. John Reed and Clive Wake (London: Heinemann, 1976), p. 10.

5. Aimé Césaire, *Return to My Native Land*, trans. John Berger and Anna Bostock (Baltimore: Penguin Books, 1969), p. 75.

6. Appiah, *In My Father's House*, p. 41.

7. Lucius Outlaw, "Philosophy, Ethnicity, and Race," *I Am Because We Are*, ed. Fred Lee Hord and Jonathan Scott Lee (Amherst, Mass.: University of Massachusetts Press, 1995), p. 325.

8. *Ibid.*, p. 315.

9. W. E. B. Du Bois, "The Conservation of Races," *W. E. B. Du Bois: A Reader*, ed. David L. Lewis (New York: Henry Holt and Company, 1995), p. 22.

10. Léopold Sédar Senghor, "Constructive Elements of a Civilization of African Negro Inspiration," *Présence Africaine*, 24–25 (1959), p. 264.

11. *Ibid.*

12. *Ibid.*

13. *Ibid.*, p. 268.

14. Senghor, *Prose and Poetry*, p. 50.

15. Abiola Irele, *The African Experience in Literature and Ideology* (Bloomington, Ind.: Indiana University Press, 1990), p.70.

16. Senghor, "Constructive Elements of a Civilization," p. 269.

17. Césaire, *Return to My Native Land*, p.86.

18. Léopold Sédar Senghor, "Negritude: A Humanism of the Twentieth Century," *I Am Because We Are*, ed. Fred Lee Hord and Jonathan Scott Lee (Amherst, Mass.: University of Massachusetts Press, 1995), p. 45.

19. Senghor, *Prose and Poetry*, p. 98.

20. Senghor, "Constructive Elements of a Civilization," p. 268.

21. Césaire, *Return to My Native Land*, p. 75.

22. Senghor, *Prose and Poetry*, p.43.

23. Senghor, "Constructive Elements of a Civilization," p. 282.

24. Senghor, *Prose and Poetry*, p. 34.

25. *Ibid*.

26. Jean-Paul Sartre, *Black Orpheus*, trans. S. W. Allen (Présence Africaine: Paris, 1963), p. 43.

27. Senghor, "Constructive Elements of a Civilization" p. 293.

28. Irele, *The African Experience in Literature and Ideology*, p. 83.

29. Christopher L. Miller, "Alioune Diop and the Unfinished Temple of Knowledge," *The Surreptitious Speech: Présence Africaine and the Politics of Otherness*, ed. V. Y. Mudimbe (Chicago: The University of Chicago Press, 1992), p. 429.

30. Léopold Sédar Senghor, "What Is Negritude?," *The Idea of Race*, ed. Robert Bernasconi and Tommy L. Lott (Indianapolis: Hackett Publishing Company, 2000), p. 138.

31. Abiola Irele, "In Praise of Alienation," *The Surreptitious Speech*, ed. Mudimbe, p. 213.

32. Senghor, *Prose and Poetry*, p.73.

33. Senghor, "Constructive Elements of a Civilization," p. 291.

34. Senghor, *Prose and Poetry*, p. 57.

35. See Claude Wauthier, *The Literature and Thought of Modern Africa* (Washington, D.C.: Three Continents Press, 1979), p. 177.

36. Aimé Césaire, "Culture and Colonisation," *Présence Africaine*, 8–10 (1956), p. 206.

37. Senghor, "Constructive Elements of a Civilization," p. 291.

38. *Ibid.*, p. 292.

39. Senghor, *Prose and Poetry*, p.49.

40. Senghor, "Negritude: A Humanism of the Twentieth Century," p. 48.

41. *Ibid.*, p. 51.

42. *Ibid.*, p.50.

43. Senghor, *Prose and Poetry*, p.70.

44. Senghor, "Constructive Elements of a Civilization," p. 290.

45. *Ibid.*, p. 290.

46. Irele, *The African Experience in Literature and Ideology*, p. 71.

47. Edward W. Blyden, *Christianity, Islam, and the Negro Race* (Edinburgh: Edinburgh University Press, 1967), p. 277.

48. Henri Bergson, *The Two Sources of Morality and Religion*, trans. R. Ashley Audra and Cloudesley Brereton (Notre Dame, Ind.: University of Notre Dame Press, 1986), p. 118.

49. *Ibid.*, p. 249.

50. Robert W. July, *The Origins of Modern African Thought* (New York: Frederick A. Praeger, Publishers, 1967), p. 475.

51. Senghor, *Prose and Poetry*, p. 52.

52. Léopold Sédar Senghor, "The Spirit of Civilisation or the Laws of African Negro Culture," *Présence Africaine*, 8–9–10 (1956), p. 51.

53. Césaire, "Culture and Colonisation," p. 132.

54. Aimé Césaire, "The Man of Culture and his Responsibilities," *Présence Africaine*, 24–25 (1959), p. 129.

55. Léopold Sédar Senghor, *The Foundations of "Africanité" or "Negritude" and "Arabité,"* trans. Mercer Cook (Paris: *Présence Africaine*, 1971), p. 83.

56. See Pierre Pradervand, *Listening to Africa* (New York: Frederick A. Praeger, Publishers, 1989), p. 200.

57. Melville J. Herskovits, *The Human Factor in Changing Africa* (London: Routledge & Kegan Paul, 1962), p. 4.

58. *Ibid.*, pp. 418–419.

59. Césaire, "Culture and Colonisation," p. 205.

60. Sartre, *Black Orpheus*, p. 60.

61. Bergson, *The Two Sources of Morality and Religion*, p. 271.

62. Senghor, *The Foundations of "Africanité" or "Negritude" and "Arabité,"* p. 37.

63. *Ibid.*

64. Senghor, "What Is Negritude?" p. 138.

65. Outlaw, "Philosophy, Ethnicity, and Race," p. 325.

66. *Ibid.*

67. *Ibid.*, p. 326.

68. John S. Mbiti, *African Religions and Philosophy* (New York: Frederick A. Praeger, Publishers, 1986), p. 14.

69. John S. Mbiti, *Introduction to African Religion* (New York: Frederick A. Praeger, Publishers, 1975), p. 14.

70. Mbiti, *African Religions and Philosophy*, p. 1.

71. *Ibid.*, pp.1–2.

72. *Ibid.*, p. 2.

73. *Ibid.*, p. 268.

74. *Ibid.*, p. 3.

75. *Ibid.*, p.15.

76. *Ibid.*, pp. 7–8.

77. *Ibid.*, p. 33.

78. D. A. Masolo, *African Philosophy in Search of Identity* (Bloomington, Ind.: Indiana University Press, 1994), p. 106.

79. Mbiti, *African Religions and Philosophy*, 70.

80. *Ibid.*, p. 10.

81. *Ibid.*, p. 16.

82. *Ibid.*, p. 269.

83. Masolo, *African Philosophy in Search of Identity*, p. 119.

84. Mbiti, *African Religions and Philosophy*, p.17.

85. *Ibid.*

86. *Ibid.*

87. Henri Bergson, *Creative Evolution*, trans. Arthur Mitchell (New York: Random House, 1944), p. 7.

88. Mbiti, *African Religions and Philosophy*, p. 17.

89. *Ibid.*

90. *Ibid.*, p. 19.
91. *Ibid.*, p. 19.
92. Theophilus Okere, *African Philosophy* (Lanham, Md.: University Press of America, 1983), p. 10.
93. Masolo, *African Philosophy in Search of Identity*, p. 109.
94. Mbiti, *African Religions and Philosophy*, p. 4.
95. *Ibid.*, p. 5.
96. *Ibid.*
97. *Ibid.*, p. 98.
98. *Ibid.*, p. 213.
99. *Ibid.*, p. 99.
100. *Ibid.*, p. 26.
101. Pradervand, *Listening to Africa*, p. 70.
102. Mbiti, *African Religions and Philosophy*, p. 218.
103. *Ibid.*, p. 219.
104. *Ibid.*, p. 28.
105. *Ibid.*, p. 222.

Chapter Four

1. Paulin J. Hountondji, *African Philosophy: Myth and Reality* (Bloomington, Ind.: Indiana University Press, 1983), p. 55.
2. *Ibid.*, pp. 55–56.
3. *Ibid.*, p. 66.
4. Marcien Towa, "Conditions for the Affirmation of a Modern African Philosophical Thought," *African Philosophy: The Essential Readings*, ed. Tsenay Serequeberhan (New York: Paragon House, 1991), p. 189.
5. Hountondji, *African Philosophy: Myth and Reality*, p. 98.
6. *Ibid.*, p. 45
7. *Ibid.*, p. 61.
8. *Ibid.*, p. 67.
9. *Ibid.*, p. 63.
10. *Ibid.*, p. 60.
11. Paulin J. Hountondji, "The Particular and the Universal," *African Philosophy: Selected Readings*, ed. Albert G. Mosley (Englewood Cliffs, N.J.: Prentice-Hall, 1995), p. 193.
12. Hountondji, *African Philosophy: Myth and Reality*, p. 69.
13. Hountondji, "The Particular and the Universal," p. 191.
14. Hountondji, *African Philosophy: Myth and Reality*, p. 53.
15. *Ibid.*
16. Hountondji, "The Particular and the Universal," p. 173.
17. Hountondji, *African Philosophy: Myth and Reality*, p. 61.
18. Towa, "Conditions for the Affirmation of a Modern African Philosophical Thought," p. 191.
19. Abiola Irele, "Introduction," Hountondji, *African Philosophy: Myth and Reality*, p. 26.
20. Kwame Gyekye, *An Essay on African Philosophical Thought* (New York: Cambridge University Press, 1987), p. 24.

21. *Ibid.*, p. 25.

22. Samuel Oluoch Imbo, *An Introduction to African Philosophy* (New York: Rowman & Littlefield Publishers, 1998), p. 87.

23. Lucius T. Outlaw, *On Race and Philosophy* (New York: Routledge, 1996), p. 72.

24. Henry Odera Oruka, "Sagacity in African Philosophy," *African Philosophy: The Essential Readings*, ed. Serequeberhan, p. 48.

25. *Ibid.*, p. 51.

26. Imbo, *An Introduction to African Philosophy*, p. 26.

27. Odera Oruka, "Sagacity in African Philosophy," p. 49.

28. D. A. Masolo, *African Philosophy in Search of Identity* (Bloomington, Ind.: Indiana University Press, 1994), p. 235.

29. Odera Oruka, "Sagacity in African Philosophy," p. 49.

30. *Ibid.*, p. 50.

31. Masolo, *African Philosophy in Search of Identity*, p. 244.

32. Peter O. Bodunrin, "The Question of African Philosophy," *African Philosophy: The Essential Readings*, ed. Serequeberhan, p. 72.

33. Masolo, *African Philosophy in Search of Identity*, p. 243.

34. Lansana Keita, "Contemporary African Philosophy: The Search for a Method," *African Philosophy: The Essential Readings*, ed. Serequeberhan, p. 139.

35. Frantz Fanon, *The Wretched of the Earth,* trans. Constance Farrington (New York: Grove Press, 1982), p. 210.

36. Frantz Fanon, *Black Skin White Masks*, trans. Charles Lam Markmann (New York: Grove Press, 1967), p. 16.

37. Georg Wilhelm Friedrich Hegel, *The Phenomenology of Mind*, trans. J. B. Baillie (New York: Humanities Press, 1971), p. 232.

38. *Ibid.*, p. 233.

39. *Ibid.*, p. 239.

40. *Ibid.*, p. 237.

41. D. A. Masolo, *African Philosophy in Search of Identity*, pp. 34–35.

42. Fanon, *Black Skin White Masks* p. 229.

43. Fanon, *The Wretched of the Earth*, p. 147.

44. Fanon, *Black Skin White Masks*, p. 30.

45. *Ibid.*, p. 231.

46. *Ibid.*, p.13.

47. Fanon, *The Wretched of the Earth*, p. 94.

48. Tsenay Serequeberhan, *The Hermeneutics of African Philosophy* (New York: Routledge, 1994), p. 71.

49. Abiola Irele, "Contemporary Thought in French Speaking Africa," *Africa and the West*, ed. Isaac James Mowoe and Richard Bjornson (New York: Greenwood Press, 1986), p.138.

50. Jean-Paul Sartre, "Preface," Fanon, *The Wretched of the Earth*, p. 21.

51. See Martin Green, *Gandhi: Voice of a New Age Revolution* (New York: Continuum, 1993), p. 230.

Chapter Five

1.   Cheikh Anta Diop, "The Birth of the 'Negro Myth'," *African Politics and Society*, ed. Irving Leonard Markovitz (New York: Free Press, 1970), p. 23.
2.   Jeffrey Crawford, "Cheikh Anta Diop, the 'Stolen legacy,' and Afrocentrism," *African Philosophy: Selected Readings*, ed. Albert G. Mosley (Englewood Cliffs, N.J.: Prentice-Hall, 1995), p. 129.
3.   Cheikh Anta Diop, *The African Origin of Civilization: Myth or Reality?* (New York: Lawrence Hill & Company, 1974), p. 4.
4.   *Ibid.*, p. xv.
5.   *Ibid.*, p. 1.
6.   See Cheikh Anta Diop, "*Existe-t-il une philosophie africaine?*," *Proceedings of the Seminar on African Philosophy*, ed. Claude Sumner (Addis Ababa: Chamber Printing House, 1980), p. 36.
7.   *Ibid.*, p. 30 (my translation).
8.   *Ibid.* (my translation).
9.   *Ibid.*, p. 36 (my translation).
10.   Cheikh Anta Diop, *The Cultural Unity of Negro Africa* (Paris: Présence Africaine, 1962), p. 7.
11.   Abiola Irele, "Contemporary Thought in French Speaking Africa," *Africa and the West*, ed. Isaac James Mowoe and Richard Bjornson (New York: Greenwood Press, 1986), p. 133.
12.   Cheikh Anta Diop, "African Cultural Unity," *Présence Africaine*, 24–25 (1959), pp. 68, 71.
13.   Diop, *The African Origin of Civilization*, p. 23.
14.   Diop, *The Cultural Unity of Negro Africa*, p. 183.
15.   Claude Wauthier, *The Literature and Thought of Modern Africa* (Washington, D.C.: Three Continents Press, 1979), pp. 91–92.
16.   Diop, "The Birth of the 'Negro Myth'," p. 22.
17.   See Wauthier, *The Literature and Thought of Modern Africa*, p. 85.
18.   *Ibid.*, p. 86.
19.   Samuel Oluoch Imbo, *An Introduction to African Philosophy* (New York: Rowman & Littlefield Publishers, 1998), p. 59.
20.   Mamadou Diouf and Mohamad Mbodj, "The Shadow of Cheikh Anta Diop," *The Surreptitious Speech: Présence Africaine and the Politics of Otherness*, ed. V. Y. Mudimbe (Chicago: The University of Chicago Press, 1992), p. 128.
21.   V. Y. Mudimbe, *The Invention of Africa* (Bloomington, Ind.: Indiana University Press, 1988), p. 97.
22.   Diop, *The African Origin of Civilization*, p. xiii.
23.   Kwame Anthony Appiah, *In My Father's House: Africa in the Philosophy of Culture* (New York: Oxford University Press, 1992), p. 101.
24.   Kwasi Wiredu, *Cultural Universals and Particulars* (Bloomington, Ind.: Indiana University Press, 1996), p. 115.
25.   Kwasi Wiredu, "How Not to Compare African Thought with Western Thought," *African Philosophy*, ed. Richard A. Wright (Lanham, Md.: University Press of America, 1984), p. 150.
26.   *Ibid.*, p. 153.
27.   *Ibid.*, p. 149.

28. *Ibid.*, p. 153.
29. Wiredu, *Cultural Universals and Particulars*, p. 1.
30. Appiah, *In My Father's House*, p. 95.
31. D. A. Masolo, *African Philosophy in Search of Identity* (Bloomington, Ind.: Indiana University Press, 1994), pp. 204–205.
32. Wiredu, *Cultural Universals and Particulars*, p. 1.
33. *Ibid.*
34. *Ibid.*
35. *Ibid.*, p. 46.
36. *Ibid.*, p. 30.
37. *Ibid.*, p. 113.
38. Kwasi Wiredu, "Problems in Africa's Self-Definition in the Contemporary World," *Person and Community*, ed. Kwame Gyekye and Kwasi Wiredu (Washington, D.C.: The Council for Research in Values and Philosophy, 1992), p. 65.
39. *Ibid.*, p. 66.
40. *Ibid.*
41. Wiredu, "How Not to Compare African Thought with Western Thought," p. 151.
42. Wiredu, *Cultural Universals and Particulars*, p. 35.
43. Immanuel Kant, *Critique of Pure Reason*, trans. Norman Kemp Smith (New York: St. Martin's Press, 1965), p. 29.
44. Theophilus Okere, *African Philosophy* (Lanham, Md.: University Press of America, 1983), pp. ii–iii.
45. Imbo, *An Introduction to African Philosophy*, p. 27.
46. Tsenay Serequeberhan, *The Hermeneutics of African Philosophy* (New York: Routledge, 1994), p. 7.
47. *Ibid.*, p. 6.
48. *Ibid.*, p. 5.
49. *Ibid.*, p. 6.
50. *Ibid.*, p. 22.
51. *Ibid.*, p. 16.
52. *Ibid.*, p. 23.
53. Mudimbe, *The Invention of Africa*, p. 185.
54. Manthia Diawara, "Reading Africa through Foucault: V. Y. Mudimbe's Re-Affirmation of the Subject," *Quest*, 4:1 (June 1990), p. 82.
55. Mudimbe, *The Invention of Africa*, p. 37.
56. *Ibid.*, p. 20.
57. Masolo, *African Philosophy in Search of Identity*, p. 179.
58. Henri Maurier, "Do We Have an African Philosophy?" *African Philosophy*, ed. Richard A. Wright (Lanham, Md.: University Press of America, 1984), p. 25.
59. V. Y. Mudimbe, *The Idea of Africa* (Bloomington, Ind.: Indiana University Press, 1994), p. xv.
60. *Ibid.*, p. xiv.
61. Mudimbe, *The Invention of Africa*, p. 3.
62. Manthia Diawara, "A Dialogue on *Présence Africaine*," *The Surreptitious Speech*, ed. Mudimbe, p. 384.
63. Mudimbe, *The Invention of Africa*, p. 189.
64. Masolo, *African Philosophy in Search of Identity*, p. 179.

65. Jean-Paul Sartre, *Black Orpheus*, trans. S. W. Allen (Paris: Présence Africaine, 1963), p. 15.

66. Masolo, *African Philosophy in Search of Identity*, p. 185.

67. Sartre, *Black Orpheus*, p. 39.

Chapter Six

1. Paulin J. Hountondji, *African Philosophy: Myth and Reality* (Bloomington, Ind.: Indiana University Press, 1983), p. 59.

2. Marcien Towa, *Essai sur la problématique philosophique dans l'Afrique actuelle* (Yaoundé, Cameroon: Editions Clé, 1971), p. 32 (my translation).

3. Kofi Buenor Hadjor, *Africa in an Era of Crisis* (Trenton, N.J.: Africa World Press, 1990), p. 12.

4. Paulin J. Hountondji, "The Particular and the Universal," *African Philosophy: Selected Readings*, ed. Albert G. Mosley (Englewood Cliffs, N.J.: Prentice-Hall, 1995), p. 191.

5. Abiola Irele, "In Praise of Alienation," *The Surreptitious Speech: Présence Africaine and the Politics of Otherness*, ed. V. Y. Mudimbe (Chicago: The University of Chicago Press, 1992), pp. 208–209.

6. *Ibid.*, p. 207.

7. See D. A. Masolo, *African Philosophy in Search of Identity* (Bloomington, Ind.: Indiana University Press, 1994), p. 167.

8. Georg Wilhelm Friedrich Hegel, *The Philosophy of History*, trans. J. Sibree (New York: Dover Publications, 1956), pp. 54–55.

9. David Carney, *Soul of Darkness* (New York: Adastra, Ltd, 1991), p. 67.

10. Friedrich Engels, *Socialism: Utopian and Scientific*, trans. Edward Aveling (New York: International Publishers, 1935), p. 75.

11. Plato, *Meno*, trans. W. K. C. Guthrie, in *The Collected Dialogues of Plato*, ed. Edith Hamilton and Huntington Cairns (Princeton, N.J.: Princeton University Press, 1978), p. 364.

12. Carney, *Soul of Darkness*, p. 64.

13. *Ibid.*, p. 63.

14. Robert W. July, *The Origins of Modern African Thought* (New York: Frederick A. Praeger, Publishers, 1967), p. 254.

15. Peter F. Sugar, "From Ethnicity to Nationalism and Back Again," *Nationalism*, ed. Michael Palumbo and William O. Shanahan (Westport, Conn.: Greenwood Press, 1981), p. 68.

16. July, *The Origins of Modern African Thought*, p. 255.

17. Oyeka Owomoyela, "Africa and the Imperative of Philosophy: A Skeptical Consideration," *African Philosophy: The Essential Readings*, ed. Tsenay Serequeberhan (New York: Paragon House, 1991), p. 178.

18. Kwame Anthony Appiah, *In My Father's House: Africa in the Philosophy of Culture* (New York: Oxford University Press, 1992), p. 144.

19. V. Y. Mudimbe, *The Invention of Africa* (Bloomington, Ind.: Indiana University Press, 1988), p. 185.

20. *Ibid.*, p. 192.

21. Appiah, *In My Father's House*, p. 145.

22. *Ibid.*, p. 107.

23. *Ibid.*, p. 176.

24. *Ibid.*

25. *Ibid.*, p. 32.

26. *Ibid.*, p. 175.

27. Lilyan Kesteloot, "A Dialogue on *Présence Africaine*," *The Surreptitious Speech*, ed. Mudimbe, p. 389.

28. Michael Paul Gallagher, *Clashing Symbols: An Introduction to Faith and Culture* (New York: Paulist Press, 1998), p. 88.

29. V. Y. Mudimbe, *The Idea of Africa* (Bloomington, Ind.: Indiana University Press, 1994), p. 69.

30. Appiah, *In My Father's House*, p. 106.

31. Henri Bergson, *The Two Sources of Morality and Religion*, trans. R. Ashley Audra and Cloudesley Brereton (Notre Dame, Ind.: University of Notre Dame Press, 1986), p. 211.

32. Janheinz Jahn, *Muntu: An Outline of Neo-African Culture* (London: Faber and Faber Limited, 1961), p. 17.

33. Karl Marx and Friedrich Engels, *The German Ideology*, ed. R. Pascal (New York: International Publishers, 1965), p. 15.

34. *Ibid.*

35. Friedrich Engels, "Letters on Historical Materialism," *Basic Writings on Politics and Philosophy*, ed. Lewis S. Feuer (Garden City, N.Y.: Anchor Books, 1959), p. 408.

36. Marx and Engels, *The German Ideology*, p. 197.

37. Immanuel Kant, *Critique of Pure Reason*, trans. Norman Kemp Smith (New York: St. Martin's Press, 1965), p. 20.

38. *Ibid.*, p. 46.

39. July, *The Origins of Modern African Thought*, p. 277.

40. Molefi Kete Asante, *Afrocentricity* (Trenton, N.J.: Africa World Press, 1991), p. 1.

41. Aziz Al-Azmeh, "The Discourse of Authenticity: Islamist Revivalism and Enlightenment Universalism," *Culture and Modernity*, ed. Eliot Deutsch (Honolulu: University of Hawaii Press, 1991), p. 474.

42. *Ibid.*, p. 476.

43. Abiola Irele, *The African Experience in Literature and Ideology* (London: Heinemann, 1981), p. 113.

44. *Ibid.*

45. See Mudimbe, *The Invention of Africa*, p. 62.

46. Tsenay Serequeberhan, "African Philosophy: The Point in Question," *African Philosophy: The Essential Readings*, ed. Serequeberhan, p. 19.

47. Cheikh Anta Diop, *The African Origin of Civilization: Myth or Reality?* (New York: Lawrence Hill & Company, 1974), p. xv.

48. *Ibid.*, p. xiv.

49. Asante, *Afrocentricity*, p. x.

50. J. K. Nyerere, *Ujamaa—Essays on Socialism* (London: Oxford University Press, 1971), p. 8.

51. Léopold Sédar Senghor, "On African Homelands and Nation-States, Negritude, Assimilation, and African Socialism," *African Philosophy*, ed. English

Parker and Kibujjo M. Kalumba (Upper Saddle River, N.J.: Prentice-Hall, 1996), p. 49.

Chapter Seven

1. Placide Tempels, *Bantu Philosophy*, trans. A. Rubbens (Paris: Présence Africaine, 1952), p. 20.
2. *Ibid.*, p. 117.
3. *Ibid.*, p. 118.
4. *Ibid.*
5. *Ibid.*, p. 116.
6. Basil Davidson, *Let Freedom Come* (Boston: Atlantic Monthly Press Book, 1978), p. 298.
7. Paulin J. Hountondji, "The Particular and the Universal," *African Philosophy: Selected Readings*, ed. Albert Mosley (Englewood Cliffs, N.J.: Prentice-Hall, 1995), p. 182.
8. *Ibid.*, p. 189.
9. Bruce J. Berman, "African Capitalism and the Paradigm of Modernity: Culture, Technology, and the State," *African Capitalists in African Development*, ed. Bruce Berman and Colin Leys (Boulder, Colo.: Lynne Reinner Publishers, 1994), p. 237.
10. V. Y. Mudimbe, *The Invention of Africa* (Bloomington, Ind.: Indiana University Press, 1988), p. 160.
11. *Ibid.*, p. 49.
12. *Ibid.*
13. *Ibid.*
14. Niamkey Koffi, *"L'impensé de Towa et de Hountondji,"* Proceedings of the Seminar on African Philosophy, ed. Claude Sumner (Addis Ababa: Chamber Printing House, 1980), p. 167 (my translation).
15. *Ibid.*, p. 173 (my translation).
16. *Ibid.*, p. 195 (my translation).
17. Niamkey Koffi and Toure Abdou, *"Controverses sur l'existence d'une philosophie africaine,"* Proceedings of the Seminar on African Philosophy, ed. Sumner, p. 213 (my translation).
18. Davidson, *Let Freedom Come*, p. 148.
19. Berman, "African Capitalism and the Paradigm of Modernity: Culture, Technology, and the State," pp. 250–251.
20. P. O. Bodunrin, "the Question of African Philosophy," *African Philosophy: The Essential Readings*, ed. Tsenay Serequeberhan (New York: Paragon House, 1991), p. 67.
21. F. Eboussi-Boulaga, *La Crise du Muntu* (Paris: Présence Africaine, 1977), p. 8 (my translation).
22. Paulin J. Hountondji, *African Philosophy: Myth and Reality* (Bloomington, Ind.: Indiana University Press, 1983), p. 174.
23. *Ibid.*, p. 60.
24. *Ibid.*, p. 61.
25. J. K. Nyerere, *Ujamaa—Essays on Socialism* (London: Oxford University Press, 1971), p. 12.

26. Kwame Nkrumah, *Consciencism* (New York: Monthly Review Press, 1964), pp. 104–105.

27. Frantz Fanon, *The Wretched of the Earth,* trans. Constance Farrington (New York: Grove Press, 1982), p. 211.

28. *Ibid.,* p. 212.

29. See Rupert Emerson, "Pan-Africanism," *African Politics and Society,* ed. Irving Leonard Markovitz (New York: Free Press, 1970), p. 458.

30. Fanon, *The Wretched of the Earth,* p. 214.

31. *Ibid.,* p. 158.

32. *Ibid.,* pp. 163–164.

33. *Ibid.,* p. 94.

34. Shaheen Mozaffar, "The Institutional Logic of Ethnic Politics: A Prologomenon," *Ethnic Conflict and Democratization in Africa,* ed. Harvey Glickman (Atlanta, Georgia: African Studies Association Press, 1995), p. 37.

35. Nkrumah, *Consciencism,* pp. 100–101.

36. D. A. Masolo, *African Philosophy in Search of Identity* (Bloomington, Ind.: Indiana University Press, 1994), pp. 36–37.

37. Plato, *The Republic,* trans. Desmond Lee (New York: Penguin Books, 1987), p. 263.

38. Daniel Chirot, *Modern Tyrants* (Princeton, N.J.: Princeton University Press, 1996), pp. 16–17.

39. V. I. Lenin, "What Is To Be Done?" in *Selected Works,* vol. 2, ed. J. Fineberg (New York: International Publishers, 1955), p. 53.

40. Patrick Chabal, *Amilcar Cabral* (New York: Cambridge University Press, 1983), p. 178.

41. Amilcar Cabral, *Revolution in Guinea* (New York: Monthly Review Press, 1972), p. 110.

42. V. I. Lenin, *Imperialism the Highest Stage of Capitalism* (New York: International Publishers, 1972), p. 99.

43. Chirot, *Modern Tyrants,* p. 22.

44. See *ibid.,* pp. 373–390; and Thomas E. O' Toole, "Jean-Bedel Bokassa: Neo-Napoleon or Traditional African Ruler," *The Cult of Power,* ed. Joseph Held (New York: Columbia University Press, 1983).

Chapter Eight

1. Abiola Irele, *The African Experience in Literature and Ideology* (London: Heinemann, 1981), p. 84.

2. Kwame Gyekye, *Tradition and Modernity* (New York: Oxford University Press, 1997), p. 235.

3. Kwame Anthony Appiah, *In My Father's House: Africa in the Philosophy of Culture* (New York: Oxford University Press, 1992), p. 105.

4. *Ibid.,* p. 171.

5. Francis Mading Deng, "Cultural Dimensions of Conflict Management and Development: Some Lessons from the Sudan," *Culture and Development in Africa,* ed. Ismail Serageldin and June Taboroff (Washington, D.C.: The International Bank, 1994), p. 508.

6. Crawford Young, "The Dialectics of Cultural Pluralism: Concept and Reality," *The Rising Tide of Cultural Pluralism*, ed. Crawford Young (Madison, Wisconsin: University of Wisconsin Press, 1993), pp. 29–30.

7. Robert Bates, *Ethnicity in Contemporary Africa* (Syracuse, N. Y.: Syracuse University Press, 1973), p. 2.

8. Bruce J. Berman, "African Capitalism and the Paradigm of Modernity: Culture, Technology, and the State," *African Capitalists in African Development*, ed. Bruce J. Berman and Colin Leys (Boulder, Colo.: Lynne Rienner Publishers, 1994), p. 236.

9. George Dalton, "Introduction," *Economic Development and Social Change*, ed. George Dalton (Garden City, N.Y.: Natural History Press, 1971), pp. 25–26.

10. Alfred Schutz, "The Social World and the Theory of Social Action," *Philosophical Problems of the Social Sciences*, ed. David Braybrooke (New York: Macmillan Company, 1965), p. 56.

11. Thierry G. Verhelst, *No Life without Roots* (London: Zed Books, Ltd, 1990), pp. 19, 22.

12. Carl J. Friedrich, "Some Reflections on Constitutionalism for Emergent Political Orders," *Patterns of African Development*, ed. Herbert J. Spiro (Englewood Cliffs, N.J.: Prentice-Hall, 1967), p. 19.

13. John Lliffe, *The Emergence of African Capitalism* (Minneapolis: University of Minnesota Press, p. 21.

14. Pierre. L. Van den Berghe, *The Ethnic Phenomenon* (New York: Elsevier, 1981), p. 27.

15. Richard H. Thompson, *Theories of Ethnicity* (New York: Greenwood Press, 1989), p. 37.

16. Young, "The Dialectics of Cultural Pluralism," p. 23.

17. Van den Berghe, *The Ethnic Phenomenon*, pp. 16–17.

18. Richard Rosecrance, *The Rise of the Trading State* (New York: Basic Books, 1986), p. 226.

19. David Hume, *A Treatise of Human Nature*, ed. L. A. Selby-Bigge (Oxford: Clarendon Press, 1960), pp. 414–415.

20. Thompson, *Theories of Ethnicity*, p. 4.

21. Young, "The Dialectics of Cultural Pluralism," p. 22.

22. See Benedict Anderson, *Imagined Communities* (New York: Verso, 1991).

23. Young, "The Dialectics of Cultural Pluralism," p. 24.

24. Harvey Glickman, "Issues in the Analysis of Ethnic Conflict and Democratization Processes in Africa Today," *Ethnic Conflict and Democratization in Africa*, ed. Harvey Glickman (Atlanta, Georgia: African Studies Association Press, 1995), p. 3.

25. Harvey Glickman, "Conclusion: Managing Democratic Ethnic Competition," *Ethnic Conflict and Democratization in Africa*, ed. Glickman, p. 402.

26. *Ibid.*, pp. 27–28.

27. Shaheen Mozaffar, "The Institutional Logic of Ethnic Politics: A Prologomenon," *Ethnic Conflict and Democratization in Africa*, ed. Glickman, p. 61.

28. Glickman, "Issues in the Analysis of Ethnic Conflict and Democratization Processes in Africa Today," p. 4.

29. Karl Marx and Friedrich Engels, *The Communist Manifesto*, ed. Joseph Katz (New York: Washington Square Press, 1964), p. 95.

30. Friedrich Engels, "Letters on Historical Materialism," *Basic Writings on Politics and Philosophy*, ed. Lewis S. Feuer (New York: Anchor Books, 1959), p. 408.

31. Karl Marx and Friedrich Engels, *The German Ideology*, ed. R. Pascal (New York: International Publishers, 1965), p. 15.

32. Kofi Buenor Hadjor, *On Transforming Africa* (Trenton, N.J.: Africa World Press, 1987), p. 66.

33. Georg Wilhelm Friedrich Hegel, *Hegel's Philosophy of Right*, trans. T. M. Knox (New York: Oxford University Press, 1967), pp. 155–156.

34. Marx and Engels, *The Communist Manifesto*, p. 61.

35. Claude E. Welch, Jr., "The Challenge of Change: Japan and Africa," *Patterns of African Development*, ed. Spiro, p. 76.

36. Leonard Tivey, "Introduction," *The Nation-State*, ed. Leonard Tivey (New York: St. Martin's Press, 1981), p. 3.

37. Jean-Jacques Rousseau, *The Basic Political Writings*, trans and ed. Donald A. Cress (Indianapolis: Hackett Publishing Company, 1987), p. 148.

38. Thomas Hobbes, *Leviathan* (New York: Oxford University Press, 1996), p. 114.

39. Carnes Lord, "Aristotle," *History of Political Philosophy*, ed. Leo Strauss and Joseph Cropsey (Chicago: The University of Chicago Press, 1995), p. 147.

40. See Plato, *The Republic*, trans. Desmond Lee (New York: Penguin Books, 1974), p. 203.

41. Peter F. Sugar, "From Ethnicity to Nationalism and Back Again," *Nationalism*, ed. Michael Palumbo and William O. Shanahan (Westport, Connecticut: Greenwood Press, 1981), p. 80.

42. Lawrence Cockcroft, *Africa's Way: A Journey from the Past* (London: I. B. Tauris & Co. Ltd., 1990), p. 99.

43. James S. Coleman, "Nationalism in Tropical Africa," *The American Political Science Review* 1: 2 (June 1954), p. 419.

44. Aristotle, *On Man in the Universe*, ed. Louise Ropes Loomis (New York: Gramercy Books, 1971), p. 252.

45. Henri Bergson, *The Two Sources of Morality and Religion*, trans. R. Ashley Audra and Cloudesley Brereton (Notre Dame, Ind.: University of Notre Dame Press, 1986), p. 266.

46. *Ibid.*, p. 275.

47. *Ibid.*, p. 276.

48. *Ibid.*, p. 274.

49. *Ibid.*, p. 271.

50. *Ibid.*, pp. 276.

51. *Ibid.*, pp. 276–277.

52. *Ibid.*, p. 277.

53. Gyekye, *Tradition and Modernity*, p. 114.

54. *Ibid.*, p. 90.

55. Bergson, *Two Sources of Morality and Religion*, p. 103.

56. *Ibid.*, p. 282.

57. Rousseau, *The Basic Political Writings*, p. 142.

58. Léopold Sédar Senghor, *Prose and Poetry*, trans. John Reed and Clive Wake (London: Heinemann, 1976), p. 66.

59. *Ibid.*, p. 68.

60. *Ibid.*, p. 69.

Chapter Nine

1. Maurice Delafosse, *The Negroes of Africa*, trans. F. Fligelman (Port Washington, N. Y.: Kennikat Press, 1968), p. xxx.
2. *Ibid.*, p. 279.
3. André Gunder Frank, *Capitalism and Underdevelopment in Latin America* (New York: Monthly Review Press, 1969), p. 94.
4. Henri Bergson, *Creative Evolution*, trans. Arthur Mitchell (New York: Random House, 1944), p. 130.
5. Edward W. Blyden, *Christianity, Islam and the Negro Race* (Edinburgh: Edinburgh University Press, 1967), p. 76.
6. Bert Hoselitz, *Sociological Aspects of Economic Growth* (Bombay: Vakils, Feffer and Simons Private Ltd., 1960), p. 19.
7. Bert Hoselitz, "The Use of Historical Comparison in the Study of Economic Development," *Social Development* (Paris: UNESCO, Mouton, 1965), p. 175.
8. Norman Long, *An Introduction to the Sociology of Rural Development* (London: Tavistock Publications, 1977), p. 59.
9. Karl Marx and Friedrich Engels, *The German Ideology*, ed. R. Pascal (New York: International Publishers, 1965), p. 14.
10. Henri Bergson, *The Two Sources of Morality and Religion*, trans. R. Ashley Audra and Cloudesley Brereton (Notre Dame, Ind.: Indiana University Press, 1986), p. 102.
11. Friedrich Engels, "Ludwig Feuerbach and the End of Classical German Philosophy," in *Basic Writings on Politics and Philosophy*, ed. Lewis S. Feuer (New York: Anchor Books, 1959), p. 207.
12. Bergson, *The Two Sources of Morality and Religion*, p. 122.
13. Marx and Engels, *The German Ideology*, p. 30.
14. *Ibid.*, p. 6.
15. Georg Wilhelm Friedrich Hegel, *The Philosophy of History*, trans. J. Sibree (New York: Dover Publications, 1956), p. 457.
16. Friedrich Nietzsche, *Daybreak*, trans. R. J. Hollingdale, (New York: The Macmillan Company, 1924), p. 197.
17. Friedrich Nietzsche, "The Birth of Tragedy," trans. Clifton P. Fadiman, in *The Philosophy of Nietzsche* (New York: Random House, 1954), p. 1077.
18. *Ibid.*
19. *Ibid.*, p. 1059.
20. Max Weber, *The Protestant Ethic and the Spirit of Capitalism* (New York: Charles Scribner's Sons, 1958), p. 53.
21. See *Addis Tribune* (18 April ·2003), Addis Ababa, Ethiopia, (www.addistribune.com)
22. Bergson, *The Two Sources of Morality and Religion*, p. 43.
23. Ali A. Mazrui, *Political Values and the Educated Class in Africa* (Berkeley, Calif.: University of California Press, 1978), p. 313.
24. *Ibid.*, p. 212.
25. Stanislav Andreski, *The African Predicament: A Study in the Pathology of Modernization* (New York: Atherton Press, 1968), p. 78.

BIBLIOGRAPHY

Al-Azmeh, Aziz. "The Discourse of Authenticity: Islamist Revivalism and Enlighten-ment Universalism." *Culture and Modernity*. Edited by Eliot Deutsch. Honolulu: University of Hawaii Press, 1991.

Andreski, Stanislav. *The African Predicament: A Study in the Pathology of Modernization*. New York: Atherton Press, 1968.

Appiah, Kwame Anthony. *In My Father's House: Africa in the Philosophy of Culture*. New York: Oxford University Press, 1992.

Aristotle. *Aristotle's Metaphysics*. Translated by Hippocrates G. Apostle. Grinnell, Ia.: Peripatetic Press, 1979.

————. *On Man in the Universe*. Edited by Louise Ropes Loomis. New York: Gramercy Books, 1971.

Asante, Molefi Kete. *Afrocentricity*. Trenton, N.J.: Africa World Press, 1991.

Bates, Robert. *Ethnicity in Contemporary Africa*. Syracuse, N. Y.: Syracuse University Press, 1973.

Benedict, Ruth. *Patterns of Culture*. Boston: Houghton Mifflin Company, 1959.

Bergson, Henri. *The Two Sources of Morality and Religion*. Translated by R. Ashley Audra and Cloudesley Brereton. Notre Dame, Ind.: University of Notre Dame Press, 1986.

————. *Creative Evolution*. Translated by Arthur Mitchell. New York: Random House, 1944.

Berkeley, George. *The Principles of Human Knowledge and Three Dialogues between Hylas and Philonous*. New York: Meridian Books, 1963.

Berman, Bruce J. "African Capitalism and the Paradigm of Modernity: Culture, Tech-nology, and the State." *African Capitalists in African Development*. Edited by Bruce J. Berman and Colin Leys. Boulder, Colo.: Lynne Reinner Publishers, 1994.

Blyden, Edward W. *Christianity, Islam, and the Negro Race*. Edinburgh: Edinburgh University Press, 1967.

Bodunrin, Peter O. "The Question of African Philosophy." *African Philosophy: The Essential Readings*. Edited by Tsenay Serequeberhan. New York: Paragon House, 1991.

Boulaga, F. Eboussi. *La Crise du Muntu*. Paris: Présence Africaine, 1977.

Broce, Gerald. *History of Anthropology*. Minneapolis: Burgess Publishing Company, 1973.

Cabral, Amilcar. *Revolution in Guinea*. New York: Monthly Review Press, 1972.

Carney, David. *Soul of Darkness*. New York: Adastra, Ltd, 1991.

Césaire, Aimé. *Return to My Native Land*. Translated by John Berger and Anna Bostock. Baltimore: Penguin Books, 1969.

————."The Man of Culture and His Responsibilities." *Présence Africaine*, 24–25 (1959), pp. 125–132.

————. "Culture and Colonisation." *Présence Africaine*, 8–10 (1956), pp. 193–207.

Chabal, Patrick. *Amilcar Cabral*. New York: Cambridge University Press, 1983.

Chirot, Daniel. *Modern Tyrants*. Princeton, N.J.: Princeton University Press, 1996.

Cockcroft, Lawrence. *Africa's Way: A Journey from the Past*. London: I. B. Tauris & Co. Ltd., 1990.

Coleman, James S. "Nationalism in Tropical Africa." *The American Political Science Review*, 1: 2 (June 1954), pp. 405–423.

Crawford, Jeffrey. "Cheikh Anta Diop, the 'Stolen legacy,' and Afrocentrism." *African Philosophy: Selected Readings*. Edited by Albert G. Mosley. Englewood Cliffs, N.J.: Prentice-Hall, 1995.

Dalton, George. "Introduction." *Economic Development and Social Change*. Edited by George Dalton. Garden City, N. Y.: Natural History Press, 1971.

Davidson, Basil. *Let Freedom Come*. Boston: Atlantic Monthly Press Book, 1978.

Delafosse, Maurice. *The Negroes of Africa*. Translated by F. Fligelman. Port Washington, N. Y.: Kennikat Press, 1968.

Deng, Francis Mading. "Cultural Dimensions of Conflict Management and Development: Some Lessons from the Sudan." *Culture and Development in Africa*. Edited by Ismail Serageldin and June Taboroff. Washington, D.C.: International Bank, 1994.

Diamond, Stanley. *In Search of the Primitive*. New Brunswick, N.J.: Transaction Books, 1974.

Diawara, Manthia. "A Dialogue on *Présence Africaine*." *The Surreptitious Speech: Présence Africaine and the Politics of Otherness*. Edited by V. Y. Mudimbe. Chicago: The University of Chicago Press, 1992.

————. "Reading Africa through Foucault: V. Y. Mudimbe's Re-Affirmation of the Subject." *Quest*, 4:1 (June 1990), pp. 76–87.

Diop, Cheikh Anta. *"Existe-t-il une philosophie africaine?"* *Proceedings of the Seminar on African Philosophy*. Edited by Claude Sumner. Addis Ababa: Chamber Printing House, 1980.

————. *The African Origin of Civilization: Myth or Reality?* New York: Lawrence Hill & Company, 1974.

————. "The Birth of the 'Negro Myth'." *African Politics and Society*. Edited by Irving Leonard Markovitz. New York: Free Press, 1970.

————. *The Cultural Unity of Negro Africa*. Paris: Présence Africaine, 1962.

————. "African Cultural Unity." *Presence Africaine*, 24–25 (1959), pp. 66–72.

Diouf, Mamadou, and Mohamad Mbodj. "The Shadow of Cheikh Anta Diop." *The Surreptitious Speech: Présence Africaine and the Politics of Otherness*. Edited by V. Y. Mudimbe. Chicago: The University of Chicago Press, 1992.

Du Bois, W. E. B. "The Conservation of Races." *W. E. B. Du Bois: A Reader*. Edited by David L. Lewis. New York: Henry Holt and Company, 1995.

Emerson, Rupert. "Pan-Africanism." *African Politics and Society*. Edited by Irving Leonard Markovitz. New York: Free Press, 1970.

Engels, Friedrich. *Herr Eugen Dühring's Revolution in Science*. Edited by C. P. Dutt. N. Y.: International Publishers, 1966.

————. *Basic Writings on Politics and Philosophy*. Edited by Lewis S. Feuer. Garden City, N.Y.: Anchor Books, 1959.

————. *Socialism: Utopian and Scientific*. Translated by Edward Aveling. New York: International Publishers, 1935.

Evans-Pritchard. E. E. *Theories of Primitive Religion*. Oxford: Oxford University Press, 1966.

Fanon, Frantz. *The Wretched of the Earth*. Translated by Constance Farrington. New York: Grove Press, 1982.

————. *Black Skin White Masks*. Translated by Charles Lam Markmann. New York: Grove Press, 1967.

Frank, André Gunder. *Capitalism and Underdevelopment in Latin America*. New York: Monthly Review Press, 1969.

Freud, Sigmund. *The Freud Reader*. Edited by Peter Gay. New York: W. W. Norton & Company, 1989.

Friedrich, Carl J. "Some Reflections on Constitutionalism for Emergent Political Orders." *Patterns of African Development*. Edited by Herbert J. Spiro. Englewood Cliffs, N.J.: Prentice-Hall, 1967.

Fries, Heinrich. *Revelation*. New York: Herder and Herder, 1969.

Gallagher, Michael Paul. *Clashing Symbols: An Introduction to Faith and Culture*. New York: Paulist Press, 1998.

Glickman, Harvey. "Conclusion: Managing Democratic Ethnic Competition." *Ethnic Conflict and Democratization in Africa*. Edited by Harvey Glickman. Atlanta, Georgia: African Studies Association Press, 1995.

————. "Issues in the Analysis of Ethnic Conflict and Democratization Processes in Africa Today." *Ethnic Conflict and Democratization in Africa*. Edited by Harvey Glickman. Atlanta, Georgia: African Studies Association Press, 1995.

Green, Martin. *Gandhi: Voice of a New Age Revolution*. New York: Continuum, 1993.

Gyekye, Kwame. *Tradition and Modernity*. New York: Oxford University Press, 1997.

————. *An Essay on African Philosophical Thought*. New York: Cambridge University Press, 1987.

Hadjor, Kofi Buenor. *Africa in an Era of Crisis*. Trenton, N.J.: Africa World Press, 1990.

————. *On Transforming Africa*. Trenton, N.J.: Africa World Press, 1987.

Hegel, Georg Wilhelm Friedrich. *The Phenomenology of Mind*. Translated by J. B. Baillie. New York: Humanities Press, 1971.

————. *Hegel's Philosophy of Right*. Translated by T. M. Knox. New York: Oxford University Press, 1967.

————. *The Philosophy of History*. Translated by J. Sibree. New York: Dover Publications, 1956.

Heidegger, Martin. "Letter on Humanism." *Basic Writings*. Edited by David F. Krell. New York: Harper & Row, Publishers, 1977.

————. *The Question Concerning Technology and Other Essays*. Translated by William Lovitt. New York: Harper & Row, Publishers, 1977.

Heraclitus. *The Presocratic Philosophers*. Edited by G. S. Kirk and J. E. Raven. Cambridge, England: Cambridge University Press, 1975.

Herskovits, Melville J. *The Human Factor in Changing Africa*. London: Routledge & Kegan Paul, 1962.

Hobbes, Thomas. *Leviathan*. New York: Oxford University Press, 1996.

Hoselitz, Bert. "The Use of Historical Comparison in the Study of Economic Development." *Social Development*. Paris: UNESCO, Mouton, 1965.

———. *Sociological Aspects of Economic Growth*. Bombay: Vakils, Feffer and Simons Private Ltd, 1960.

Hountondji, Paulin J. "The Particular and the Universal." *African Philosophy: Selected Readings*. Edited by Albert G. Mosley. Englewood Cliffs. N.J.: Prentice-Hall, 1995.

———. *African Philosophy: Myth and Reality*. Bloomington, Ind.: Indiana University Press, 1983.

Hume, David. *A Treatise of Human Nature*. Edited by L. A. Selby-Bigge. Oxford: Clarendon Press, 1960.

Imbo, Samuel Oluoch. *An Introduction to African Philosophy*. New York: Rowman & Littlefield Publishers, 1998.

Irele, Abiola. "In Praise of Alienation." *The Surreptitious Speech: Présence Africaine and the Politics of Otherness*. Edited by V. Y. Mudimbe. Chicago: University of Chicago Press, 1992.

———. *The African Experience in Literature and Ideology*. Bloomington, Ind.: Indiana University Press, 1990.

———. "Contemporary Thought in French Speaking Africa." *Africa and the West*. Edited by Isaac James Mowoe and Richard Bjornson. New York: Greenwood Press, 1986.

Jahn, Janheinz. *Muntu: An Outline of Neo-African Culture*. London: Faber and Faber, 1961.

Jean, Clinton M. *Behind the Eurocentric Veils*. Amherst, Mass.: University of Massachusetts Press, 1991.

July, Robert W. *The Origins of Modern African Thought*. New York: Frederick A. Praeger, Publishers, 1967.

Kant, Immanuel. *Critique of Pure Reason*. Translated by Norman Kemp Smith. New York: St. Martin's Press, 1965.

Keita, Lansana. "Contemporary African Philosophy: The Search for a Method." *African Philosophy: The Essential Readings*. Edited by Tsenay Serequeberhan. New York: Paragon House, 1991.

Kesteloot, Lilyan. "A Dialogue on *Présence Africaine.*" *The Surreptitious Speech: Présence Africaine and the Politics of Otherness*. Edited by V. Y. Mudimbe. Chicago: The University of Chicago Press, 1992.

Kierkegaard, Søren. *Kierkegaard's Concluding Unscientific Postscript*. Translated by David S. Swenson. Princeton, N.J.: Princeton University Press, 1964.

Koffi, Niamkey. "*L'impensé de Towa et de Hountondji.*" *Proceedings of the Seminar on African Philosophy*. Edited by Claude Sumner. Addis Ababa: Chamber Printing House, 1980.

Koffi, Niamkey, and Toure Abdou. "*Controverses sur l'existence d'une philosophie africaine.*" *Proceedings of the Seminar on African Philosophy*. Edited by Claude Sumner. Addis Ababa: Chamber Printing House, 1980.

Lenin, V. I. *Imperialism the Highest Stage of Capitalism*. New York: International Publishers, 1972.

———. "What Is To Be Done?" In *Selected Works*, vol. 2. Edited by J. Fineberg. New York: International Publishers, 1955.

Lévy-Bruhl, Lucien. *How Natives Think*. Translated by Lilian A. Claire. Princeton, N.J.: Princeton University Press, 1985.

Lliffe, John. *The Emergence of African Capitalism*. Minneapolis: University of Minnesota Press, 1983.

Long, Norman. *An Introduction to the Sociology of Rural Development*. London: Tavistock Publications, 1977.

Lord, Carnes. "Aristotle." *History of Political Philosophy*. Edited by Leo Strauss and Joseph Cropsey. Chicago: University of Chicago Press, 1995.

Marx, Karl, and Friedrich Engels. *The German Ideology*. Edited by R. Pascal. New York: International Publishers, 1965.

———. *The Communist Manifesto*. Edited by Joseph Katz. New York: Washington Square Press, 1964.

Masolo, D. A. *African Philosophy in Search of Identity*. Bloomington, Ind.: Indiana University Press, 1994.

Maurier, Henri. "Do We Have an African Philosophy?" *African Philosophy*. Edited by Richard A. Wright. Lanham, Md.: University Press of America, 1984.

Mazrui, Ali A. *Political Values and the Educated Class in Africa*. Berkeley, Calif.: University of California Press, 1978.

Mbiti, John S. *African Religions and Philosophy*. New York: Frederick A. Praeger, Publishers, 1986.

———. *Introduction to African Religion*. New York: Frederick A. Praeger, Publishers 1975.

Miller, Christopher L. "Alioune Diop and the Unfinished Temple of Knowledge." *The Surreptitious Speech: Présence Africaine and the Politics of Otherness*. Edited V. Y. Mudimbe. Chicago: University of Chicago Press, 1992.

Mozaffar, Shaheen. "The Institutional Logic of Ethnic Politics: A Prologomenon." *Ethnic Conflict and Democratization in Africa*. Edited by Harvey Glickman. Atlanta, Georgia: African Studies Association Press, 1995.

Mudimbe, V. Y. *The Idea of Africa*. Bloomington, Ind.: Indiana University Press, 1994.

———. *The Invention of Africa*. Bloomington, Ind.: Indiana University Press, 1988.

Nietzsche, Friedrich. *Daybreak*. Translated by R. J. Hollingdale. New York: Cambridge University Press, 1982.

———. *The Twilight of the Idols*. Translated by Anthony M. Ludovici. New York: Russel & Russel, 1964.

———. *Beyond Good and Evil*. Translated by Helen Zimmern. In *The Philosophy of Nietzsche*. New York: Random House, 1954.

———. *The Genealogy of Morals*. Translated by Horace B. Samuel. In *The Philosophy of Nietzsche*. New York: Random House, 1954.

———. *The Birth of Tragedy*. Translated by Clifton P. Fadiman. In *The Philosophy of Nietzsche*. New York: Random House, 1954.

Nkrumah, Kwame. *Consciencism*. New York: Monthly Review Press, 1964.

Nyerere, J. K. *Ujamaa—Essays on Socialism*. London: Oxford University Press, 1971.

Odera Oruka, Henry. "Sagacity in African Philosophy." *African Philosophy: The Essential Readings*. Edited by Tsenay Serequeberhan. New York: Paragon House, 1991.

Okere, Theophilus. *African Philosophy*. Lanham, Md.: University Press of America, 1983.

O'Toole, Thomas E. "Jean-Bedel Bokassa: Neo-Napoleon or Traditional African Ruler." *The Cult of Power*. Edited by Joseph Held. New York: Columbia University Press, 1983.

Outlaw, Lucius T. *On Race and Philosophy*. New York: Routledge, 1996.

———. "Philosophy, Ethnicity, and Race." *I Am Because We Are*. Edited by Fred Lee Hord and Jonathan Scott Lee. Amherst, Mass.: University of Massachusetts Press, 1995.

Owomoyela, Oyeka. "Africa and the Imperative of Philosophy: A Skeptical Consideration." *African Philosophy: The Essential Readings*. Edited by Tsenay Serequeberhan. New York: Paragon House, 1991.

Pascal, Blaise. *Pascal's Pensées*. Translated by H. F. Stewart. New York: Pantheon Books, 1950.

Plato, *The Republic*. Translated by Desmond Lee. New York: Penguin Books, 1987.

———. *Meno*. In *The Collected Dialogues of Plato*. Edited by Edith Hamilton and Huntington Cairns. Princeton, N.J.: Princeton University Press, 1978.

Pradervand, Pierre. *Listening to Africa*. New York: Frederick A. Praeger, Publishers, 1989.

Reed, John, and Clive Wake. "Introduction." Léopold Sédar Senghor. *Prose and Poetry*. London: Heinemann, 1976.

Rorty, Richard. "Philosophers, Novelists, and Intercultural Comparisons: Heidegger, Kundera, and Dickens." *Culture and Modernity*. Edited by Eliot Deutsch. Honolulu: University of Hawaii Press, 1991.

Rosecrance, Richard. *The Rise of the Trading State*. New York: Basic Books, 1986.

Rousseau, Jean-Jacques. *The Basic Political Writings*. Translated and edited by Donald A. Cress. Indianapolis: Hackett Publishing Company, 1987.

———. *The First and Second Discourses and Essay on the Origin of Languages*. Edited and translated by Victor Gourevitch. New York: Harper & Row, Publishers, 1986.

Sartre, Jean-Paul. "Preface." Frantz Fanon. *The Wretched of the Earth*. Translated by Constance Farrington. New York: Grove Press, 1982.

———. *Black Orpheus*. Translated by S. W. Allen. Paris: Présence Africaine, 1963.

———. *Existentialism and Human Emotions*. Translated by Hazel E. Barnes. New York: Philosophical Library, 1957.

Schopenhauer, Arthur. *The World as Will and Representation*, vol. 1. Translated by E. F. J. Payne. New York: Dover Publications, 1969.

Schutz, Alfred. "The Social World and the Theory of Social Action." *Philosophical Problems of the Social Sciences*. Edited by David Braybrooke. New York: Macmillan, 1965.

Senghor, Léopold Sédar. "What Is Negritude?" *The Idea of Race*. Edited by Robert Bernasconi and Tommy L. Lott. Indianapolis: Hackett Publishing Company, 2000.

———."On African Homelands and Nation-States, Negritude, Assimilation, and African Socialism." *African Philosophy*. Edited by English Parker and Kibujjo M. Kalumba. Upper Saddle River, N.J.: Prentice-Hall, 1996.

———. "Negritude: A Humanism of the Twentieth Century." *I Am Because We Are*. Edited by Fred Lee Hord and Jonathan Scott Lee. Amherst, Mass.: University of Massachusetts Press, 1995.

———. "On Negrohood: Psychology of the African Negro." *African Philosophy: Selected Readings*. Edited by Albert Mosley. Englewood Cliffs, N.J.: Prentice-Hall, 1995.

———. *Prose and Poetry*. Translated by John Reed and Clive Wake. London: Heinemann, 1976.

———. *The Foundations of "Africanité" or "Negritude" and "Arabité."* Translated by Mercer Cook. Paris: Présence Africaine, 1971.

———. "Constructive Elements of a Civilization of African Negro Inspiration." *Présence Africaine*, 24–25 (1959), pp. 262–294.

———. "The Spirit of Civilisation or the Laws of African Negro Culture." *Présence Africaine*, 8–10 (1956), pp. 51–64.

Serequeberhan, Tsenay. *The Hermeneutics of African Philosophy*. New York: Routledge, 1994.

———. "African Philosophy: The Point in Question." *African Philosophy: The Essential Readings*. Edited by Tsenay Serequeberhan. New York: Paragon House, 1991.

Shorter, Aylward. *Revelation and Its Interpretation*. London: Geoffrey Chapman, 1983.

Smith, Gordon Hedderly. *The Missionary and Anthropology*. Chicago: Moody Press, 1945.

Sugar, Peter F. "From Ethnicity to Nationalism and Back Again." *Nationalism.* Edited by Michael Palumbo and William O. Shanahan. Westport, Conn.: Greenwood Press, 1981.

Tempels, Placide. *Bantu Philosophy.* Translated by A. Rubbens. Paris: Présence Africaine, 1969.

Thompson, Richard H. *Theories of Ethnicity.* New York: Greenwood Press, 1989.

Tivey, Leonard. "Introduction." *The Nation-State.* Edited by Leonard Tivey. New York: St. Martin's Press, 1981.

Towa, Marcien. "Conditions for the Affirmation of a Modern African Philosophical Thought." *African Philosophy: The Essential Readings.* Edited by Tsenay Serequeberhan. New York: Paragon House, 1991.

———. *Essai sur la problématique philosophique dans l'Afrique actuelle.* Yaoundé, Cameroon: Editions Clé, 1971.

Van den Berghe, Pierre L. *The Ethnic Phenomenon.* New York: Elsevier, 1981.

Verhelst, Thierry G. *No Life without Roots.* London: Zed Books, 1990.

Wauthier, Claude. *The Literature and Thought of Modern Africa.* Washington, D. C.: Three Continents Press, 1979.

Welch, Claude E. "The Challenge of Change: Japan and Africa." *Patterns of African Development.* Edited by Herbert J. Spiro. Englewood Cliffs, N.J.: Prentice-Hall, 1967.

Wiggins, James B. *In Praise of Religious Diversity.* New York: Routledge, 1996.

Wiredu, Kwasi. *Cultural Universals and Particulars.* Bloomington, Ind.: Indiana University Press, 1996.

———. "Problems in Africa's Self-Definition in the Contemporary World." *Person and Community.* Edited by Kwame Gyekye and Kwasi Wiredu. Washington, D.C.: Council for Research in Values and Philosophy, 1992.

———. "How Not to Compare African Thought with Western Thought." *African Philosophy.* Edited by Richard A. Wright. Lanham, Md.: University Press of America, 1984.

Young, Crawford. "The Dialectics of Cultural Pluralism: Concept and Reality." *The Rising Tide of Cultural Pluralism.* Edited by Crawford Young. Madison, Wis.: University of Wisconsin Press, 1993.

Zahan, Dominique. *The Religion, Spirituality, and Thought of Traditional Africa.* Chicago: University of Chicago Press, 1979.

ABOUT THE AUTHOR

Messay Kebede is Associate Professor of Philosophy at the University of Dayton in Ohio. He obtained his Ph.D. from the University of Grenoble in France. He previously taught philosophy at Addis Ababa University (Ethiopia). He is the author of two books, *Meaning and Development* (Rodopi, 1994) and *Survival and Modernization* (Red Sea, 1999). He has also published numerous articles. The most recent include: "The Rehabilitation of Violence and the Violence of Rehabilitation: Fanon and Colonialism" (*Journal of Black Studies,* 2001), "Directing Ethnicity toward Modernity" (*Social Theory and Practice,* 2001), and "Generational Imbalance and Disruptive Change" (*International Journal of Applied Philosophy*, 2003).

INDEX

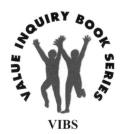

VIBS

The **Value Inquiry Book Series** is co-sponsored by:

Titles Published

75. Warren E. Steinkraus, *Taking Religious Claims Seriously: A Philosophy of Religion*, edited by Michael H. Mitias. A volume in **Universal Justice**

76. Thomas Magnell, Editor, *Values and Education*

77. Kenneth A. Bryson, *Persons and Immortality*. A volume in **Natural Law Studies**

78. Steven V. Hicks, *International Law and the Possibility of a Just World Order: An Essay on Hegel's Universalism*. A volume in **Universal Justice**

79. E. F. Kaelin, *Texts on Texts and Textuality: A Phenomenology of Literary Art*, Edited by Ellen J. Burns

80. Amihud Gilead, *Saving Possibilities: A Study in Philosophical Psychology*. A volume in **Philosophy and Psychology**

81. André Mineau, *The Making of the Holocaust: Ideology and Ethics in the Systems Perspective*. A volume in **Holocaust and Genocide Studies**

82. Howard P. Kainz, *Politically Incorrect Dialogues: Topics Not Discussed in Polite Circles*

83. Veikko Launis, Juhani Pietarinen, and Juha Räikkä, Editors, *Genes and Morality: New Essays*. A volume in **Nordic Value Studies**

84. Steven Schroeder, *The Metaphysics of Cooperation: A Study of F. D. Maurice*

85. Caroline Joan ("Kay") S. Picart, *Thomas Mann and Friedrich Nietzsche: Eroticism, Death, Music, and Laughter*. A volume in **Central-European Value Studies**

86. G. John M. Abbarno, Editor, *The Ethics of Homelessness: Philosophical Perspectives*

87. James Giles, Editor, *French Existentialism: Consciousness, Ethics, and Relations with Others*. A volume in **Nordic Value Studies**

88. Deane Curtin and Robert Litke, Editors, *Institutional Violence*. A volume in **Philosophy of Peace**

118.　Arleen L. F. Salles and María Julia Bertomeu, Editors, *Bioethics: Latin American Perspectives*. A volume in **Philosophy in Latin America**

119.　Nicola Abbagnano, *The Human Project: The Year 2000*, with an Interview by Guiseppe Grieco. Translated from Italian by Bruno Martini and Nino Langiulli. Edited with an introduction by Nino Langiulli. A volume in **Studies in the History of Western Philosophy**

120.　Daniel M. Haybron, Editor, *Earth's Abominations: Philosophical Studies of Evil*. A volume in **Personalist Studies**

121.　Anna T. Challenger, *Philosophy and Art in Gurdjieff's Beelzebub: A Modern Sufi Odyssey*

122.　George David Miller, *Peace, Value, and Wisdom: The Educational Philosophy of Daisaku Ikeda*. A volume in **Daisaku Ikeda Studies**

123.　Haim Gordon and Rivca Gordon, *Sophistry and Twentieth-Century Art*

124.　Thomas O Buford and Harold H. Oliver, Editors, *Personalism Revisited: Its Proponents and Critics*. A volume in **Histories and Addresses of Philosophical Societies**

125.　Avi Sagi, *Albert Camus and the Philosophy of the Absurd*. Translated from Hebrew by Batya Stein

126.　Robert S. Hartman, *The Knowledge of Good: Critique of Axiological Reason*. Expanded translation from the Spanish by Robert S. Hartman. Edited by Arthur R. Ellis and Rem B. Edwards. A volume in **Hartman Institute Axiology Studies**

127.　Alison Bailey and Paula J. Smithka, Editors, *Community, Diversity, and Difference: Implications for Peace*. A volume in **Philosophy of Peace**

128.　Oscar Vilarroya, *The Dissolution of Mind: A Fable of How Experience Gives Rise to Cognition*. A volume in **Cognitive Science**

129.　Paul Bube and Jefferey Geller, Editors, *Conversations with Pragmatism*. A volume in **Studies in Pragmatism and Values**

130.　Richard Rumana, *Richard Rorty: An Annotated Bibliography of Secondary Literature*. A volume in **Studies in Pragmatism and Values**

131. Stephen Schneck, *Max Scheler's Acting Persons: New Perspectives.*
A volume in **Personalist Studies**

132. Michael Kazanjian, *Learning Values Lifelong: From Inert Ideas to Wholes.*
A volume in **Philosophy of Education**

133. Rudolph Alexander Kofi Cain, *Alain Leroy Locke: Race, Culture, and the Education of African American Adults.* A Volume in **African American Philosophy**

134. Werner J. Krieglstein, *Compassion: A New Philosophy of the Other.*

135. Robert N. Fisher, Daniel T. Primozic, Peter A. Day, and Joel A. Thompson, Editors, *Suffering, Death, and Identity.* A volume in **Personalist Studies**

136. Steven Schroeder, *Touching Philosophy, Sounding Religion, Placing Education.* A volume in **Philosophy of Education**

137. Guy Debrock, *Process Pragmatism: Essays on a Quiet Philosophical Revolution.* A volume in **Studies in Pragmatism and Values**

138. Lennart Nordenfelt and Per-Erik Liss, Editors, *Dimensions of Health and Health Promotion.*

139. Amihud Gilead, *Singularity and Other Possibilities: Panenmentalist Novelties.*

140. Samantha Mei-che Pang, *Nursing Ethics in Modern China: Conflicting Values and Competing Role Requirements.* A volume in **Studies in Applied Ethics**

141. Christine M. Koggel, Allannah Furlong, and Charles Levin, Editors, *Confidential Relationships: Psychoanalytic, Ethical, and Legal Contexts.* A volume in **Philosophy and Psychology**

142. Peter A. Redpath, Editor, *A Thomistic Tapestry: Essays in Memory of Étienne Gilson.* A volume in **Gilson Studies**

143. Deane-Peter Baker and Patrick Maxwell, Editors, *Explorations in Contemporary Continental Philosophy of Religion.* A volume in **Philosophy and Religion**